HARLEY-DAVIDSON
SPORTSTER
PERFORMANCE HANDBOOK

Buzz Buzzelli

Motorbooks International
Publishers & Wholesalers ®

To the people who provide the parts and services that make it possible to transform an American legacy into a high-performance motorcycle. You make the Sportster even more fun!

First published in 1992 by Motorbooks International Publishers & Wholesalers, PO Box 2, 729 Prospect Avenue, Osceola, WI 54020 USA

© Buzz Buzzelli, 1992

Library of Congress Cataloging-in-Publication Data
Buzzelli, Buzz.
   Harley-Davidson sportster performance handbook / Buzz Buzzelli.
     p. cm.—(Motorbooks performance handbook series)
   Includes index.
   ISBN 0-87938-601-0
   1. Harley-Davidson motorcycle—Performance—Amateurs' manuals.   2. Harley-Davidson motorcycle—Maintenance and repair—Amateurs' manuals.   I. Title. II. Series.
TL448, H3B88   1992
629.227′5—dc20   92-30162

On the front cover: The Evolution Sportster is mild mannered when in stock trim, but can be modified into a real hot rod, easily and inexpensively. This Sportster is owned by Steve Kimball of El Toro, California. *Ron Hussey*

On the back cover: Top left, this XLH-883 racer sponsored by Bartels' Performance Products features the company's rearset kit and exhaust system. Upper right, the Harley-Davidson Screamin' Eagle ignition module is useful on any high-performance Sportster. Lower right, the Feuling/Rivera heads bring four-valve heads to the Sportster. Lower left, stroker kits, such as this one from S&S Cycle, boost low-end torque more than any other modification.

Printed and bound in the United States of America

Contents

Acknowledgments

This book was made possible by the many people who took the time and effort to assist me. It was their ideas, information, photos, documentation, graphs, and diagrams—and in one case, sketches on napkins—that brought this work to print. A special thanks to performance guru Joe Wiley Minton, who provided most of the information in the engine chapters; and to Joe Houpt and all the people at Suburban Harley-Davidson who turned their place of business into a photo studio; and to Dan Fitzmaurice of Zipper's Performance Products, who also gave immeasurable help and who answered many questions by relating the story of the hand grenade in the phone booth.

Thank you all.

The Harley-Davidson Sportster: Mythos in the Machine

My first motorcycle was a 1957 Sportster, so it was natural for me to acquire the 1987 Thirtieth Anniversary XLH-1100. I did not keep the '57 model, but then I also got rid of my Lionel train set. As you get older, you realize how certain possessions should never have been sold to buy useless things like an education and food.

The 1100cc Thirtieth Anniversary bike spent its first winter in my living room, where it leaned on its kickstand next to the dinning room table. During those cold Milwaukee snowstorms I could sit on it—especially at night when my family would not accuse me of being under the influence of some kind of medication—and turn on its headlamp. The brightness traveled through the window and across the snow banks, and in its beam of light my entire childhood seemed to pass by me.

When I was a kid, I lived next door to a guy who worked on a horse ranch in northern Wisconsin. He would ride a quarter horse home for lunch every day. Sometimes I would get his permission to ride the horse around the Fox River valleys near my home. On one ride, I encountered a man on a Harley-Davidson. This motorcycle had more leather gear than did the horses I saw on Saturday morning cowboy television shows. The rider wore a Stetson, and his jacket fringe flapped in the wind.

There I was, on a real horse, which I could ride for only a brief time; and here was this full-time cowboy on a chrome steed. I immediately subscribed to *The Enthusiast*, Harley-Davidson's official publication, and began pestering my father for a motorcycle, even though I was much too young to actually own one.

Through the efforts of an older pal, who had a garage in which he worked on a '39 Ford sedan with a '48 Mercury flathead, I finally acquired that first Sportster. It was used. It shook and rattled and leaked, and I loved it. I did not bother to fix anything. All I did was paint my name on the gas tank and ride. Nothing ever went wrong with that bike, and suddenly I became an American cowboy for real.

Harley-Davidson makes many different kinds of motorcycles, but the Sportster has a special appeal for those who desire a bike with a unique history and visionary potential for poetic rides:

Meditations on an XLH-1100 Sportster

the view from behind these buckhorns down
Wisconsin Highway Q with peanut tank
in the sun and this V-twin a pounding
metaphor: distant birds on a wire
along meadows and the downshift into
    second gear brings carburetion cracking
gunshots through shorty duals at sunrise.

    ★   ★   ★   ★   ★

standing on the footpegs in Milwaukee County
nearer dusk then easing back into saddle
    comfort
with a pleasing vibration through cowhide boots:
chrome headers ensure a dominant pioneer ride
upon an urban range and the duster worn against
night rain slaps the oil tank at a gallop in wind.

Sportsters are the machines that naturally get higher performance treatment, technological advancement, and sleeker modifications, all of which makes the Sportster even more so a thoroughbred and ready to gallop. The Sportster is precisely where modernity and antiquity meet. So strap on your leathers, spur your imagination, and ride into this book like a twentieth century cowboy should: with a pioneer spirit.

—*Martin Jack Rosenblum*

Martin Jack Rosenblum is a poet and recording artist. His book, *The Holy Ranger: Harley-Davidson Poems*, is available in from Motorbooks International. His music album *Free Hand*, on Flying Fish Records, is sold at music stores. He tours with his band performing in concerts, and has appeared at major Harley Owners Group rallies across the country.

Introduction

I have heard Harley riders (mostly big twin riders) call the Harley-Davidson Sportster a "girl's bike." I've even heard bikers say things like, "It's not even a real Harley."

Little do they know.

Of all the Harleys made, it is the XL Sportster that is the quickest and fastest. If the Sportster is for "girls," then girls must wanna have fun. They must love lots of power and the exhilaration of high speed and performance because the Sportster has the potential for the highest performance of any Harley-Davidson ever made.

A stock Evolution XLH-1200 stands 100lb lighter than any stock 1340cc big twin, making it the ideal foundation for building a high-performance Harley. So anyone embarking on such a high-powered venture using a 1340, starts with a 100lb disadvantage, minimum. And by changing to a few lightweight components, a Sportster's weight can easily be reduced by 30lb. Its integral engine-and-transmission case forms a lighter, stronger, more compact package than the big twin's pieced-together powertrain. The big twin's separate gearbox and primary drive add a lot of complexity, bulk, weight, frontal area, and last but not least, cost. It's also less rigid than the Sportster's unit case.

There are other reasons why the Sportster makes a perfect high-performance motorcycle. Its stiff chassis, for example, has the right steering geometry and short wheelbase to make it a natural for high-speed use. As for its engine, the XL has Harley-Davidson's hottest camshafts, which makes it more responsive than big twins to changes in the ignition, intake, and exhaust systems. To get a sizeable increase in performance from a 1340, you must change the camshaft. Not so with an XL. We'll get to all that later.

The simplicity of the V-twin Sportster makes it a joy to work on. It doesn't have a lot of parts and those that it does have are quite visible, inviting riders to enjoy the almost lost art of hot rodding. The Sportster is the Harley that's best suited for hot rodding,

making it easy for Sportster owners to indulge in the pragmatic American tradition of tinkering.

The beauty of owning a Sportster is that you can start with a $5,000 motorcycle and, for a relatively small investment, end up with a high-performance motorcycle that easily outruns the bigger modified V-twins, and can give superbikes fits.

Harley-Davidson's V-twin engines enjoy a little-acknowledged advantage over multicylinder engines. An inline engine is inherently limited in bore size by the proximity of adjacent cylinders. There are limits to how large you can make the cylinder without running into the next-door piston. That's why Japanese four-cylinder bikes can't be enlarged to more than about 85ci.

Not so with the Harley-Davidson Sportster! A Sportster engine builder has a potential cubic-inch advantage. With an individual head for each of its cylinders, a Sportster engine provides more room for creative tuning—to 110ci, and more! And there is no end to the number of component suppliers who can easily make that possible. As you will see, however, there's no need to go to all that work because for the majority of street riders, the standard stroke works just fine.

Federal noise and emission regulations put severe constraints on Harley-Davidson's powertrain engineers. As a result, they are limited in the amount of power they are able to extract from a standard-production engine. Because of this, and thanks to its standard camshafts, the XLH-883 engine is capable of generating 50 percent more power, simply by unplugging the intake and exhaust tracts and eliminating the rev limiter.

The XL responds well to just a few tricks. And the Sportster engine is strong enough to handle more power than it produces in stock form, which is why it makes a perfect project bike. In this book, you will learn how to build a light, docile, good-running, and reliable Sportster that will attain up to 70 or 75hp, for less than $1,000. Invest another $1,500 or so, and you can achieve as much as 90 to 100hp. That's amazing, considering that the Sportster was developed directly from a Harley-Davidson motorcycle that produced about 30hp—the Model K. Converting the flathead Model K to an overhead-valve engine was one of motorcycling's finest achievements.

When introduced, the brawny XL immediately proved to be a high-performance motorcycle, and it became America's prototypical superbike. Maybe "muscle bike" is a better term. It was the dominant force of the street and strip throughout the sixties and the early seventies, and projected an image of raw masculinity and power. The Sportster's endless torque and massive power made it a crowd-pleasing winner. Not only did it immediately begin winning races and setting records, it was also a favorite hot rod on the street.

Thanks to its Evolution engine, today's Sportster is as much a part of the high-performance scene as it was when introduced. It is strong and robust, and it made the American Motorcycle Association (AMA) Championship Cup Series (CCS) Twin Sports class possible. The Sportster is the chosen machine for a new form of AMA dirt-track racing inaugurated in 1993. In addition, it remains a favorite for record-breaking drag-strip and Bonneville-salt-flats assaults.

Much has changed on the Sportster during its thirty-five-plus years of production, yet it has managed to retain its timeless design.

Whether you want just a little more power, or a suspension system that works better, or a monster bike with power exceeding 100hp, this book will guide you. The first two chapters cover the Sportster's legacy. The rest of the book is devoted to the number of ways you can improve your XL.

The standard XL Sportster is a fine machine to start with. This book will explain how to make it even better!

Important!

This book is intended to help you get the best value and performance from your Harley-Davidson Sportster, as well as provide useful information about the Sportster series.

The information in this book primarily pertains to engine and vehicle usage *off public roads*, or off-highway, because federal law restricts the removal or modification of any part that affects federally required emission control systems on motor vehicles.

The Clean Air Act defines "motor vehicle" as a self-propelled vehicle designed and sold for transporting persons or property on a street or highway. Section 203(a)(3) of Title II of the Clean Air Act as amended, 42 USC Section 7522(a)(3) et seq., provides

that the following acts and the causing thereof are prohibited:

". . . for any person to remove or render inoperative any device or element of design installed on or in a motor vehicle engine in compliance with regulations under this title prior to its sale and delivery to the ultimate purchaser, or for any manufacturer or dealer knowingly to remove or render inoperative any device or element of design after such sale and delivery to the ultimate purchaser.

". . . for any person engaged in the business of repairing, servicing, selling, leasing, or trading motor vehicles or motor vehicle engines, or who operates a fleet of motor vehicles, knowingly to remove or render inoperative any device or element of design installed on a motor vehicle or motor vehicle engine in compliance with regulations under this title following its sale and delivery to the ultimate purchaser."

The phrase "element of design" includes changing a vehicle's original equipment parts, such as carburetors, camshafts, pistons, and valves, among other things. This means that installing replacement parts that vary in specification from the manufacturer's original equipment specification could be interpreted as a violation of these federal laws. Specific examples of this include, but are not limited to: changing a carburetor's jet sizes; installing a high-lift or long-duration camshaft; enlarging the dimensions of the engine's bore or stroke for the purpose of increasing cubic-inch displacement ; or altering the inlet and exhaust ports and valves. These represent a few but not all examples of "elements of design."

Furthermore, many states have enacted laws with various penalties for tampering with, or otherwise modifying, any required emission or noise control device or system. Vehicles not used on public highways may be exempt from most regulations; however, the reader is advised to check local and state laws to be certain.

Many of the procedures described in this book may result in a violation of the Clean Air Act. In addition, many parts described or listed are merchandised for off-highway application *only*, and are tagged with a special notice to the effect that "the part has been designed specifically for off-highway application only."

Motorcycles that are modified with high-performance parts may be difficult to ride. Extreme caution should be exercised when operating a modified vehicle—especially on the first test ride! The recommendations in this book are intended strictly for the experienced rider.

This book is *not* intended to replace factory-produced service manuals or parts catalogs, but rather to provide supplemental information.

Chapter 1

Model K and the Early Sportster

The 1957 Model XL Sportster—the motorcycle that has been produced for more than thirty-five years—was not the motorcycle that Harley-Davidson had originally planned to produce. Harley-Davidson engi-neers had been working to develop an all-aluminum, high-cam, ohv V-twin, known as the Model KL.

Chris Spexarth, Harley's chief engineer at the time, headed the KL project. According to Spexarth,

The Sportster engine could have looked like this KL's, a prototype ohv machine, had the KL's development been completed. The KL featured aluminum cylinders and heads, a 60deg V angle, and a single high-mounted camshaft. Note that the engine looks much different than that of the K model and the Sportster. Its chassis was identical to the production K, and used standard-produc-tion components. Harley-Davidson

the KL looked promising. So promising, in fact, that orders for production machinery were placed. The company appeared poised to move ahead with it.

"We priced it out," Spexarth said, "and it cost considerably less than the K model [referring to an ohv version of the Model K]. The KL project was a go from every aspect, except time. It needed time to develop."

Harley-Davidson management wanted new models, and wanted them quickly. Development of the KL, however, moved at a slower pace than management was willing to tolerate. After a high-level board meeting one afternoon, William H. Davidson, the company's president, came to Spexarth.

"Chris, we're going with the four-cam," he said, which meant that the KL project was replaced with a plan to convert the four-cam, flathead Model K to an ohv machine. Thus, the KL was dead and the XL was born.

Harley-Davidson's development committee directed William J. Harley, who headed the engineering department (and was the son of cofounder William S. Harley), to proceed with a quick-paced ohv conversion of the Model K .

An ohv conversion of the K was a logical step. After all, the ohv big twin, which began with the 1936 Knucklehead, had already passed into its second configuration, in the form of the Panhead, with its aluminum alloy heads. In addition, Harley's ohv involvement dates to the single-cylinder Peashooter and the eight-valve twin of the 1920s.

Which raises the question, why didn't Harley make the Model K as an ohv to begin with? That's an interesting story.

Harley-Davidson's experience with flatheads dates from 1926, when a 21ci (cubic inch) single was introduced. In the V-twin arena, the first 45ci (750cc, or cubic centimeter) side-valve engine appeared in 1929, with the introduction of the Model 29D. The Model D evolved into the W series, which became one of the most popular in the company's history. Additional flathead experience came from the 61 and 74ci V model series, produced in large numbers between 1930 and 1948. For five years, between 1931 and 1935, Harley models were flatheads exclusively .

In addition to thousands of civilian W models, Harley supplied some 90,000 WLA military motorcycles to the US government during World War II. The WLA's 45ci engine also powered the three-wheeled Servi-Car until it was discontinued in 1974, seventeen years after the ohv Sportster was introduced. The forty-five-year production of the "45" engine may be

The Sportster's earliest ancestors—the predecessors to all Harley-Davidson V-twins—were machines like this three-speed 1915 twin. Like current-model Sportsters it had the same 45deg V configuration, as well as the same knife-and-fork style of connecting rods. The first Harley V-twin was displayed at a show in late 1907. Ironically, its displacement of 53ci (869cc) was only 0.86ci (14cc) less than the original Sportster that was to follow fifty years later. Harley-Davidson

the longest production run of a motorcycle engine in history.

So the decision to develop a new flathead to replace the W series made perfect sense to an American company like Harley-Davidson. At the time, Detroit was still cranking out flatheads as well. Harley's enormous pool of side-valve knowledge made The Motor Company one of the most experienced in this technology. There were also economic reasons for building a flathead Model K. Harley had looked at the possibility of developing a smaller ohv model in 1939, when a couple of prototypes of the 45ci Model WL were built. In the final analysis, the production cost of the 45ci ohv engine was nearly the same as for the 61ci ohv EL. The high cost of the 45 ohv couldn't be justified.

Still, some people question Harley's wisdom in producing the Model K as a flathead in the first place. After all, the rest of the world had moved on to develop and produce ohv powerplants following World War II. Logical as a flathead may seem to some people, in the context of world history, developing a brand-new flathead appeared to be a step backwards. Backwards, that is, until you look at the American Motorcycle Association rule book.

The AMA Class C rule book provided another compelling argument for a new flathead. Since 1933, standard-production 750cc (45ci) side-valve machines competed with 500cc (30ci) ohv types. To Harley-Davidson, a new, more compact side-valve twin-cylinder motor seemed like a perfectly logical and simple step to take in 1952. The company took advantage of its extensive experience by making the Model K's bore and stroke identical to the WL.

Traditionally, Harley-Davidson has never been comfortable about going head-to-head with other competing manufacturers. The British were fielding 500cc ohv singles and twins, and something different, like a flathead, was seen as a safe and cautious approach to racing. In some people's minds, if they

During World War II, Harley-Davidson supplied the army with 88,000 WLAs, and enough parts to built 30,000 more.

It was powered by the same type motor as all 45ci Harley-Davidson motorcycles since 1929. Harley-Davidson

lost, it was because of the flathead handicap; if they won, it was because they overcame the ohv advantage!

Now we find ourselves with a new question: How, then, was the overhead XL justified? That resulted from a combination of things. First, major development and tooling costs had already been amortized in the Model K; and second, the choice of cylinder head material provided the key.

The ohv Sportster was a virtual carbon copy of the Model K, with different cylinders and heads. For five years, the K benefited from constant improvement, both in chassis and powerplant. As you will see, this continuous refinement shaped the K into a well-proven design that formed a solid foundation for a new ohv Harley.

Model K Design

Today, the Model K seems like a very conventional, ordinary motorcycle. But when introduced, it incorporated innovative designs and surprising technology. It was the first all-new Harley in sixteen years, since the 1936 Model E.

The "prodigy Sportster" 45deg V-twin engine set a precedent by integrating the transmission assembly into the engine crankcase. This was the first of its kind, preceding the earliest British unit-construction twins of 1961 by nearly ten years. In fact, the unit British bikes wouldn't hit American shores until eleven years after the K was introduced.

Unlike other Harleys, the clutch was disengaged by using a "modern" hand-operated lever, and the four-speed gearbox was shifted with a foot-operated

The original 1930 74ci VL model proved to be poorly developed. William H. Davidson, president of Harley-Davidson from 1942 to 1971, recalled that its initial performance was poor. The flywheels were too small, the engine and clutch didn't work, the frames broke, and the mufflers became so clogged with carbon that the engines lost power. Eventually, the VL's problems were ironed out. Harley was fortunate that the new 45ci D series, introduced the year prior, proved to be relatively trouble free. Still, Harley engineers learned a lot from the VL, and technological advances bled over into other programs. Harley-Davidson

lever. Although Harley already had some experience with this in the 125cc Model S of 1947, the ratcheting foot-shift mechanism was a unique feature among large American motorcycles at the time. The K was the first big Harley to replace the conventional tank-mounted hand-shift lever and foot-operated clutch pedal.

The gearbox had a direct-drive top gear, with primary drive on the left-hand side and final drive on the right. This meant that the gearbox output sprocket could be changed without disturbing the primary driveline or the clutch, which was unique compared to the big twin models. Big twins had their output sprockets buried behind the primary drive and clutch assembly. Thus, Sportster transmission sprockets could be quickly and easily changed—a definite racing advantage.

Harley has always been an "engineering company," and one of the reasons for the indirect gearbox ratios in the lower gears was strength. It was felt that spreading the loads across the two gearshafts increased the strength of the transmission unit, an important consideration in an assembly that combined the gearbox in the same case as the crankshaft.

The K's row of camshafts was a carry-over from the side-valve WL, which had its origins in the 1929 DL. (The evolution of the DL/WL series is an interesting story in itself, covered in detail by Allan Girdler in *Harley Racers*.) The train of gears was a natural for an engine with side valves, with an individual cam to directly operate each valve. This gear train remains with the Sportster—and the XR-750 racing engine—to this day. While this layout has inherent disadvantages, such as increased manufacturing costs and noise emission, it offers several major advantages for high-performance applications.

Compared to the single-cam big twin, the four-cam Sportster layout offers a tuner two very distinct high-performance benefits. First, the pushrod angles provide a straighter load path to the rocker arms (especially to the front exhaust), which reduces many front-cylinder exhaust valve timing problems compared to those experienced by the big twins. Second, it allows tremendous flexibility in adjusting cam timing for high-performance use. For example, a minor change in inlet timing can be made without grinding and installing a completely new camshaft. A tuner can adjust the inlet or the exhaust cams

The standard DS-45 engine provided economical and reliable power for thousands of Servi-Cars over a forty-two-year period. The original Sportster had the same stroke as the DS engine, which was produced until 1974, *seventeen years after the Sportster was introduced. The 3.813in stroke was fashionable in 1951, when this photo was taken. Harley Davidson*

The appearance of the Model K (bottom) contrasts sharply with the WL's older styling, which it replaced (1941 model shown at top). Harley-Davidson

individually to make changes in valve overlap or duration. In addition, the short camshafts, supported at both ends by bearings only a few inches apart, are rugged.

Unlike other motorcycles of its time, the Model K's oil pump was enclosed in the crankcase, and the generator was mounted remotely in front of the component. All of this made it an easy bike to work on. Compared to separate engine and gearbox designs, its simple overall layout and the reduced number of parts make it a natural choice for racing.

The Model K's chassis design was also innovative: it used hydraulically damped rear shock absorbers to control its pivoted swing arm. It was the first Harley, and one of the first mass-produced motorcycles in the world, to incorporate this technology.

The K also had a hydraulically damped front fork. The frame's steering geometry was designed around the use of narrow 19in wheels, a radical departure from the traditional use of balloon-type 5.00x16in tires of other Harley models. Wheel sizes had evolved from using skinny 28in rims with 2.25in-wide tires on the earliest models, to 3in tires during the 1920s, then to 4in widths on 19in rims in the 1930s, and finally to 5.00x16in tires on the 1949 Hydra-Glide.

The fat balloon tires of this era helped to compensate for little or no suspension—the large tires could soak up some of the road bumps. With springs and dampers at both ends, the balloon tires

---

Why a Flathead K? Why an Iron XL?

At a time when the world migrated to overhead valves and aluminum heads, Harley-Davidson introduced the flathead Model K, followed by the iron-head XL. While these may appear to be two steps backwards, there are reasons behind Harley's decision to develop these products . . . but they are not the reasons most people think.

The WL, which was more than twenty years old at the time, clearly needed upgrading. Hey, it was *old,* having begun life in 1929. Racing regulations accommodated 45ci flatheads, pitted against 500cc ohvs. The half-liter bikes were mainly BSA and Norton singles, and the Triumph was a twin. Harley's twenty-five years of flathead experience, combined with the utter simplicity and durability of the Harley-Davidson side-valve engine, surely influenced the company's decision to upgrade the flathead. The main reason, however, was that Harley management has made it a policy never to go head-to-head with other manufacturers. Thus, a 500cc ohv was out. Better to field something nobody else had.

Some people have argued that there may be another explanation for the Model K's cylinder head and valve layout: Harley's ohv Panhead experience—a bad experience. The Panhead was introduced in 1948, four years prior to the K's introduction, at a time when the K was in its incubation stage. During that time, the Panhead was plagued with more than a few cylinder head problems, such as valve guides that loosened and hydraulic lifters that didn't lift valves. (The lifters were originally located in the head, or rocker box area, and didn't get enough oil. Eventually, Harley moved them to their current location.)

Indeed, the Panhead troubles theory states it wasn't until 1953—when Harley-Davidson engineers adapted Chrysler automotive valve lifters and iron guides—that management finally felt they had a handle on the aluminum ohv woes. When it came to the concept of an ohv engine, management was gun shy.

The reason the foregoing theory doesn't fly is the KL. While the KR models were being raced in competition and used on the streets of America, a concurrent program was under way to develop the KL overhead-valve street machine. In addition, the KL, because it was an ohv, did not qualify to compete under AMA Class C rules. In the final analysis, the flathead K was a solution to the problem of bringing a more competitive racer to dirt tracks, while quickly plugging a temporary hole in the marketplace until the KL was ready.

The Panhead theory explains the XL's iron heads, though. With the death of the aluminum-head KL, when it came to the concept of ohv heads, management was gun shy of *aluminum.* The original iron-head ohv, the 1936 EL, experienced virtually no problems related to its iron cylinder heads. Iron was a known and stable element, in more ways than one, and it virtually guaranteed instant success. Why gamble on aluminum then?

The question of whether management made the right choice was answered in the mid-seventies, in the form of the little-known V-880/1100. After several styling mock-ups, and over a dozen prototypes in several variations during a six-year period—not to mention the demise of several project managers—AMF (American Machine and Foundry) drove a stake into the heart of the all-aluminum project. The would-be replacement Sportster project was eliminated in 1976.

But did the V-880's demise indicate that Harley was unwilling to develop aluminum heads? Perhaps not. In fact, it may again only prove that we are trying to build a theory around the wrong premise. Harley already had two families of twins during the mid-1970s, including the successful XR-750 racer, at a time when the world wanted multicylinder engines. Development of the (ill-fated) V-four Nova subsequently began with the end of the V-880 program. Had this proceeded with proper funding, the Harley V-four would have been the first V-four motorcycle in the world. But when the time came to invest capitol on tooling, AMF balked, and Honda introduced the first V-four.

were not needed to smooth the ride. Additionally, the Model K's tire size attributed greatly to its ease of handling and light steering response. It clearly set a precedent that would become a Sportster hallmark.

The engine had a typically undersquare bore and stroke of 2.75x3.813in The 3.813in stroke has remained common to Harley-Davidson middleweight machines ever since.

The Model K weighed around 440lb, produced about 30hp, and could reach 80mph—maybe, depending on which way the wind was blowing, how heavy the rider was, and how much the rider had for breakfast. Although an average ohv 500cc twin could outrun it, the 30hp Model K looked and rode more like a sleek European motorcycle than a traditional American bike.

When the Model K was unveiled on November 18, 1951, at a Harley-Davidson national dealers' convention in Milwaukee, representatives from more than 880 dealers, from forty-six states and several Canadian provinces, reacted enthusiastically. Factory literature of 1952 proclaimed, "Its performance qualities have been outstanding. . . . It has speed, power, acceleration and beauty of design."

Elvis Presley's first Harley was a 1956 KH. The young singer went on to own many Harleys. The story appeared in Harley's magazine, The Enthusiast. *Harley-Davidson*

Which brings us to some conflicting claims. Acceleration was slow, and with a top speed of barely 80mph, its performance was nothing to boast about. After all, this was a time when Chuck Yeager proved that it was possible to fly faster than sound could travel, more than 700mph. In the motorcycle world, 650cc British twins, which were becoming very popular at this time, could easily run away from it with quarter-mile speeds of over 80mph and top speeds of 100mph.

Building a Sportster Base

The Model Ks experienced more than a few problems, as any new design does. The most notable was transmission gear breakage. Although these problems were eventually solved (temporarily, then re-solved), the K's uninspiring performance remained.

Only a few minor changes were introduced for 1953, most notably a faster-acting throttle. Other new features included a new Standard Solo Group, offered at no extra charge, and optional new saddlebags and Buddy Seat.

The big news, however, involved the Model KK, which featured a special speed kit. This included hotter cams, polished combustion chamber and ports, less chrome, and flatter handlebars. With proper gearing, it could reach 95mph.

There was bigger news yet for 1954—the Model KH, with a longer stroke, was introduced with an advertised displacement of 55ci. This was the Golden Anniversary model, bearing a special medallion on its front fender.

Needle-bearing hubs were introduced on the 1954 Model K. While the rest of the motorcycling world went to wheel bearings using ball-type bearings, Harley stuck with needle bearings, and today uses tapered roller-type wheel bearings exclusively. Harley-Davidson

The KH's swept volume was actually 54.1ci. The larger displacement resulted solely from a 0.75in increase in stroke—to 4.5625in—which yielded an astounding bore and stroke ratio of 1.66:1. It had a compression ratio of 6.8:1, and the factory claimed it produced 38hp at 5200rpm. Many other changes in the 1954 Model KH improved its overall performance and durability. The crankshaft featured taper-fit flywheel shafts secured with a nut, similar to the flywheels of the ohv 74ci big twins. The big-end bearing had seventeen rollers, and a new retainer that promised improved reliability at high engine speeds. It also featured new U-flex oil control rings and cam-ground pistons. The cylinders were lengthened to accommodate the longer stroke.

Harley-Davidson engineers paid special attention to the heads by reshaping both inlet and exhaust ports, and increasing the intake valve size by 0.11in. Valve spring changes helped to reduce valve float at high rpm.

Both the K and the later XL had a long history of gearbox changes, especially following an increase in power output. For 1954, the transmission cases were made of heavier material, and the gearbox, shift mechanism, kick starter, and primary drive received many detailed refinements. Although only three screws secured the primary-drive chain cover, four dowels were used to locate it, and the case was made thicker. The gear case and front chain cover were polished.

Other engine areas that received attention were cam gears, primary-drive tensioner, carburetor, oil pump, and bearings. It certainly wouldn't be the first time Harley engineers directed their attention to these areas.

Many chassis improvements were also introduced in 1954. Stamped-steel brake shoes replaced the original aluminum shoes, and new pad material and hardened cams helped to improve durability while decreasing squeal. New fork covers helped to hide, but not reduce, fork-oil leaks.

Frame geometry was altered slightly, as well. The steering head angle was changed, giving 29.75deg of rake and 3.22in of trail. Although standard wheel size was 19in, with 3.50x19in Goodyear or Firestone tires as standard, riders could order optional 18in rims with 3.50x18in tires at no charge. A 4.00x18in Goodyear Grasshopper tire proved to be a popular option, even at a slight additional charge.

A total of sixteen engineering changes were made in 1955. Among them was a change in steering geometry, in an effort to further improve stability. Trail was increased a full inch, and the fork legs were shortened an inch. Appropriate changes were also made to the spring and damping rods.

One of the most unusual—and advanced—details about the 1955 model was its frame, made from chrome-moly steel rather than carbon steel.

Another unique 1955 feature remains with today's Sportster: An access door was added to the transmission so that the entire gearbox assembly could be serviced without removing the engine and splitting the cases.

Among other improvements for 1955 were a rubber-mounted speedometer, stronger wheel hub flanges, and new front fender medallion, in addition to new colors.

In 1956, additional changes were made to some of the same areas that had been updated two years prior. The Model K had always experienced some problems with transmission gear breakage, especially the 1954 and 1955 models. An experimental-department employee, Art Kauper, discovered flaws in the bar stock from which the gears were machined. Harley-Davidson engineers switched to a forging process to eliminate this. The second gear mainshaft and third gear countershaft were made from these forgings. The other second and third gears were also redesigned with thicker tooth sections. The engagement dogs on mainshaft second gear were increased from four to five.

A Speed Kit was also offered for an additional $68. The base KH listed for $935, bringing the KHK's price tag with a Speed Kit to $1,003.

The 1956 Model K experienced a change that is still implemented on today's models: Harley lowered the saddle height. The steering-head casting and rear-shock forgings were changed, and the shocks were shortened by $9/16$in. The shock's outer diameter and oil capacity were increased, and the rear wheel could travel farther into the rear fender area.

Despite the rear shock absorber's shorter damping rod, the factory claimed the travel remained the same and, according to factory literature, ". . . the same good riding quality is retained."

The oil pump was redesigned, eliminating the relief valve and replacing the shaft's pin with a woodruff key.

Roller-type wheel bearings appeared on the 1956 K, replacing the double-row ball bearings in the rear wheel to increase load capacity. Other changes to improve durability included a thicker kick-starter gear, spring-steel control wire guides, and a carburetor support bracket.

The most visible component change was a streamlined taillamp that had been introduced on the FL the previous year. This fender-mounted taillight became another Sportster hallmark.

The XL Program

It is not generally known that Harley was experimenting with ohv Model Ks as early as 1953. In fact, ohv middleweights were investigated while the K was being developed. A young cross-country racer, Don Brown, was one of two riders who rode experimental machines at the Catalina Grand Prix in May of 1953. Brown had raced factory KRM machines in

The original KRM, intended for cross-country racing, had a two-into-one exhaust system, something shared by the production street machine. Harley-Davidson

Here's a "racing does improve the breed" photo. Later KRMs, like this 1954 model, were similar to—yet different and improved from—the original types. Notice the enlarged shock absorbers and oil tank. Racing in the southwestern deserts, KRMs suffered crushed exhaust pipes. Re-routing the front pipe to a higher location and enlarging the skid plate addressed the problem. The lesson would not be lost on the original XLCH's exhaust system, which was routed in much the same way. Harley-Davidson

Racing Ks: KR, KR-TT, and KRM

Model K derivatives achieved enormous success on America's racetracks. The KR racing machines were offered for sale from the factory, and could be purchased at any Harley dealership.

A 1953 brochure pictures the Model KR Track Racing, Model KR-TT (Tourist Trophy), and Model KRM Scrambles and Trials. These racers were used in every form of competition: oval dirt tracks, TT steeplechase, enduro, hillclimb, road race, and cross-country scrambles in the deserts of southern California.

The basic KR had a rigid frame and no brakes. It was the consummate dirt-track vehicle and dominated professional dirt-track racing for two decades.

The KR-TT came equipped with front and rear brakes. It was intended for TT races, and served as the basis for a successful road racer.

The KRM, a cross-country mount, was essentially a KR-TT, except for changes in its fenders, and the addition of a two-into-one exhaust system. It also had a skid plate to protect the engine's sump when used in desert races and enduros.

Port side of a KRM racer. Picture the word "Sportster" in raised letters on the primary- drive case, and what do you see? Harley-Davidson

The KR-TT (1954) served as a scrambles and road racer. It featured a larger oil tank, something the later XLs could not handle because of their bulkier ohv heads and rocker boxes. This formed the basis of road racers, present and future. Harley-Davidson

In 1965, Reiman (No. 1) and Mert Lawwill finished this close (Reiman won)! Reiman still competes in road races today. The KR simply ran away with AMA Class C pro racing, and although the XL never slipped into the professional AMA racing slot that was occupied by the KR, it became a formidable and popular racer in many other pro and amateur fields. Harley-Davidson

Later models included the larger displacement 55ci KHR-TT. This was a stroker to compete with the British-made ohv 650cc vertical twins in certain forms of AMA racing, such as Tourist Trophy. (For a complete history of KR racing machines, see Allan Girdler's excellent book *Harley Racers*.)

The KR competed successfully until the XR-750 was introduced in 1970. Roger Reiman won the first 200 Mile race at Florida's new Daytona International Speedway on a 1961 KR. He won again in 1964 and in 1965. The KR's last big victory came at Daytona in

1969, when Calvin Rayborn won the 200 Mile race for the second year in a row at more than 100mph. During the seventeen years between 1953 and 1969, KRs recorded thirteen wins at Daytona, countless dirt-track wins, and all but three Grand National Championships.

A contrast in the evolution of road racing. Roger Reiman rode a KR to victory in the 1961 Daytona 200 Mile race. Harley-Davidson

The Sportster's resemblance to the Model K is obvious: the original 1952 K is above, and the premier 1957 Sportster is below. Harley-Davidson

southern California desert and scrambles races. (Ironically, Brown went on to become the president of one of Harley's competitors, the BSA-Triumph group.)

Brown, along with top-ranked cross-country champion Del Kuhn, was given experimental Model K-based ohv machines that had been prepared in Milwaukee especially for the Catalina race. Brown saw the machine a couple of times in the back of his sponsoring dealer's shop, but never rode it until race day.

"I was doing very well," Brown says. "I passed a zillion riders in the first lap and nobody passed me. It was awfully fast."

As Brown was passing a slower rider on a high-speed fire road, the rider turned into Brown as he went by, knocking Brown's right handlebar loose. "To this day," he adds, "I don't know how I managed to avoid going over the cliff." He was forced to retire, and the factory took the machine back to Milwaukee for analysis. He never saw another ohv machine like it until the Sportster was introduced more than three years later.

The Model K, which originally sold for $750, cost Harley-Davidson $125,000 to develop. The total cost of getting it to the production line, including tooling,

was $750,000. The money invested on the Model K was well spent, however. It would earn dividends later in the XL program.

Early prototypes, designated "X," had a low 7.5:1 compression ratio. Engineers wanted to assure themselves that the basic machine possessed a good measure of durability to perform and complete their test programs. Later in the testing, when compression was increased to 9:1, the model was designated "XL."

The 9:1 compression ratio came as a result of an extraordinarily high domed piston, needed to fill the cavernous chamber. The wide-splayed valves were laid out at an angle ninety degrees from each other, which created a deep chamber. And the deep chamber allowed Harley-Davidson engineers to use very large valves. During this era, the trend was toward wide valve angles and large valves.

For a 1957 design, the Sportster certainly was, as factory literature touted, "a modern, up-to-date power plant . . . with engineering and design features that set the pace for motorcycling pleasure and performance."

Like the side-valve engines before it, the Sportster engine used roller valve lifters. Factory literature

This sight greeted dealers who attended Harley-Davidson's annual sales conference in Milwaukee, Wisconsin, in the fall of 1956. The introductory 1957 Sportster stands at center. Trademarked names hyping the product's features—real or imagined—were beginning to come into use. Such names as Hummer and Hydra-Glide and Ramped Cams can be seen on the Sportster's stand. Being an engineering company, Harley traditionally gave its products a letter or number designation, if nothing more than to indicate its displacement size; VL 61 and WL 45

are examples. The 1947 Hummer and 1949 Hydra-Glide are two of the company's first vehicles to be given factory names. Interestingly, the later Model K never received a name, but the Sportster did. During the 1980s, Harley's marketing department deliberately attempted to move away from designations. Ironically, except for two other Sportster models, the 1983 XLX-61 and XR-1000, every model and submodel was christened with an official birth name right from the factory. Harley-Davidson

21

1959 Jack Pine Enduro

The Jack Pine Enduro was considered one of the most grueling cross-country events. Harley riders usually rode Model Ks or big twins, but when riders entered Sportsters, it created quite a stir. Gerald McGovern said that it helped establish the Sportster's credibility. Harley-Davidson

Rider Ernest Kimball and passenger Robert Kircher, of Grand Rapids, Michigan, cross the Tobacco River during the 1957 Jack Pine. They entered this novel Sportster-engined three-wheeler and took the sidecar class honors. The Sportster's competition legacy was being forged. Harley-Davidson

Less than a year after the Sportster's introduction, riders showed up at the Jack Pine Cowbell Classic Enduro in Michigan riding XL Sportsters. One rider was Gerald McGovern, a Michigan Harley dealer who had won the 1950 event. He went on to win the 1957 event as well. A total of 414 riders were entered; however, only 115—less than 30 percent—finished the two-day 500 mile event. Harley-Davidson

referred to these as, "high speed racing tappets." Other high-performance features included the stel-lite-faced exhaust valves, aluminum-alloy push rods, and cam-ground aluminum pistons with chrome-plated top compression ring.

But it was the Sportster's cams that would continue to capture the attention of performance-minded riders. The cams were described as, "ramped cams," and again quoting the literature, ". . . ramped on both the closing and opening sides, making for quieter, smoother motorcycling. Another 'years ahead' mechanical feature." The cams were central to the Sportster's mystique. Later Sportsters would offer "P" and "Q" cams—high-performance cams that enthusiasts reveled in. Sportster riders of the era talked about high-performance and racing cams that were believed to turn tame street Sportsters into wild road-burners.

In 1958, the Sportster embarked on its evolutionary trail. To improve the rigidity and durability of the camshaft gears, the gears were made integral with the shafts, eliminating the need for woodruff keys. The drive gearshaft diameter was enlarged by 0.125in.

Meanwhile, the saga of the gearbox's evolution continued in 1958. The diameter of the shaft that supported the drive gear and second gear was enlarged 0.125in and was provided with eight instead of six splines. This was done in hopes of solving service problems in the field.

Other changes for 1958 included a choke control lever located on the air cleaner (it was formerly operated by a left-side lever); a heavier clutch cover and new gasket; new oil-resistant clutch hub seal and gearshaft O-ring; and a two-brush generator similar to generator used on the Duo-Glide. Minor changes included thicker brake-shoe spring wire, stiffer oil pump check-valve spring, and new oil-tank cap gasket.

Directional signals—similar to the type offered for 1958 Duo-Glides—were optional, in addition to 1in extended suspension units for increased ground clearance. Notice that a major modification for 1955 and 1956 was to lower the seat height; now, two years later, an optional high-riding package was offered.

This up-down-up trend in seat height follows Harley-Davidson throughout its history. In the early

Those famous cams and gears, the Ramped Cams, were left over from side-valve days. The gear train is the last remaining link to the early days of motorcycle production. Like today's Harley-Davidson models, the Sportster cams and their designations have a legacy. Enthusiasts who prided themselves in being Sportster aficionados could recite cam types, like the P cam which was touted to be a *hot factory racing grind that improved power above 4000rpm. Although the "P" designation was created to distinguish it from other cam variations, Harley marketing people took advantage of the P cam's increasing popularity and featured it in factory brochures and dealer literature. Before long, it was legendary. Harley-Davidson*

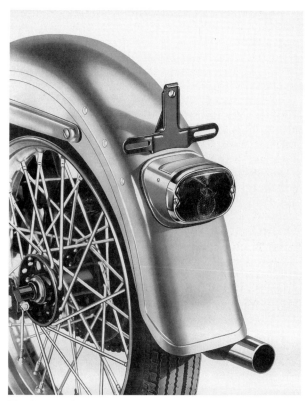

The famous Sportster taillight became a standard feature on all Harleys. The Sportster's influence goes beyond other Harley-Davidson models, as foreign manufacturers took aim at XL styling features. The Kawasaki Vulcan, for example, incorporates Harley styling features introduced as long as forty years ago. Harley-Davidson

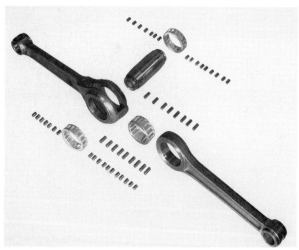

The knife-and-fork connecting rod with roller bearings, as typified by these components from a 1953 Model K, is still at the heart of all Harley-Davidson V-twins, making them unique among today's motorcycles. Other twins not only use plain-type bearings, they've also discontinued using the rod system that centers both front and rear rods on a common plane. The purpose is to eliminate secondary balance forces, which would be amplified if the rods were aligned on offset planes. Harley-Davidson

days, while 28in wheels were standard, optional 26in wheels could be ordered to reduce the saddle height. In later years, after lowering the 1984 Low Glide, an optional suspension package model—with a higher seat height—was offered in 1985. The factory always juggled its machines between taller, better riding bikes, to bikes with lower seat heights. The ever-porpoising ride height truly was, and remains, an engineering compromise and a distinct Harley phenomenon.

In the Sportster line, this compromise culminated in the Hugger of today, which is a lower version of the standard bike. Ironically, in the FXR line, the FXR-SP (Sport Edition) is a taller version of a lower model!

A factory brochure that was produced around March 1958 features "The Thrilling Scramblers," the

The Model K's "trap door" gearbox, introduced in 1954, became a standard feature on all Sportster variants, including XR series racers. Even today, factory racers of all kinds—including exotic international Grand Prix road racers—use this type of system. In addition to providing quick access, the doorway allows tuners to change internal gearbox ratios without pulling the motor and splitting the cases. Critics of the Sportster who have called it primitive and hard-edged, have often failed to note the many advanced engineering features it ushered in, features that other machines of its era lacked. The original reason for the trap door, however, should not be overlooked. The K was plagued with gearbox problems, and prior to the advent of the door, dealer mechanics were forced to remove the engine from the frame to repair the transmission. Harley Davidson

XLCH and XLC racing versions. The engines had larger ports and valves, high-domed pistons, lightened tappets, and magneto ignition. These machines also wore a new fuel tank—the now-famous "peanut" tank.

About six months later, when the 1959 models were rolled out in the fall of 1958, the XLCH street machine appeared with its high two-into-one exhaust system. The "CH" designation is generally believed to stand for Competition Hot. The C version—created at the request of California dealers—with its wide-ratio gearing was intended for cross-country racing use in California. Some say the "C" stands for Competition, while others insist it means California.

The year of 1959 set many style precedents, and some features proved to be both interesting and proverbial, especially in the areas of exhaust systems and overall styling. For example, a new dual exhaust system appeared on the XLH model (a more powerful XL with higher compression ratio and larger valves introduced in 1958) with twin mufflers stacked one above the other along the right side. This was destined to later become restyled as the legendary "shorty duals" in 1963.

The headlamps of 1959 are also noteworthy. The XLH's "bullet" type headlamp was restyled into a sheet-metal nacelle. This style of nacelle became a standard feature of the FL and FLH big twins in 1960. Meanwhile, the 1959 XLCH came on the scene with a tiny, almost off-road type of headlamp—only 5¾in diameter—that hung beneath an eyebrow mount. Actually, the idea was lifted from the 125 two-stroke design of 1947. Of course, this was to become a Sportster standard, one that all later 1340cc big twin sport models would eventually inherit.

In other words, in several areas, the 1959 Sportsters led the way for many future Harley models to follow.

The XLCH also featured a unique "trip-o-meter" for checking distances between two points. This was essential for enduro competition. It may be hard to imagine that in these days of 200lb competition machines, a near 500lb machine was used for off-road competition. Yet, during this period of American motorcycling, a typical off-road mount weighed up to 700lb. How times change!

The XLCH was perhaps the first dual-purpose or dual-sport motorcycle on the American scene. The XLCH was intended for both on-road and off-road use, and its overall appearance was decidedly different from other American street motorcycles of its

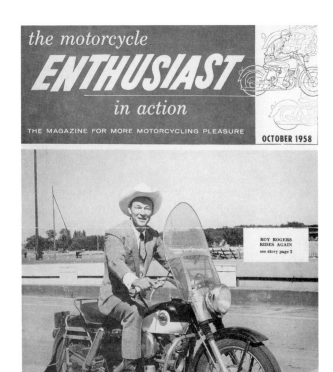

Popular singing cowboy and TV and movie star Roy Rogers owned several Harley-Davidsons. He tried out a new XL Sportster during a performance at Milwaukee's State Fair Park. Harley-Davidson

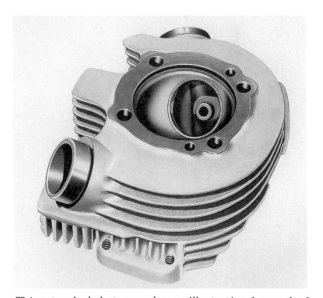

This retouched photo served as an illustration for much of the Sportster sales literature. Brochures referred to the head as having "over size power ports." When the Sportster was introduced, the cylinder head technology in vogue at the time held that a 90deg included valve angle allowed the largest possible valves, and therefore the largest ports, and therefore the optimum flow. This resulted in two problems. First, the tall combustion chamber roof required a high-dome piston to keep compression up. This meant that the dome provided an obstacle for the incoming charge, thus the shape of the inlet port tract was not direct. Harley-Davidson

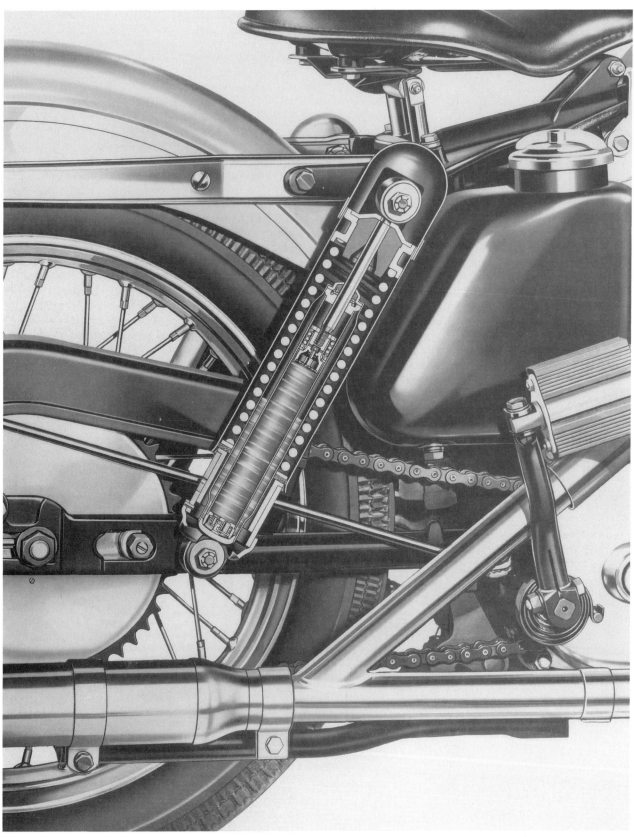

The 1960 Sportsters featured larger, improved shock absorbers. Some riders who have been around long enough to experience them claim that, not only were they far better performers than today's imported units, but they also lasted longer. However, these long-time riders also admit the shocks leaked. Harley-Davidson

day. Ironically, in the sixties—a decade later—Honda and Yamaha would re-introduce this concept with high-pipe models (the Honda 250cc and 305cc Scrambler and Yamaha 250cc DT-1 Enduro) and reap enormous commercial success.

While the XLCH sported shortened and thinned fenders, the XLH had deep fender panels. With its large fuel tank, bulbous cast-aluminum primary-drive cover, and "headlight nacelle with its modern, futuristic styling," as factory literature described it, the XLH looked more like a Duo-Glide than its more sporting sibling.

The XLCH created excitement among enthusiasts. With its peanut tank, stamped-metal primary cover, barely noticeable lighting equipment, thinned fenders, and small-section tires, the XLCH Sportster presented racy lines that not only were strikingly different than traditional American motorcycles and Harley big twins, but whose appearance rivaled the smaller import models.

Imagine that look, combined with light weight and ohv power, and you've got the "Original American Superbike."

Everything about the 1959 Sportster reeked of high performance. One of the less obvious features that impressed the cyclists of that era, for example, was the speedometer, mounted front-and-center directly behind the handlebars. Factory literature

A basic single instrument—the speedometer—first appeared on the original XL, housed in the fork shroud's sheet metal. Today's XLH-883 (the one that spent three years wearing a $3,995 price tag after its introduction in mid-1985) continues the legacy. Sportsters may evolve into deluxe versions from time to time, but they always return to the basics. Harley-Davidson

The most awesome racing machines ever put into the hands of dirt-track racers were the Sportster CH and C models, offered in 1958. This is the earliest version of the factory-made racing Sportster. Note the magneto beneath the carburetor. The XLR-TT racing versions had the Fairbanks-Morse mag mounted in front of the engine, in the place of the generator. Harley-Davidson

The 1960 XLCH presented a fine profile of the world's original superbike, right down to its checkered-flag tank graphics. The machine was all steel and aluminum, and its massive engine, wedged into an all-steel chassis, gave an impression of a solid, rugged motorcycle. And when the rider opened the throttle, the XLCH's acceleration was the most heart-pounding, arm-stretching experience in the motorcycling world. Harley-Davidson

pointed out that this was "similar to the location of the tachometer on racing models." Even the gas tank logos, which featured the company's racing emblem of the era, added to the machine's mystique.

Within two years of its introduction, the Sportster had become unanimously recognized as a superbike. The motorcycle magazines raved about its outstanding performance. Its brute torque, arm-yanking acceleration, and relatively light weight (for its era) made it a trendsetter. American engineering and ingenuity had prevailed.

The Sportster got its brute force the American way—from pure cubic inches. Yet, even in its relatively mild state of tune, its performance impressed not only Americans, but the foreign press as well. When the British magazine *Motor Cycling* tested a 1960 XLCH, it was impressed, calling it "Breathtakingly fast, ruggedly simple, massively built, functional to the nth degree." The report stated that the Sportster could "spin its 4-inch tyre when taking off on dry tarmac and top 100 mph less than 35 seconds later!" It went on to say that its "shattering acceleration" was perhaps the machine's most impressive capability; that its 14.5sec, 90mph quarter mile was "outstanding"; and that "a rapid departure produced tyre-smoking, wheel-standing starts."

The XLCH, a dual-purpose on- and off-road motorcycle, preceded by several years a later trend among Japanese imports. Many traditional Sportster features that became legendary first appeared during this time, such as the eyebrow headlamp mount, single instrumentation, peanut tank, and in 1963, the shorty dual exhaust system. That's Harley-Davidson employee Clyde Denzer riding a 1962 model. Denzer spent more than twenty-five years with Harley-Davidson, and became racing manager following Dick O'Brien's retirement. Harley-Davidson

This 1960 photo shows the big-tank version of the XLR-TT. The XLR-TT was a stripped, racing-only version of the XLCH. You could order the XLR with a standard or close-ratio gearbox, and Speedster or Laconia handlebars. Overall, the machine appears to be nothing more than a stripped-down street bike, but it had special equipment. It came with eighteen-, nineteen-, twenty-, and twenty-two-tooth mainshaft sprockets (it was equipped with a twenty-one), two Champion A-12 spark plugs, and a plug wrench. Some additional equipment, at extra charge, included larger brakes, twenty- and thirty-tooth engine sprockets with chains, and fifteen-, sixteen-, seventeen-, and twenty-three-tooth mainshaft sprockets. Although the bike was pictured in Harley literature with a front fender, the fender was not included as standard equipment. Harley-Davidson

The only update for 1960 was the addition of new shock absorbers, similar to the Duo-Glide's, with completely revised compression and rebound damping rates.

You can always tell the 1961 XLH from a 1960 by the creased edge of the newer model's fuel tank. This was Harley's idea of Jet Age styling. Other than an aluminum upper fork triple crown on the 1962 model, Sportster styling remained nearly unchanged for three years.

In 1963, both models got a new third-gear ratio, from 1.381 to 1.323:1. Because the final-drive gearing was different, this gave an overall third-gear ratio of 5.56:1 on the H and 5.85:1 on the XLCH. Also, the XLCH now sported the famous shorty duals, an addition that made it seem more like a hot rod.

Another progressive feature, in addition to a rubber-mounted sealed-beam unit, was the improved magneto with higher output coil and, of all things, an ignition key lock. Formerly, no provision was made for an ignition key. Now, at last, you could lock the ignition of your XLCH Sportster!

When *Cycle World* journalists road tested the XLCH, they proclaimed it the "fastest mass-produced motorcycle we have tested," and, "the fastest thing the expert rider is likely to find for sale, anywhere." It turned a quarter mile in 14.3sec at 92mph, and reached 60mph in only 6.0sec. In those days, that was quicker and faster than just about any high-performance vehicle on the road. The Triumph Bonneville and the Norton Atlas came close, and depending on who was riding and track conditions, the British twins made a good accounting of themselves, but lacked the shear roll-on propulsion of the 55ci Harley-Davidson.

The stock street Sportster certainly enjoyed the prime of its life during the sixties. It was, as they say, "a lean, mean, fightin' machine" that could take on any other bike it ran up against. But when the Japanese introduced large-displacement multicylinder bikes,

The XLCH's peanut tank became as much of a Harley legacy as its V-twin configuration. Harley-Davidson

beginning with the four-cylinder single overhead camshaft (sohc) 1969 Honda, the picture changed dramatically. (More about that later.)

Most changes for 1964 were minor, such as a chrome panel for the XLCH's lower fork bracket, and a new graphic for the H model's oil tank. A more visible improvement, however, was the full-width diecast aluminum front brake hub. It was Italian-made, from the newly acquired Aermacchi group, and it showed. Its styling was decidedly European in origin. Aluminum tappet guides were another significant advancement.

In 1965, the big twins got electric starting. In preparation for electric starting, both XLH and XLCH models were outfitted with a twelve-volt electrical system. The XLH had an automatic spark advance, while the XLCH retained its manually controlled advance system.

Previous to this, the Sportster had two twist grips. The left controlled the ignition advance, while the right provided conventional throttle control. To start a CH or an H model, the rider twisted the left-hand grip to retard the ignition timing. This helped to reduce the odds that the rider would be launched over the bars if—some would say *when*—the engine kicked back during the starting ritual.

With its powerful battery-and-coil-fired ignition system, the XLH was easy enough to start, usually a one- or two-kick proposition. With its weak, magneto-fired ignition system, the XLCH often proved to be a challenge for any rider to start. After spectating at a race or having a few beers at the local pub, Saturday afternoon entertainment often took the form of betting on how many kicks it took Roy to get his XLCH fired up. When traveling in a group, the standard procedure among battery-ignition riders

The XLCH's high exhaust pipe, however, didn't enjoy such a fate, and was replaced with the classic shorty duals in 1963. The high-mounted exhaust pipe and muffler was a unique feature for a street motorcycle, though, and explored uncharted territory in street styling. The high *pipe gave it a particularly macho appearance: It looked all-outdoors and all-performance. The letter "H" on the oil tank, indicates a high-compression, high-output engine.* Harley-Davidson

In today's world of 200lb single-cylinder motocross racers, it's hard to imagine that 450lb Sportsters were regularly used for cross-country, enduro, and scrambles racing. After its introduction, riders entered Sportsters in every type of racing that they qualified for, and began winning important events in unprecedented numbers. Sportsters completely outclassed big twins that were used in compe-

tition, and although slightly heavier than the K model, their abundant power more than made up any weight handicap. The XLCH had gobs of torque, and its power-band was easy to manage. Riders could idle through streams and mud holes as easily as they could level hills and traverse deserts. Shown here is a 1959 XLCH. Harley-Davidson

The Sportster, which could be used in TT scrambles, became a lethal weapon against British 650 and 750cc twins. With its tremendous torque, riders could kick the rear end sideways anytime they wished, and although the vertical twins could beat it, none could put on such a spectacular show. In the hands of riders like Dick Hammer, shown clearing the Spencer Park jump on January 15, 1962, the Sportster clearly was the crowd pleaser. Harley-Davidson

was to wait until all the XLCH Sportsters were started before cranking up their bikes.

For better or worse, those days are gone forever.

Racing-type ball end levers were introduced on 1965 Sportsters, along with a "high-fidelity horn" and new shocks. The XLCH's shocks had covered springs, and the XLH had a new adjusting cam for setting the preload.

Sportsters were advertised to have 15 percent more power in 1966, a horsepower punch that, according to factory literature, "will wipe up anything on or off the road."

The *big* news was the use of a P cam (a racing cam with hot valve timing) along with race-developed intake ports and jumbo valves. The cams were designed to boost power in the 3500 to 5500rpm range. A new, larger throat Tillotson diaphragm carburetor had an accelerator pump, and a patented insulator helped to isolate the carburetor from engine heat.

Power was claimed to be 60hp. This probably was the most powerful XL, however, because the best

the factory could do with later Environmental Protection Agency (EPA) restrictions was a claimed 58hp on the 1969 model. It's interesting to note that both of these claims exceed the claimed 55hp of the more efficient 1986 Evolution XL. Guess there really was some magic in those old iron heads!

That may have been the high-performance swan song of Sportsters. A few years later, in 1969, Honda introduced the first multicylinder street machine, the CB-750. The technological explosion that followed was unlike anything ever experienced in the motorcycle industry.

Electric starting came to the Sportster world in 1967. The program had begun in mid-1963. Three systems were developed through the preliminary design stage, when one was dropped. Another was dropped in the experimental phase.

The remaining system went through considerable debugging. Engineers found excessive drag in the jackshaft's plain bearings, so they changed to needle bearings; and the gear ratio had to be changed to get the right cranking speed.

During the late fifties and early sixties, 418 Sportsters were enlisted for Shore Patrol and military police units.

They were all H models, like this 1964 variant. Harley-Davidson

In the early sixties, Harley-Davidson also developed police model Sportsters in hopes of attracting business from departments with limited budgets. Although a Sportster-based police bike easily outperformed the big twins, they were never popular with law enforcement agencies. Shown is a 1961 model. Harley-Davidson

Later government contracts called for additional prototypes, such as this XLA for a contract dated 16 February 1970. Harley-Davidson

According to a story that appeared in *The Enthusiast*, Harley-Davidson's publication, "Over 90 percent of everything the engineers needed to know for the XLH starting had been learned from the FL program." Despite the knowledge gained from experience in the FL program, it took Harley-Davidson engineers more than two years to get the XL electric starting program into production.

The Sportster's shock absorbers were changed again in 1967. According to factory information, the only purpose for the change was to allow easier adjustment. For 1968, the Sportster's fork was given new internals with revised damping and 1in additional travel. The fork boots were deleted to expose the fork leg and give it a leaner look.

As planned, Harley dropped the kick starter from the XLH for that year. The left engine cover was restyled on both the XLH and XLCH so they had identical covers, and the peanut tank became an XLH option. The year 1968 predicted the XL's future. Except for the XLS Roadster, all Sportsters would inherit the legacy of this model year's peanut tank.

Another legacy, not necessarily appreciated by Harley aficionados, was the exhaust pipe crossover tube, fitted for the first time in 1969. This helped to balance the exhaust pulses, sending them through both mufflers, which did a couple of beneficial things. It helped to reduce emissions, while at the same time it increased power output by 5hp. Although most Harley riders would rather not see this cross tube, the modern world—according to the EPA—required it.

New head castings also appeared on 1969 models. These had larger racing valves and black cylinder fins, and the engine was said to produce 58hp. Safety bead wheel rims also appeared for the first time, with wide-profile tires.

Finally, the H model got the XLCH eyebrow headlamp treatment, and the sheet-metal headlamp nacelle disappeared, probably forever. You'll always be able to tell a pre-1970 XLH Sportster by its sheet-metal headlight shroud.

If 1968 and 1969 were banner years for the Sportster, 1970 stands out as a year of genetic mutation. In fact, most would call it a step backwards because nobody appreciated the optional "boat tail" body that was offered. Available only in 1970 and 1971, it disappeared from the options list, to the applause of most Harley enthusiasts. But before we condemn the boat-tail styling, we should consider it in its historical context. There was nothing like it. The boat tail was clearly too far ahead of its time. But like other aspects of Sportster styling, it would influence future motorcycle manufacturing for years to come.

Meanwhile the XL-family engineers busied themselves with a new program, the Model 1000, or 61, engine introduced on the 1972 Sportster. That, and the story of the Evolution engine, are the subjects of the next chapter.

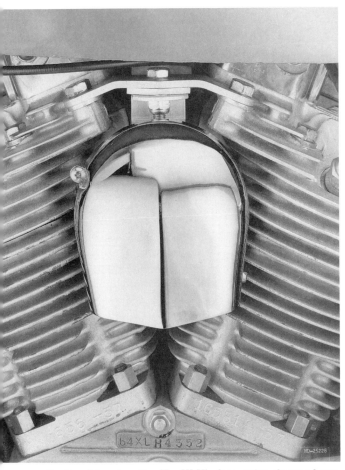

Destined for eternity: The XLH's decorative chrome horn, shown here on a 1964 model, has become the symbol of upgraded, deluxe Sportsters. During the Sportster's history, it suffered an identity crisis. At first, there was a clear definition between the more civilized, luxurious XLH and the almost primitive, basic XLCH. Later, during the seventies, both models shared nearly identical features, to the point that it became difficult to tell an H from a CH. For example, they had the same peanut tank, primary case, and electric starting. Harley-Davidson capitalized on this when the 1986 Evolution was introduced in 1985. To justify the higher price for the XLH-1100 (and later 1200) models, they where adorned with extra chrome and paint. Although the bigger model added only pennies to manufacturing costs, it carried a significant price premium. Blame it on the horn! Harley-Davidson

The 1964 model's front brake had a definite European influence. The original equipment manufacturer (OEM) Firestone and Goodyear tires that were offered, while popular with riders of that era, offered little road grip compared to today's tires. Harley-Davidson

The two-into-one-muffler exhaust system of this 1964 XLH soon gave way to the classic shorty duals that the Sportster wears to this day. The XLCH already wore the duals, and the XLH took a step closer to looking like a XLCH. In fact, the distinctive differences between the H and CH, which made them so easy to tell apart at a glance, gradually disappeared. Harley-Davidson

Michael Parks, who played the title character on the television series Then Came Bronson, giving Buffy Saint Marie a ride on his Sportster during filming of the episode "Mating Dance for Tender Grass." They ride alongside Eddie Blue Sky. The Bronson show aired weekly during 1969 and 1970 for seventy-eight episodes. Parks played a lone drifter who traveled through dusty towns aboard his Sportster. MGM

In 1968, Harley introduced the new crossover-style twin mufflers, which stuck around for three years before reverting back to the shorty duals. This had an interesting effect on weight. Factory literature quoted a 1967 XLCH's weight at only 452lb, while the electric-starting XLH weighed 530lb, a hefty 78lb difference. In 1978 literature, the weight difference between the twin-muffler XLCH and XLH was 452 vs. 508lb, only a 56lb difference.

Countless speed records at the Bonneville salt flats were set with machines powered by the iron engine. Drag race champion Leo Payne, shown during a run in October 1968, was a long-time campaigner of the ferrous-metal XLs, and set many class records. Motorcyclist

Daytona Beach, 1969: The Harley team proudly lines up for a group photo. It was Harley's road racing climax, and the beginning of the end. The team fared well, and Cal Rayborn won the event for the second consecutive year. But the AMA had changed the rules, allowing machines of equal displacement, regardless of the number of cylinders—be they ohv, ohc, or two-strokes—to compete in the same class. Harley adapted what basically, in crude terms, could be described as mounting an iron Sportster top end to the KR cases. The horsepower wasn't there. The next year, 1970, the team proudly lined up for another team photo along the start-finish line, which turned out to be quite ironic. In terms of race results, it might as well have been a firing squad—the glory days were over for Harley-Davidson. The new XR-750 iron engine, using standard Sportster barrels that were shortened 0.30in and highly modified iron heads, proved to be too slow. Gene Romero set fast time (157mph) on a Triumph triple, and Dick Mann won the race on a four-cylinder Honda while the Harley team struggled. When Yamaha fielded its four-cylinder TZ-700, it became the dominant racing force, and four-strokes never challenged it. Harley ran the iron XR for two years and although it turned in disappointing results, the street-based engine provided a good testing base for the future aluminum-alloy XR. And why not? Didn't the same thing happen when the XL replaced the K model? Harley-Davidson

Guy Leaming was the 1969 drag racing champion. Drag racers have always liked the V-twin Harleys because, among other things, the V-twin is relatively free from bore and stroke constraints. Other engine types, with crank throws adjacent to each other, have limitations due to the close proximity of the cylinder bores and heads. John Kinker

Ron Fringer is one of the all-time Top Gas racers who set many records during the seventies. He sometimes teamed with engine builder Warner Riley, using Riley's Bonne- ville motors. A rider, builder, and tuner, Fringer knows how to observe and evaluate the bike, and make the correct changes to get the most performance. John Kinker

Ray Price pioneered the "funny bike" class, which was nothing more than a top-fuel-burning dragster that looks almost streetable. The closest thing to this class today is the Pro Stock gas class. Price was one of those wizards who could get more horsepower than nearly anyone else out of an iron-head XL. John Kinker

Rarely seen, a Sportster in sidecar road racing. This shot was taken at a 1969 American Federation of Motorcyclists (AFM) race at Orange County (California) International Raceway (now a shopping center). The driver is Dean G. Hummer—for whom the H-D Hummer was named—and hanging off is Rulon G. Gulbranson. Mahony

By 1970 the Sportster had become a homologated and legal contender in AMA racing in the form of the original XR-750, with iron barrels and heads. The rules required 200 machines to be manufactured. Although they were alleged to have been made, only about 100 were actually reported sold. The original XR-750 suffered more than a few problems, and had little success. After the alloy XR, introduced two years later, had weathered its development woes, it went on to become a most successful racing motorcycle. It continued the tradition of Harley racers in the spirit of the JD twin-cams, the Peashooter, the WL, and the KR. The XR machines were developed by racing boss Dick O'Brien, who has forever left his signature on Harley's racing heritage. Harley-Davidson

Harley-Davidson's West Coast sales manager, Malcolm Wood (currently southeastern area manager), went to Bonneville Speed Week in August, 1970. He was impressed with the efforts of Harley riders like Leo Payne, Warner Riley and Denis Manning, who were contending and setting Bonneville speed records. When Don Vesco set the ultimate land-speed record for motorcycles of 251.924mph in September, Wood contacted factory people and suggested that with the help of these speed merchants, Harley could take the record. John Davidson, then president, got involved, and so did Harley-Davidson's racing manager, Dick O'Brien.

All of the ingredients to do this were laying around— trouble was, they were laying all over the country. O'Brien phoned Warner Riley, who had just established two new speed records for Sportsters, and asked Riley to supply the engine. O'Brien also contacted Denis Manning, who had built a streamliner that had just been through its shakedown runs at Bonneville in August, and Manning's assistants Craig Rivera and John Yeates. George Smith was asked to provide his fuel expertise, and O'Brien supplied two other Harley factory people, Clyde Denzer and John Pohland. To complete the team, expert road racer

and dirt tracker Cal Rayborn, of Spring Valley, California, was asked to ride the streamliner. Within four weeks, they would have the record.

But not without a fight. Rayborn had his hands full, with engines that were on the edge of exploding each second he kept the throttle open, inside an aluminum tube on wheels that weaved like a drunk. The streamliner crashed and rolled several times during the week-long effort, and the pulverized body looked like a potato chip.

By the time Rayborn coaxed the fatigued and depleted machine across the timing lights in the final run on October 16, 1970, the last engine blew, and there were not enough spares and salvageable pieces for another run. But Rayborn had managed to steer the spooky thing through the speed traps in two consecutive runs in opposite directions for an average speed of 265.492mph. It is the fastest speed a Sportster-powered two-wheeler ever went, anywhere, in any configuration. This record still stands today, over twenty years later.

In the photo, left to right: Pohland, Denzer, Rivera, Riley, Manning, Rayborn, Smith, O'Brien. Yeates took this picture, prior to running the streamliner.

Chapter 2

The One-Liter Sportster, and Beyond

The Sportster, especially the XLCH "Competition Hot" version, was king of the performance hill during the sixties; however, the introduction of larger displacement multicylinder bikes from Japan brought an end to the Sportster's domination. Several significant vehicles marked the turning point. First, in 1969 the Honda CB-750 amazed motorcyclists with its single-overhead-cam, four-cylinder engine. Then the Kawasaki KZ-900 astonished riders with its performance. Even the British got into the act with the Triumph and BSA triples.

Few industries had ever experienced such a technological explosion. Like a chain reaction, all of the Japanese Big Four—Honda, Kawasaki, Suzuki, and Yamaha—introduced newer and better machines. Each raced the other manufacturers to field faster bikes, to sell more of them, to beat them on the racetracks—to be Number One.

Except for the shorty dual exhaust system and seat style obviously influenced by imports, there's no major difference between the look of a 1974 XL-1000 compared to a 1970 55ci model equipped with stacked mufflers. The ignition has been moved inside the cam gear case, which is restyled. The steel safety bead rims and front disc brake set a new standard. Harley-Davidson

And the "little" 883 Sportster? The once brawny, muscular performance leader was left in the dust, literally. So in 1972, Harley-Davidson set out to improve the XL's performance the old-fashioned way, by adding cubic inches. Retaining the stroke established decades before, the bore size was enlarged 0.188 in, to 3.188in. The goal was one liter, or 61ci. Ironically, this was the same displacement as the company's original ohv engine, the 1936 E Knucklehead.

Harley-Davidson typically uses nomenclature to designate a new model or improvement. In this case, the model retained its "XL" letters; however, rather than refer to this model as a 61 (using the American standard) it was called a 1000, using the metric system to designate its 1000cc displacement.

It was rated at 61hp, and its top speed was over 110mph. *Cycle World* magazine road tested a 1972 Sportster and reported a quarter-mile time of 13.38sec at 97.7mph. It reached 60mph in 5.5sec, with a top speed of 116mph. Even with the muffler restrictions required in California that year, the reported mileage was 43mpg.

The magazine focused its attention on the Sportster's traditional problems. The editors pointed out that the new wet clutch was far superior to the dry one, although lever pressure was slightly stiffer. The first three gears were nicely spaced, but the fourth-gear switch presented a big gap, dropping rpm considerably. The new shift drum improved gear-change action. Even with its bare-bones seat, this was the first XL on which the editors could ride for more than 400 miles in one day. And the new oil pump

didn't leak when the bike was parked on its kick stand.

The Sportster showed its age, though. The younger, new-generation motorcycles coming to America from foreign lands had aluminum cylinders and heads. Soon they would mature, sprouting three-valve and four-valve (and eventually five- and eight-valve) cylinder head designs. Three, four, and six cylinders became the norm, and motorcyclists came to expect plastic body parts instead of steel.

The XL, on the other hand, had real steel fenders that the seat bolted directly to, and cylinder heads made of iron. The XL's frame, basically the same as the 1952 K model's, was twenty years old. It used cast-iron lugs at major junctions. Located about mid-arm, the rear shock geometry put the dampers at a disadvantage. Even boasting a big one-liter engine, in 1972—the same year of the double-overhead-cam KZ-900—the Sportster was a technological dinosaur, plodding along among thoroughbred quarter horses.

But the factory continued to upgrade and improve the Sportster, and despite its aging, it continued to sell well. In 1972, the company produced 7,500 XLH and 10,650 XLCH models. Production jumped to a total of 19,960 in 1973, the year in which turn signals became mandatory. Compared to the XL, only 8,775 Electra Glides and 7,625 Super Glides were made. The iron XL may have been archaic, but its was still a tremendous sales success.

For 1973, Harley-Davidson switched to Japanese-made Showa forks with aluminum sliders.

Government regulations began to alter the bare-bones Sportster, however. In 1974, the throttle control

What Harley-Davidson anticipated as a dream turned into a nightmare when riders unanimously rejected the look of the new 1979 model. In a quick-fix move, the factory hung shorty duals on the 1980 model, but the straight-tube frame required a redesign that would not appear in dealer *showrooms until 1982. Many lessons were learned from this and, for better or worse, some Harley corporate leaders still use this as an example to resist any radical attempt at change. Harley-Davidson*

XLCR Cafe Racer

We can't talk about the Sportster Cafe Racer without first discussing the 1971 FX Super Glide. A product of Willie G. Davidson's styling department, the Super Glide resulted from the marriage of the FL chassis and the XL front end.

Although the original FX had boat-tail rear-end treatment, subsequent models featured the Sportster-style rear fender. The Sportster has influenced the big twin family ever since.

WIllie G. talks fondly of the FX: "It was the most important thing I did in twenty years, as far as keeping the company going," he says. "The FX became the foundation of all sport-model big twin Harleys."

The FX was a "Skunk Works" project, completed far away from the hustle and bustle and red tape of the corporate offices. Like the FX, the Cafe Racer was the work of a few people operating in an off-company shop.

Jim Haubert, whose father owned a local machine shop, played a key role. His machine shop became the studio for the entire XLCR project, and he worked with Willie G. and his assistant, Lou Netz. All the pieces remained at his shop until the complete machine was finished.

"Jim had experience in our racing department, and he had a tremendous knowledge of things," says Willie G. "He was an avid motorcyclist, and he could take a clock apart—anything—and make it better. We would go over to Jim's shop every day.

"Our goal was an XR-ish looking Sportster with some of the original FX influence [referring to the original model with bodywork]. I wanted to come up with a departure for the Sportster, something that reflected performance. That's why we developed the exhaust system, with a muffler on each side."

The XLCR was the first production motorcycle to use a black-on-black paint scheme. The exhaust system's high-gloss porcelain finish, along with the other gloss-black paint, contrasted the texture of the engine's wrinkle finish. (Unfortunately, the porcelain was prone to chipping, so only a few rare early-production examples were made. Willie G. owns one.)

Willie G. continues: "We had a young engineer who was running exhaust system tests on the dyno. He came up with the siamese-type system. We spent a lot of time on it, and it added 5hp. It was the most powerful Sportster we ever had."

The Cafe Racer was the first Harley-Davidson to sport the upside-down taillight, something that remains on the sport models to this day.

"No one ever saw the Cafe Racer until we brought it here to show management," says Willie G. "We took it to the State Fair Park, which has a paved half-mile oval, to ride, because it was not a standard sit-up Harley-Davidson. Charlie Thompson and my

The 1979 XLCR is the most collectible of all Cafe Racers. Factory records indicate that nine Cafe Racers were built in 1979. Notice the Ham Can air cleaner, a product of ever-tightening EPA regulations; all 1979 models featured this "bread box." Harley-Davidson

brother John [then-president John Davidson] rode it. It was well liked. They saw it as progress, as a new direction to go. We decided to show it at Daytona."

The XLCR's Daytona debut generated a lot of excitement, and the motorcycle press gave it enthusiastic reports. Production, however, was delayed for nearly a year. The company had begun its efforts to improve quality, and resources were being diverted. By the time production models began to emerge from factory doors a year after its showing, customer anticipation had dwindled.

Jerry Wilke, current Harley-Davidson vice president of sales and marketing, was a district sales manager at the time. "I remember towing a trailer around with two Cafe Racers on it as I visited the dealers in my district. We tried to sell them right off the trailer, but dealer's didn't want 'em," recalls Wilke.

According to factory records, a total of 1,923 XLCRs were made in 1977; 1,201 in 1978; and 9 in 1979, for a total of 3,123. Many of them cluttered dealer showrooms for years, despite rock-bottom prices, and dealers were still trying to get rid of them in the early eighties. It was not unusual to see a 1979 model on a showroom floor in 1982.

Although many Harley-Davidson vice presidents, directors, and managers are enthusiastic about an Evolution Cafe Racer, a modern version has never been given a go-ahead by product planners. Too many management people remember the painful sales experience of the original, and are reluctant to attempt another.

"I think it was too early," says Willie G., "too far ahead of its time. But even so, it remains a cult bike today."

In 1986, Nick Ienatsch (far left), an editor on the staff of Motorcyclist magazine, brought his hand-made Cafe Racer replica to Milwaukee, which was based on a 1986 Evolution Sportster. He had volunteered to leave it in the hands of The Motor Company for a few weeks so that engineers and product planners could evaluate it. A group of Cafe Racer enthusiasts rendezvoused with Ienatsch at Harley's engine and transmission manufacturing plant for a ride to the road races at Road America in Elkhart Lake, Wisconsin. The machines are all variations of the XLCR: There's Ienatsch's Evolution 1200, several XR-1000 conversions, including a couple of factory-looking full-race types, and a few stockers. Yes, the friendly ride turned into a high-speed race, and citations were issued by local law enforcement agencies along the way. From left to right: Ienatsch; unidentified rider; Harley-Davidson vice president Clyde Fessler (with lowered and customized XR-1000); H-D licensing manager Joel Weiss (with XR-1000 customized with XLCR parts); H-D public relations manager John Gaedke (with an ex-racing XR-1000); and artist Mike Davidson and Harley Owners Group (HOG) manager Bill Davidson. Dave Gess was given return springs and cables. By 1975, federal mandates required motorcycles to have common gearshifting, on the left-hand side with a down-for-low pattern. Harley-Davidson fitted the Sportster with a linkage system that ran from the right-hand side, rearward behind the engine, then forward to the left-hand shift lever. Obviously, the brake pedal moved to the right side, operating the rear drum brake by another linkage mechanism, but this was a straight shot from front to rear. In 1977, new cases accommodated the left-side shifting, and the awkward linkage was trashed.

With few changes, the Sportster's sales continued to maintain levels that satisfied management. Disc brakes were added in 1973. The frame was altered in the oil pump area so that the pump could be removed without pulling the engine from the frame.

In 1977, a touring XLT model appeared. It was equipped with saddlebags, windshield, a heavily padded seat, and handlebars to put the rider into a proper touring posture. Its 3.5gal fuel tank, based on the design of the FX's Fat Bob tanks, gave it a useful 150-mile range. It was also equipped with a higher overall top-gear ratio. Most of the XLT's amenities had already been designed and tested long before,

when the company developed XL prototypes for the military and for possible police use (see chapter 1). But despite its practicality, the touring XL never became popular with riders.

When the XLCR first appeared at Daytona in March 1977, it sported a brand-new frame which had a rear area that mimicked the XR-750 racer with rear-set shocks. Its all-new siamese exhaust system, with a muffler on each side of the bike, improved power by about 5hp.

While the XLCR continued production into 1978, the standard XL Sportsters kept their old frames. Both models visually appeared identical, with only subtle differences. They shared the same fuel and oil tank, seat, wheels, gear ratios, and exhaust system. The once powerful image of the XLCH had been diffused, and its super-muscular appearance lost its exclusivity.

Harley-Davidson engineers busied themselves with the task of bringing the Sportster into the modern era. All XL models were to get the XLCR's new frame and power-improving exhaust system, which they did in 1979. The frame was a tremendous improvement. The swing-arm geometry was, well, modern. The straight-frame tubes followed the load

A rare sight: an exhaust pipe and muffler on the left-hand side of an XL. This is the 1979 Roadster, with upgraded features and styling patterned after the Low Rider. Despite the fact that the split exhaust improved power dramatically, riders never appreciated the header. In fact, it was common practice among dealers to remove the standard siamese system and install shorty duals or aftermarket systems on new bikes before putting them on the sales floor. For years afterward, dozens of siamese systems hung from the rafters of dealers' attics and back rooms. Harley-Davidson

paths, which helped make it stiffer. There was even ample room for the oil tank and battery. The modernized Sportster was a great engineering achievement.

It was also a marketing disaster. Riders and dealers alike complained that it looked too "foreign," with its straight-frame tubes and side panels. After all, you couldn't see all the parts that made up the whole. Even the exhaust system's name, that of a cat originating in the Orient, turned off the All-American Faithful.

Pity the bewildered Harley-Davidson management, who were ambushed. Years of development perceived as "improvement" went down the tubes. Corporate officers immediately ordered engineers and Willie G. Davidson's styling people to retreat to the drawing room.

Although seemingly a disastrous situation, it did bring long-term benefits. The company had learned an important lesson: Thou shalt not mimic the competition. The sudden unpopularity of the Sportster, combined with the flat-line marketing charts of Cafe Racer sales, all added up to one thing for Harley-Davidson management: radical change is dangerous. From that day on, Harley has embraced its heritage,

and eschewed swift and dramatic changes. Meanwhile, Harley-Davidson engineers discovered a temporary solution: the right side panel was restyled to expose the battery on 1980 and 1981 models.

A special seventy-fifth anniversary edition of the Sportster was announced in 1978, replete with custom paint and limited-edition status. Dealers were encouraged to hold open houses. A spec sheet reported the Sportster's fourteen new features, explaining the benefits of each. The company wanted to position itself to compete with the Japanese companies, which were importing record numbers of heavyweight motorcycles.

The cast wheel option, introduced in 1978, continued in 1979 and beyond. There was no XLT model for 1979, however, and the touring version has not been produced since. The kick starter was dropped, and in its place was a new brake master cylinder. Now the XL had discs front and rear.

Several other important changes occurred in 1979. The new XLS model appeared, with upgraded features and styling patterned after the Low Rider. The XLS, even with its XLCR-style frame, was a step forward for Harley-Davidson. It evolved into a machine with a completely different identity than the standard model.

Based on the XLH, the XLS was a natural extension of the Super Glide, Low Rider, and Sportster style. Its fork legs were extended 2in, and with its flat, drag-style handlebar mounted on 3.5in risers, it continued the sharp-edged custom tradition that Harley-Davidson had been honing over the years. It

A matter of style: different handlebar shapes influence rider comfort. Some riders get cramps and fatigue with one type and not the other, while the reverse may true of other riders. The Buckhorn-style handlebar has long been the favorite of Harley riders; however, the flat dragster bar, seen here on a 1979 Roadster, is preferred by other riders. There's enough demand for each to keep them both in production, and today, you can fit whatever style suits you on any Sportster model. Harley-Davidson came with a two-tone paint scheme, sissy bar with a leather stash pouch, and a fat-section 16in rear tire.

The fat tire contributed to the bike's intended look: heavy rear end and light front end. This design clearly differentiated it from the XLH, which retained its 18in rear wheel. It lasted only one year, however, because in 1980 the XLH got the 16in wheel also.

Despite its lengthened legs and 60in wheelbase, the XLS' seat height was only 29in. It weighed in at 515lb with its 2.25gal fuel tank, the lightest electric-start Sportster in years. This was due to the new, lighter frame.

The company produced only 141 XLCH models in 1979. As mentioned earlier, the once-distinctive identity of the CH had dissipated. In its place was the 1980 XLS, now named Roadster through a national contest. The 1980 Roadster got the Super Glide's 3.3gal fuel tank, which helped to distinguish it from the standard XLH. At first glance, the Roadster appeared more like a big twin than its siblings.

Meanwhile, Harley-Davidson powertrain engineers busied themselves with the Evolution program, while the XL chassis group put the finishing touches on the new frame. In June 1981 the new frame was rolled out for the media at the York, Pennsylvania, final-assembly plant, in the midst of a media circus that hyped the buy-back from AMF.

Although the Evolution engine occupied Harley-Davidson's powertrain engineering department during the early 1980s, much of Harley's engineering resources were being spent on emissions research. In fact, about a quarter of working hours in 1982 were invested in meeting ever-tightening regulations. The company understood that its corporate future lay in the new, improved powerplant that was being designed to cope with proposed EPA emissions regulations.

One of the effects of the heightened environmental consciousness that grew out of the seventies was the varying qualities of gasoline available. Oil companies were constantly changing their formulation (something they have continued to do for years). Gasoline octane ratings dropped severely. Chevron had long offered its White Pump fuel, a 100 plus octane gas that allowed high compression ratios in inefficient engines. It and other high tests with ethyl were eventually withdrawn, to be replaced with low-octane, low-lead, and no-lead fuels. As a result, Harley-Davidson engineers, as well as Detroit companies, have been hard pressed to keep pace.

So it was no surprise that 1982 model Sportsters wore thicker head gaskets, lowering compression from 9.0 to 8.8:1. The motorcycle magazines that tested the 1982 and 1983 models were getting to the

Except for its engine, the 1983 XLX-61 looks just like the later Evolution 883. Harley-Davidson

quarter-mile lights in about 14.2sec, nearly a full second slower than the 883 of ten years prior. Top speed was about 100mph.

In 1983, the essence of the bare-bones XLCH was reincarnated in the XLX-61. Interestingly, in an apparent defiant display of independence, the factory dropped the metric 1000 name. Ironically, when the Evolution came along a few years later, the metric label returned.

The XLX was positioned perfectly for the market. The factory had noticed that as the Sportster exceeded the $4,000 retail price mark, sales seemed to drop. Apparently, the Sportster buyer was very price conscious. What the bean counters discovered over the next few years was that the $4,000 price barrier was critical. This lesson was later applied to the Evolution XLs.

As brilliant a move as the XLX was, it appeared to come at an awkward time. Dealers already had a surplus of carry-over models, some as old as 1979! The motorcycle market was softening, and new-bike sales were beginning an ever-increasing downward spiral—a trend that would continue for the foreign manufacturers throughout the decade. Although the XLX promised to move new bikes, from the dealers' viewpoint, it didn't help clear out the old models.

As it turned out, 1982 proved to be the bottom for Harley-Davidson. Sales actually increased in 1983.

Factory management may have wondered if t. a one-year fluke. After all, indicators pointe major slump. Worse yet, the Japanese were bri in massive quantities of motorcycles, which thr ened to weaken Harley's position.

As you know, those worrisome early years for The Motor Company were rewarded. The overall new-bike market did, indeed, nose-dive. But, as amazing as it seemed—especially in those desperate times—Harley's sales actually increased . . . again and again each year!

Like the Battle of Midway was during World War II, Harley's performance in the marketplace in 1983 proved to be the turning point. It was a year that brought exciting changes and new models. The XLX-61 appeared; the XLS got the Fat Bob-style fuel tank; the XR-1000 was introduced; and in the big-twin world, the rubber-mount FXRS gained acceptance.

As rosy as this picture may seem, Harley-Davidson suffered cash-flow problems. Harley-Davidson dealers wanted to spend money only in the spring and not the fall, but the bankers wanted the payments on their loans year-round. Harley-Davidson generated some tricky schemes to keep the dealers' cash flowing, but still needed products with high profit margins.

One approach to achieving a high profit margin while guaranteeing to move units was to produce

The 1983 XLS Roadster evolved into a Low Rider-styled machine, one that eventually began to gain acceptance before the factory canceled it. Harley-Davidson

The XR-1000: More than a Machine

In June of 1981 "The Eagle Soared," and Harley-Davidson broke away from AMF. A struggle for survival followed.

Sportster sales had been dwindling for several years. In 1982 XL production had been cut in half, to less than 8,000 units. even counting about 1,700 anniversary editions. Worse, sales had plummeted to less than 4,000 units, leaving thousands of unsold vehicles in the pipeline.

This alarmed corporate management, who understood that the XL traditionally had been a strong seller, sometimes accounting for more sales than all other models combined! For some corporate insiders, the downward trend in sales was the beginning of the end, predicting the death of the Sportster.

Consequently, the need to boost Sportster sales, and especially profits, was vitally important to Harley-Davidson at this time. For Clyde Fessler, then marketing director and later sales manager, this meant that he needed to find a way to get more Sportsters out on the street. He considered the strategy of creating a new model that appealed to a nontraditional market niche.

Engineering and styling resources were limited, however. Harley-Davidson was focusing on rebuilding the company and improving quality. In addition, the engineers had their hands full with the Evolution engine design and development programs. Whatever Fessler produced, it had to be put together very quickly, and with a minimum of resources.

Fessler had been traveling to motorcycle rallies and races throughout the country. He noticed that riders were commenting about street-legal XR-750s. "At every race," he says, "a rider would come up to me and say something like, 'Boy, I wish I could buy an XR for the street!'"

There was another reason for building an XR-engined street bike: Battle of the Twins racing. A competitive machine was needed to go up against the Ducatis and BMWs in the GP class because the iron-head XL could not complete.

Fessler got together with racing manager Dick O'Brien and asked what it would take to make an XR road legal. They began brainstorming, and came up with the idea to make the XR-750 street legal by adding an electrical and starting system. But the XR, designed for thirty-minute dirt-track races, used a total-loss battery ignition and had to be bump-started. There were no provisions for kick starting or charging a battery. After analyzing the idea, they realized that tooling costs and engineering demands were prohibitive, especially considering the relatively low projected sales volume.

The XR-1000 was as stripped as the XLX-61 was but more powerful than any previous Sportster. Harley-Davidson

"That didn't stop us," says Fessler. "We figured that rather than making the XR street legal, we could 'XR-ize' the standard XL."

Either way, they were left with the prospect of reproducing racing-type cylinder heads in relatively high volume. Contracting with an outside vendor took the load off factory resources. Jerry Branch, a long-time racing tuner and cylinder head expert, solved that dilemma. The cylinders had to be shortened a half inch to squeeze the tall heads under the top frame tube, which required a new connecting rod and piston. Other than that, it was a piece of cake.

Meanwhile, as Fessler points out, Harley-Davidson employees had been experiencing bad times. Sales were down, dealers were complaining, and the banks applied relentless pressure on management. In short, this was a dismal time for everyone at Harley-Davidson.

But, the XR-1000 was a ray of hope.

"I remember the first day they pulled it out of the test lab," says Fessler. "A test engineer revved the engine and took off. People were hanging out the windows, and there was a super energy level. When I came back inside, there was electricity in the air. People were saying, 'Hey, now we're doing something!' It was highly motivational."

Today, the consensus of Harley-Davidson enthusiasts is that the company *didn't* do it right, that the XR-1000 should have been styled as a racing XR-750 or a Cafe Racer. But does that mean it was a failure? As a vehicle, it was a disaster. Although it's the most powerful production Sportster ever made—at a claimed 70hp it was more powerful than the iron-head XR-750—compared to the performance level offered by foreign machines, the XR is nothing but "a sheep in wolf's clothing." It's not comfortable to ride, the engine sounds like it's grinding rocks, and with a 2gal fuel supply it has a range that couldn't get it outside a major metropolitan area without refueling.

Success can be measured in a number of ways, however. As a marketing product it achieved its objectives, although it took more than two years. But Harley-Davidson was more interested in profit margins, and the XR's margin brought in substantial revenue. On the other hand, the XLX-61, introduced at a retail price of $3,995 in 1982, did not enjoy a good margin; despite sales numbers, it never generated the revenues of the XR-1000.

But the XR-1000, perhaps more than any motorcycle of its era, did something very important. It boosted morale. To factory workers, dealers, and customers who saw the Harley-Davidson world crumbling, the XR plugged a hole in the dike.

History will show that despite its shortcomings and disappointments, the XR-1000 stands as a symbol of the Harley-Davidson legacy. It was created by determined, gutsy people who struggled under constraints in a difficult situation. In the end, they produced a machine that stands as one of the company's greatest achievements.

The XR-1000's exhaust exited through two high pipes on the left side of the bike. Harley-Davidson

special editions. Unique models were developed to commemorate special events, such as the Sportster's Twenty-Fifth Anniversary in 1982. Buyers were willing to pay an incremental price for these exclusive machines. A limited number of orange-and-black Milwaukee Edition models was also offered. The practice of generating special editions proved so successful that it continues to this day.

The XR-1000 represented another approach to higher profit margins. It was developed through what could be described as a grass-roots effort by a small number of people. Normally it's the big twins that bring in the higher profits, but the XR-1000's $7,000 price tag guaranteed incremental profit margins unrivaled by other models.

Several prototype XR-style street bikes were looked at during the seventies, but could never be justified due to limited market appeal. The reason the XR-1000 was so profitable was because it was put together with limited resources. *Cycle World* reported the XR's quarter-mile elapsed time of 12.88sec, the quickest Sportster ever and the first to break into the 12sec bracket. To get that kind of power, buyers had to ante up $3,000 more than for an XLX.

The XR shared the XLX's satin-textured engine cases, but the XLH and XLS had polished cases. The XR got the satin-textured case to maintain a race-bike

appearance. But the XLX, which was intended to present a bare-bones look, got the surface treatment to help distinguish it from its upscale counterparts that commanded a higher price. The XLH's 3gal fuel tank made its brief appearance, only to disappear the next year.

Mechanically, 1984 changes included a diaphragm spring clutch. Harley's powertrain engineer, John Favill, had formerly worked for AJS and Norton where he designed the first motorcycle diaphragm spring clutch on the AJS 250, and later for the Norton Commando. Applying his considerable experience, the external generator was replaced by an alternator contained inside the primary-drive case, behind the clutch basket. The diaphragm spring reduced clutch lever pressure considerably.

Externally, 1984 XLHs got the little peanut tank back, and the XLX and XLS chugged along without major changes. A larger diameter single disc front brake replaced the twin disc brake system in 1984.

Because the Evolution Sportster program was expected to be completed for the 1986 model year, no major changes were incorporated in the 1985 Sportsters. All models, however, received the Allied Industrial Workers of America and International Association of Machinists and Aerospace Machinists (AIW and IAM) union labels. The unions' seal of approval

The XLH sported the 3.3gal tank that appeared on an earlier Roadster, but it met with lukewarm approval.

Since the 1986 Evolution, no Sportster has worn a large tank. Harley-Davidson

symbolized their reassurance to consumers that the workers who built them put their confidence in the products.

Harley-Davidson planners deliberately trimmed back production of 1985 models in anticipation of an early Evolution XL introduction.

Evolution Sportster

Major development work on the all-new Sportster engine, with aluminum-alloy cylinders and heads, began in 1978. Harley-Davidson management was

Clear lineage: Except for its distinctive Blockhead rocker boxes and chromed exhaust pipes, the 1986 Evolution XLH-883 is a carbon copy of the 1983 XLX-61—and both shared the same $3,995 price tag. After three years, the company announced a price increase for the XLH-883: It would be raised from $3,995 to $3,999, a total of $4. As of the 1993 model year, the basic XLH-883 was priced at $4,775. Harley-Davidson

Although Harley-Davidson had the opportunity to completely reshape the exterior of the Evolution Sportster engine, the marketing and styling departments agreed to retain the engine's traditional outward appearance. They used the 1340's cylinder shape to help commonize tooling, which improves manufacturing efficiency, but the rocker box shape was changed to help give the XL its own identity. Harley-Davidson

Although the Evolution frame was based on the 1982 frame, there were significant enough differences to prevent retrofitting a few of the pre-1986 accessories and parts, such as fuel tanks. The Evolution had a new upper forward engine mount, although the rear bracket remained unchanged. The backbone in the seat area was revised so that the rear cylinder could be removed without removing the engine from the frame, allowing more convenient top-end work. Most important, beginning with the 1986 XLH-883, Harley-Davidson frames received the new powdercoat finish. This dry charged-particle process, which involves baking the parts in an oven, produces a finish so durable that you can (practically) hit it with a hammer without chipping.

From a rider's viewpoint, the XLH-883's speedometer-only single-instrument cluster harkens back to the bare-bones Sportster of yesteryear. The 1986 models had lock-down turn signal switches. So many riders complained about them that the factory dropped them the next year. The front turn lights doubled as running lights, a feature introduced on the 1986 XLH-883 and that remains today. Harley-Davidson

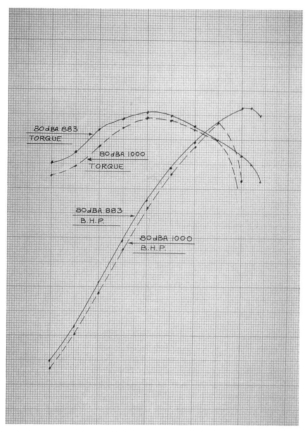

80dBA 883 TORQUE

80dBA 1000 TORQUE

80dBA 883 B.H.P.

80dBA 1000 B.H.P.

In an undimensioned engineering chart, the factory demonstrated that the new, smaller 55ci engine actually produced more power than the old, larger 61ci iron head. This comparison was made with each engine equipped for an 80dBA noise level rating. Harley-Davidson

only too aware that the iron Sportster was a dinosaur living in a modern era.

The original Evolution program called for the simultaneous development of both the XL and the big twin powerplants. By January 1981, both programs passed through the design stage and entered the prototype phase. Resources were strained, however. Considering the immense task of completely re-designing both existing powerplants, and the ongoing quality improvement efforts, the engineering department's work load and that of its support groups was overwhelming.

This was also at the time when AMF agreed to sell its motorcycle division to a group of investors. The new management group realized the importance of the Evolution projects. The new Harley-Davidson Motor Company, with its highly leveraged finances, could not afford a mistake. They were betting the farm on this project, and a mistake would spell death to America's last motorcycle manufacturer, as well as the financial futures of the investors.

The Evolution Sportster endured other pressures as well. The company's cash flow was in critical condition: bankers and investors alike hounded management for prompt payment. Workers feared the so-called Black Fridays, when massive numbers arrived at work to find a "pink slip" informing them of a layoff. Programs had to be slashed to operate the business within parameters that were acceptable to the bankers.

As a result, after the buy-out in 1981 the Evolution Sportster project was shelved while all engineering resources were concentrated on the big twin. The "New Motor Company" made a new commitment to

The 883 was a preintroductory model, meaning that it preceded Harley's regular 1986 model introduction. Once introduced, the XLH-1100 joined the full line and remained an 1100 for two years before Harley-Davidson enlarged it to 1200cc. Engineers were concerned about the cylinder wall thickness, which they felt needed to be increased for a 1200. They were also concerned about—guess what!—the gearbox, which was near its power-handling limits. Harley-Davidson

quality—a drive that had its origins five years earlier —and invested in improving all phases of marketing, manufacturing, and engineering.

Harley's recommitment to quality included the development of a computer program for designing valve gears; it had an enormous impact on the Evolution engines' overall development. This newly developed software program which mathematically modeled the valve gear dynamics helped engineers to analyze the destructive forces in the valvetrain. Using simultaneous studies of lab testing and computer modeling, engineers learned to predict valve dynamics. After nearly a dozen versions of the 1340 cam and valve gear combinations, by mid-1983 the 1340cc Evolution engine was ready for production.

After launching the 1340cc Evolution big twin, engineering efforts quickly shifted to the Sportster Evolution program in early 1984. The refined valve dynamics software allowed engineers to predict and control the Sportster's valvetrain dynamics. Bill Erdman, a Sportster program engineer, remembers it well.

"We were able to hit our target quicker," says Erdman, "based on the previous development work on the 1340. With our slick computer program, we finalized the XL valvetrain after only three iterations."

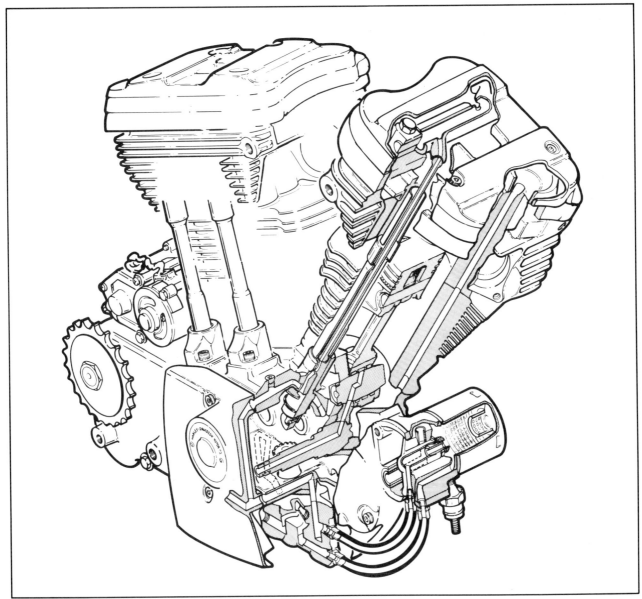

The Evolution's oil system was completely redesigned. While the previous system filtered the oil before returning it to the tank, the Evolution's delivers oil from the sump, through the filter to the engine, then siphons it back to the tank. Feed capacity is 50 percent higher, mainly to feed the hydraulic valve lifters. For the 1990 five-speed, the return routes from the rocker boxes were again altered. Drawing by Harley-Davidson; photo courtesy Joe Ford

Other areas that benefited from the Evolution big twin program were pistons, rings, lifters, cylinders, and heads. But the Sportster faced its own challenges. Environmental Protection Agency regulations were tougher than before, and Harley-Davidson found itself devoting one out of every four engineering work hours to the effort to reduce noise and exhaust emissions.

With a train of five gears, controlling tolerance build-up in the cam gear case became a major obsession. Normal manufacturing tolerances can cause excessive backlash between the cam gears. During a study on the problem, Harley-Davidson engineers placed a miniature microphone inside the case to monitor the noise. With the aid of Mister Mic, as they called it, they came to a solution. Installed inside the cam gear case at various locations, the tiny mic aided engineers in detecting and solving noise emission sources.

Other efforts were made to reduce noise. One change was to shorten the connecting rods by 0.50in. One of the reasons for this was valve cover clearance in the Sportster frame. The three-tiered cover needed a little extra space so that mechanics could remove the heads and cylinders without removing the engine from the frame. A shorter engine height was essential to take advantage of what was seen as a major benefit of the Evolution program.

The people charged with creating the Evolution Sportster engine faced challenging directives. In keeping with the company's new-found search for quality, the Evolution Sportster had to be improved in every way. But there were other parameter's that

complicated the picture: In addition to improvements, it also had to carry a price tag of $3,995. That was $700 less than the existing iron model.

The $4,000 retail price was important for many reasons. Historically, as the price of a Sportster rose above the $4,000 mark, the number of Sportsters sold was reduced dramatically. A lower price meant more sales. Second, from a psychological aspect, a price tag under $4,000 would give the company, its dealers, and its customers a badly needed morale boost. Product quality had reached an all-time low during the late seventies, and although the company had steadily improved quality during the eighties, sales continued on a downward spiral.

One other not-so-minor issue emerged during the International Trade Commission hearings in the fall of 1982. In order to impose a tariff on foreign motorcycles the company had to prove that progress was being made to both upgrade the quality of existing models, and to develop a marketable new product line. Once the tariffs were imposed by President Ronald Reagan the company needed some hard evidence, like a $3,995 price tag on a new, improved Sportster.

As Don Valentine, Harley's chief powertrain engineer, says, "The $3,995 price tag was as much an engineering objective as were the latest improvements in pistons, cylinders, valve gear heads, and crankshaft. A low price is a consumer benefit, just like hydraulic lifters."

The low price put pressure on everyone, and nobody applied the pressure more than vice president Pete Profumo. At program review meetings,

A new oil pump provided increased oil supply to the new hydraulic lifters. The return side (left) has 50 percent greater capacity than the delivery side. Although the self-adjusting hydraulic lifters are a major consumer benefit, the oiling requirements of the lifters provide a major problem for high performance. Feeding 50 percent more oil into the system requires drawing more out of the sump. While not a problem for street riding, at sustained high speeds the sump tends to fill up with excess oil, causing internal drag and power loss. Joe Ford

Profumo repeatedly refused to authorize any change until "the numbers" (a financial analysis) were refined. In one instance, when faced with a $7.44 cost penalty for a component, he asked how much of the price was estimated and how much of it was really known. He requested an explanation and further investigation. Through his relentless haggling, Profumo demonstrated that he certainly understood the objective, and he made sure no one else forgot.

The 883cc displacement was chosen for several reasons. The smaller displacement meant less insurance for the owner, making it more affordable. That was in keeping with the original $3,995 objective: to make it affordable for the buyer. Also, returning to the original displacement (and bore and stroke, for that matter) was viewed as a means of capitalizing on the Sportster's legacy.

The design objectives were to incorporate low-maintenance features and new technology, such as the newest in pistons, valve gear, and combustion chambers, in a package that would meet current and proposed EPA noise and exhaust emission regulations. Another primary goal was to make servicing easier, and to double the recommended service interval, from 2,500 to 5,000 miles.

The 883cc engine also had to embody the essence of Sportster styling. Essentially, the engineers left most exterior elements untouched, while they gutted the interior to install new technology. Of the 426 parts in the Evolution Sportster engine, 206 were totally new. The new Evolution engine had twenty-nine fewer parts (including fasteners) than the iron engine.

Compared to the iron XL-1000 it replaced, the Evolution XL-883 was mechanically quieter, cooler running, more durable, less polluting, and required lower maintenance. With new hydraulic lifters and electronic ignition, the only major engine-related service task was to clean the air cleaner.

The Evolution's oil system was completely redesigned as well. The previous system filtered the oil before returning it to the oil tank. The Evolution engine delivers oil from the tank, through the filter to the engine, then it is pumped back to the tank. Oil flow is 50 percent higher, mainly to feed the hydraulic valve lifters.

The Evolution Sportster cams, like the 1340cc Evolution lobes, feature the polynomial COMPUCAM design. The cam profiles were developed using a computer-aided design program to model valvetrain dynamics. The design closely matched port velocities to efficiently fill the cylinders despite the relatively short valve opening and overlap durations. Joe Ford

Although the self-adjusting hydraulic lifters are a major consumer benefit, the oiling requirements of the lifters present a major problem for high performance. Feeding 50 percent more oil into the system requires drawing more out of the sump. While not a problem at low engine speeds, at sustained high speeds the sump tends to fill up with excess oil, which causes internal drag and a loss of power. (More on this in later chapters.)

By the time the Evolution XLH-883 Sportster was introduced in the summer of 1985, more than 276,000 Sportsters had rolled out of the factory's doors. That's more than a half-million iron cylinders and heads. The aluminum update was long overdue.

In the entire history of the Sportster, this was its biggest redesign since the original XL of 1957 (it certainly could be argued that it was the biggest ever). Like the original, the Evolution benefited from years of prior-model development. The Evolution's

chassis, introduced four years earlier, had proven to be an excellent handler. Just as the Model K passed along its well-proven and well-developed foundation, so too would the iron XL.

Thankfully, there was one thing the alloy XL did not inherit from its iron predecessor: weight. At 466lb, the XLH 1100 was one of the lightest electric-start Sportsters ever to roll out of Harley's doors.

Evolution of the Evolution

As mentioned earlier, the Evolution 883cc Sportster was premiered several months in advance of the regular 1986 model introduction. The XLH-1100, with its larger 3.35in bore, came along with the other 1986 Harley-Davidson models in the fall of 1985. To justify a higher retail price, the bigger XL was gussied up with chrome trim and two-tone paint. Twenty-eight percent of the 1986 Sportsters—4,041 units—were 1100s. A total of 10,348 XLH-883 models were made. In

Harley-Davidson design engineers worked closely with manufacturing engineers and managers to develop a system for reducing or controlling gear lash in the cam gear case. The objective was to quell noise emissions to comply with EPA regulations. To accomplish this, an elaborate process was developed to match gears to individual cases. The temperature of the cam cover and gears is held constant during the matching process. After measuring the case's cam-to-cam running centers in a controlled environment of 68–70deg Fahrenheit, the data are fed to a computer to pick the correct gears for the case. This preassembly selection process ensures exact fit between each gear. Joe Ford

addition, 954 Liberty Edition XLH-1100s were produced. This was part of a fund raising program for the 200th anniversary of the Statue of Liberty and Ellis Island. For each Liberty Edition sold, Harley-Davidson donated $100 to the restoration fund.

An upgraded Deluxe model was also among the 1986 line-up. This was essentially a two-seater with passenger footpegs, wire wheels, and steel rims. It accounted for only about 16 percent of Sportster production.

The Sportster celebrated its 30th anniversary in 1987. Per Harley-Davidson practice, an Anniversary Edition XLH-1100 was created. These were sequentially numbered limited edition models. The factory planned to build only 650 of them, and released a certificate to each owner indicating the sequence of each machine within the run of 650 (number 381 of 650, for example). However, according to factory records, a total of only 600 were actually made, making this an even more collectible machine.

At mid-year, a lowered Sportster model appeared, dubbed Hugger. This was designed to appeal to riders who wanted a lower seat height. Evaluations and rider feedback had determined that most riders (including large numbers of women) preferred the buckhorn-style handlebar, so that became a major feature. Harley was careful not to position the new machine as a "woman's bike," although appealing to women was a major motivator. The Hugger's advertising only stressed the low seat height, for fear of losing sales to men.

To get the seat lower, the fork tubes were shortened two inches. The swing arm was lengthened, with the axle slots located 0.50in rearward, which changed the rear shock geometry. In addition, engineers had discovered that a loose-fitting seat cover allowed the foam cushion material to displace in a way that effectively lowered the rider another 0.75in, while improving long-term comfort. The overall result was a seat height 1.75-in lower than the standard XLs, at 26.75-in.

The Hugger was a big success, and despite its mid-year introduction, accounted for 22.5 percent of all 1987 XLH-883s—only a few units short of the Deluxe model's total of 2,260 units.

For 1988, new 39mm fork tubes replaced the older 35mm tubes. Harley makes the upper and lower fork triple crowns, so only the inner and outer tube

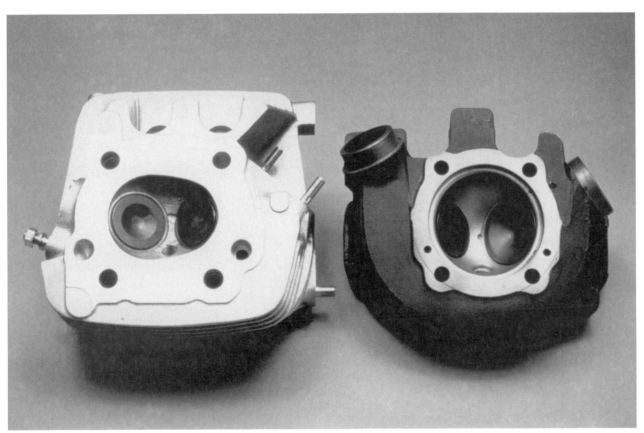

The Evolution 883cc Sportster's unique bathtub-shaped combustion chamber (left) contrasts markedly with the iron Sportster's hemispherical combustion chamber. While the 1340 combustion chamber was designed with the aid of Detroit-based consultants, the 883 head was designed exclusively by Harley-Davidson engineers. Decreasing the included valve angle helped to lower the roof of the Sportster's combustion chamber, which improved combustion efficiency. Joe Ford

assembly came from the Showa suspension company in Japan. The new fork not only added stiffness, but its design was more contemporary. It could be assembled more efficiently at the factory, and it offered easier maintenance for the owner.

Other 1988 changes included an enricher circuit in the new 40mm carburetor, which helped to improve throttle response and to reduce lean stumbling. The 1988 models also featured two rear-view mirrors as standard equipment for the first time in Harley history.

The kickstand on Evolution Sportsters presented a bit of a problem when trying to raise it while seated. It was located so far forward that even a tall rider had to exercise a bit of contortion. This was finally resolved in the 1989 model year, when it was repositioned rearward. Also for 1989, although hardly noticed, was a price increase of the basic XLH-883, from $3,995 to a whopping $3,999. For four years, the price of an entry-level Harley had remained below $4,000. This was a cause of great frustration for the importers of Japanese-made motorcycles at the time, which faced a depreciating dollar.

Except for a new paper air filter and paint options, the 1990 Sportsters did not change. Part of the reason is that engineers were busying themselves with the new five-speed gearbox, among other things,

to be introduced in 1991. The lack of significant upgrades had no affect on sales. Another 15,163 units rolled out of York during the 1990 model year, of which 70 percent were 883s.

The four-speed gearbox with its flat shifter plate disappeared in 1991, replaced with a more contemporary drum-type shifter and five speeds. In attempts to commonize production as well as improve shift action, the new shifter mechanism and transmission gears were similar to the Big Twin types. The newsstand publications that road tested the 1991 models were unanimous in their praise of their slick shifting operation.

Another important upgrade for the XLH-883 Deluxe and XLH-1200 models was the addition of Gates Polychain belt final drive. A belt-drive kit had been offered by Harley-Davidson Parts and Accessories. In addition, both the standard and Hugger models boasted new O-ring chains.

To take advantage of the XLH-1200's additional power output, its primary drive ratio was changed from 1.735:1 to 1.600:1, by using 35/56 sprockets in place of 34/59 sprockets. This lowered engine speeds by about 8 percent at equivalent road speeds.

There were many other changes for 1991. The hydraulic lifters were replaced with automotive type units, and the oil pump was given internally cast feed

Exterior of Evolution and iron Sportster cylinder heads. Even in a photo, the Evolution head's (left) decreased valve angle is evident. Joe Ford

lines. The breather system included new umbrella valves in the rocker boxes to vent directly into the air cleaner, eliminating the vent hose from the gear cover. The alternator was moved from behind the clutch to the crankshaft, which improved its output at low engine speeds. Oil inspection plugs were changed from screw-in types with the "Chevrolet bow tie"-looking tool sockets to plugs secured with two small flush screws. The rider footrest mounts were changed to accept the rubber-isolated type used on Big Twin FXRs. And finally, the old Dunlop K-291 tires were replaced with new style K402s.

This last change was quite significant. Harley-Davidson engineers worked closely with Dunlop tire engineers to develop matched sets of tires specifically for Harley-Davidsons. The K-291 is a fine tire, but the newer 402s offer the improved wear qualities of a high-mileage touring tire, combined with the high-performance characteristics of a more sporting tire.

They retrofit previous model Sportsters, as long as they are fitted as a set (it is not advisable to mix a 291 with a 402).

The only big news for 1992 was a lower-than-low Hugger. Harley-Davidson engineers found a way to bring the seat height even closer to the ground. They did this by reducing suspension travel and by reshaping the seat. This brought the ride height to 26in.

Belt drive came to all Sportsters, with the addition of the Gates Polychain, on the 1993 standard XLH-883 and Hugger models. For a high-performance Sportster, this is a mixed blessing. The belt system does provide advantages in reduced maintenance,

Harley's patented tiered rocker box assembly allows the entire top end to be removed while the engine is in the frame. Although this creates extra mating surfaces, thanks to improved quality, it does not pose the oil-leakage problems it would have ten years earlier. Joe Ford

XLH 883 Sportster® Hugger™

XLH 1200 Sportster®

You can compare any of the latest Sportsters—like these 1991 five-speeds—with any other model year and still see a family resemblance. In the midst of rapid change, some things never change, and that can be a good thing. Harley-Davidson

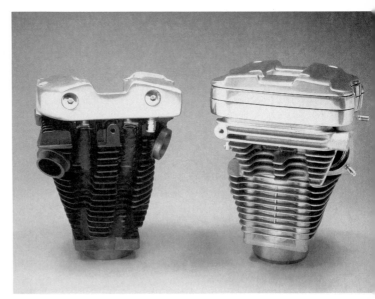

Sportster cylinders (right) incorporated Evolution-big-twin technology. The iron liner is cast into the aluminum-alloy cylinder and held fast by knurled ridges called Spiney-Lok. Joe Ford

wear, noise emission, and improved smoothness; but it also includes some compromises, most notably increased rear wheel unsprung weight and limited gearing options. It is ironic that for several years, many Sportster riders had been installing after-market belt kits; now the high-performance rider will be considering the installation of chain and sprockets.

Production figures show that as of the end of the 1991 model year, Harley-Davidson manufactured 94,755 Evolution Sportsters. Of these, seven out of ten were 883cc models (65,914), while the balance com-

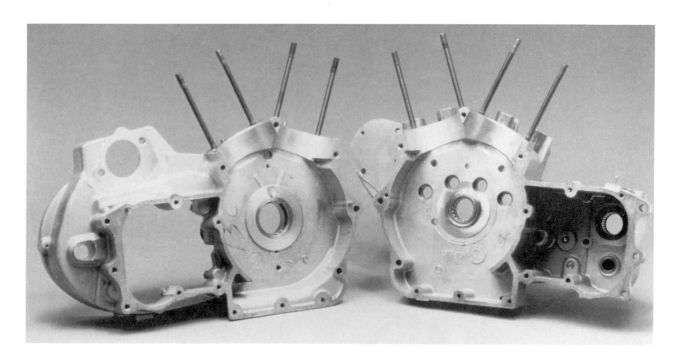

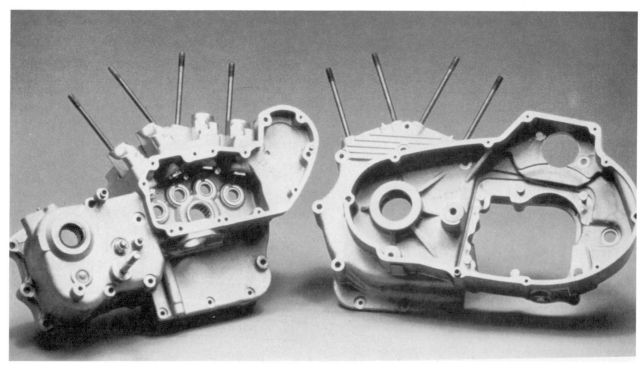

The Evolution Sportster's central crankcase halves were totally new to incorporate hydraulic lifters and a new camshaft gear train. Although the cases were completely reengineered, it's obvious that the designers did not veer too far from the original. Joe Ford

prised 1100cc and 1200cc models. During these six years, Evolution Sportsters comprised 21.3 percent of all Evolution production.

Evolution Production Line

In October 1991, Harley-Davidson designed and installed an all-new assembly line dedicated exclusively to build Sportster engines. The goals were to expand overall factory efficiency. Once the decision was made in October, a new extension was added to the building, and the computer system was installed. Only three months later, the first engine came off the line, on January 2, 1992.

The output of the twenty-one-station line, located adjacent to the 1340cc engine line, can be varied. It can be expanded to forty-one stations, which would double capacity to a maximum of about 600 units per day, or 30,000 annually. All line operations are monitored and controlled by the computer system.

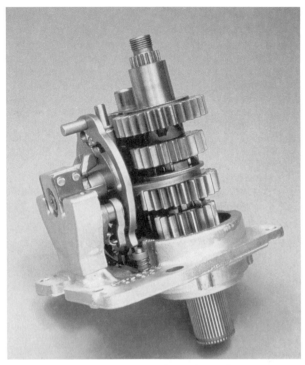

Harley-Davidson engineers tightened up tolerances in the Evolution Sportster's shifting mechanism. The entire gearbox benefited from Harley-Davidson's new gear manufacturing equipment. The company continues to heat treat its gears at the Capitol Drive engine and transmission plant in Wauwatosa, Wisconsin. Joe Ford

The 883's connecting rods contributed to the Evolution's easy maintenance. They were 0.50in shorter than the XL-1000 rods, which helped keep the heads under the top frame tube. The forged rods, with hardened bearing inserts, attached to two forged-steel flywheel halves with integral mainshafts. This three-piece assembly had increased rigidity, and less tendency to spin on its mainshafts. Joe Ford

Evolution Sportster crankcases are machined by a CNC computer-controlled milling machine. Closer tolerances and fewer rejects result from performing all the drilling, boring, tapping, and milling operations on a single machine.

The Buell: The Other Sportster

Erik Buell is a former engineer at Harley-Davidson. He came to The Motor Company in 1979, and played a key role in the design and development of the FXR rubber-isolated chassis. Buell also became owner of another operation, when he acquired the rights and tooling for an experimental British motorcycle, the Barton, that was in its initial stages of development.

The Barton was supposed to be a "Yamaha Killer." At the time, the awesome TZ-750—an inline, two-stroke, four-cylinder road racer—dominated racing. The "square-four" Barton was created to compete with it. It had rotary disc inlet valves, which gave it a technological advantage over the piston-port competition.

The machine was a long way from being ready for competition, though. Its engine needed development to improve rideability and reliability. As for the chassis, Buell designed his own. The whole effort required nearly full-time work, so in 1985, he left Harley-Davidson to go on his own.

After years of development, the Buell racer was ready for production. Unfortunately, the AMA decided to change the rules to the current Superbike concept, and the need for the Buell racer vanished overnight. Without a market, Buell was out of business.

But the inventive Erik Buell proposed to Harley-Davidson that a "production" Sportster be built to qualify it for racing in the Battle of the Twins. Homologation required fifty production units. Harley-Davidson had that many XR-1000 engines in stock, and agreed to sell them to Buell. Within months, Buell's new factory was chugging out XR-engined RR-1000 Battle Twin motorcycles.

The Buell motorcycle's most unique engineering feature is its four-point engine mounting system, which isolates the Sportster engine's vibration from the rider. In addition, it features a single rear shock slung under the crankcases, which helps to provide a low center of gravity. The chrome-moly chassis is very light and stiff, and the steering geometry was patterned after international contemporary Grand Prix racers. Many of the components are machined from billet or are specially cast, and a high quality of workmanship is apparent.

Once the fifty XR engines were gone, it was only natural to switch to the new Evolution engine. This required some redesigning. The Evolution-engined RR-1200 first appeared in 1988 with the full body-work of the previous model. Although it attracted praise from motorcycle magazine product testers, many Harley-Davidson dealers and customers ex-

Willie G. Davidson, Harley-Davidson's vice president of styling, analyses the new RS-1200 model during the 1989 Harley dealer meeting in Milwaukee. Willie G. was responsible for creating the 1977 XLCR Cafe Racer. Harley-Davidson has publicly stated that it has no interest in entering the high-performance market; and further, because of the small number of sport bike buyers, The Motor Company cannot justify the resources necessary to develop and manufacture a machine like the Buell. The radical Buell RR and RS series vehicles take the concept of factory-made sport bikes well beyond the limits of Harley's conservative philosophy. Dave Gess

Erik Buell, with the original RR-1000. The RR-1000 evolved into the RR-1200 when Buell switched engines from the XR-1000 to the 1200cc Evolution. While purists loved it, the full-coverage body and racing-style seating position did not appeal to the vast majority of riders. Dave Gess

Erik Buell's experience with high-performance Sportsters includes many years of road racing an XR-1000. This photo was taken at Road America, in Elkhart Lake, Wisconsin, in 1985. In 1978, he was the fastest qualifying rookie expert at Daytona—aboard a Yamaha TZ-750. Wanting to compete on an American-made motorcycle prompted Buell to acquire the Barton project. Dave Gess

Buell manages all aspects of the business, including the design and development of new products. During model development, Buell (left) works directly with fabricators, Jim Schnieder (center) and Brian Mclaughlin. Dave Gess

pressed a strong desire for minimal bodywork to expose more of the engine and intricate components. This led to the current RS-1200 model.

The RS retains all of the RR's performance features, in a package designed to accommodate both rider and passenger in relative comfort. The location of the RS's handlebar grips and footrests position the rider more comfortably than do the RR's. In addition, a passenger seat cover, which acts as a driver backstop when retracted, doubles as a backrest when flipped up. A new version for 1992, the RSS-1200, features a single seat.

The Buell Motor Company currently builds about 200 units per year.

With its passenger backrest in the retracted position, the RS-1200 seat forms a backstop for the rider.

When extended, it becomes the passenger's backrest (right). Dave Gess

An off-line transfer system allows a line operator to detour a defective engine and park it in the center of the U-shaped line, rather than stopping the entire line. While the line continues running, a repairperson attends to the problem.

The carriers that the cases are mounted on provide a stable support. They stop completely when at their stations, which adds stability while the work is being performed.

Every day, Harley-Davidson Transportation Division fleet eighteen-wheelers carry engines to the final-assembly plant in York, Pennsylvania.

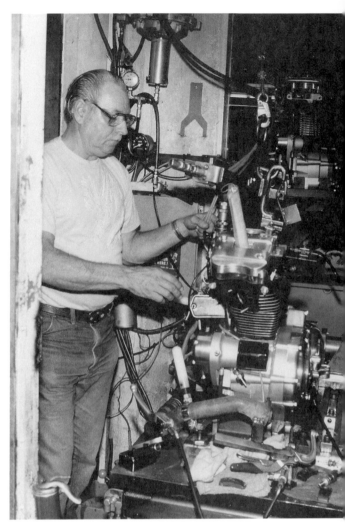

Each Evolution Sportster engine is run on a dyno and tested against a long check list before being sent to the York, Pennsylvania, final-assembly plant.

All Evolution Sportster cylinder studs are torqued by a computer-controlled machine in one operation. Digital readouts tell an operator the exact torque on each stud.

Chapter 3

The Stage I and Stage II Sportster Engine

The Evolution Sportster, the quickest and fastest standard Harley-Davidson made, has the potential of outperforming the best-running modified big twins. As a 1200, the Sportster motor can be made to produce virtually as much power as a modified big twin motor. With parity of power, combined with lower weight and less air resistance, a hopped-up Sportster is indeed the definitive high-performance Harley-Davidson.

There are many approaches to this subject. The variety of sources for cams, exhaust systems, carburetors, head work, and so forth is enormous, and many capable performance shops provide machining and modification services. The trick, however, is to get the right combination of components and modifications. For example, cams are designed to work with a certain cylinder head flow volume. The cubic-foot-per-minute flow capacity of a particular head may require a certain valve timing. Let's consider a particular cam that works on an engine with a combustion chamber, porting, and piston supplied by Jerry Branch of Flowmetrics. This cam may result in slightly different power characteristics with a head

and piston combination used by Carl Morrow of Carl's Speed Shop, or Dan Fitzmaurice of Zipper's Performance Products.

Although the procedures and equipment described here work well and have had successful and well-documented results, it is not the only way to go. If you choose, for instance, to have work performed by a local or different source than described here, be open to their advice as well. Proven professionals such as Carl Morrow and Dan Fitzmaurice are well qualified to help you build a good motor.

In this chapter, Joe Minton and I will describe the combinations that he has found to work well. We will also try to guide you in more extensive modifications in the next chapter. Minton has been modifying Evolution Harley-Davidsons since 1984, and probably has as much experience with Evolution Sportsters as anyone.

In this chapter we will refer to a Stage I and a Stage II engine. The difference between these stages has been arbitrarily set. Stage I is simply "bolt on"— installing items such as an exhaust system and air cleaner, without major machining or internal mod-

The many faces of Sportster pistons (left to right): a modified, dished piston for use in an 883 that has been bored to 1200cc; a 20deg domed piston for a 100hp *Sportster; a moderate compression big-bore piston for street use; and a 30deg high-compression, big-bore piston for drag racing use.* Zipper's Performance Products

Many performance shops offer their own proven combination of components in kit form. This is the Stage II 1200cc conversion kit from Zipper's. It includes modified 9.8:1 heads with big valves and dual-plug ignition; Red Shift or Andrews cams with solid lifters and high-performance valve springs; S&S Super E carburetor with ThunderJet; large-diameter high-flow exhaust system; and your choice of several ignition systems. With its 20deg domed pistons, the engine gives you 1.5hp per cubic inch—110hp at the crank. You can benefit from companies that spend a lot of time and effort matching various components for optimum performance. A comprehensive package takes the guesswork out of trying to match components. If you doubt your technical ability to work with engines or to build from scratch the engines described in this book, it's easy enough to find a performance company that will install a complete matched package. If you choose not to use a proven kit, and elect to do it yourself, stick with the combination of parts and modifications that have been tested and proven to work. Zipper's Performance Products

ifications. Stage II involves more extensive (and expensive) modifications, as well as new cams, carburetor, and other components. Not so coincidentally, all the basic elements described in our Stage I engine (except for enlarging the displacement form 883 to 1200cc) are the same modifications that are available to AMA CCS Harley-Davidson 883 Twin Sports competitors.

The exception to Stage I "no machining" is boring the cylinders of an XLH-883 to 1200cc displacement. It is assumed that anyone interested in high performance will not be satisfied with the performance of an engine displacing only 55ci, especially considering that a 74ci engine is so easily attainable. This bored-out 883, using the stock heads, cams, and carburetor, is referred to here as the 883/1200. (Still, the principles and information concerning components that work on a 1200 also apply to the 883 with its stock displacement.)

Stage I Costs

Component	Cost (approx. '92 $)
Piston kit	200
Screamin' Eagle air cleaner	60
Exhaust system	350
Ignition module	120
Gaskets, etc.	50
Total parts	780

Even more impressive than the great power increases possible from an XL is the low cost and ease with which the required modifications can be made. The 70hp 883/1200 conversion mentioned earlier can be built by any rider with competent mechanical skills. The total is much less than $1,000, including the cost of boring the cylinders. For a few hundred dollars more, the 1200 valves can be installed in the 883 head for about a 5hp gain and 1000rpm. This is actually a better value than changing carburetors, and your total cost barely exceeds $1,000.

What is called the Stage II engine—and again this has been arbitrarily set—involves opening the cam cover and installing new cams, porting the head, changing the carburetor, and so on. Some performance shops offer their own proven packages in stages. These may or may not correspond to what we are talking about here. As mentioned, there is more than one way to get successful results.

With the addition of proper cams, carburetor, and expert porting work, an Evolution Sportster develops ninety or more horsepower. It will cost around $2,000 to $2,500 to build yourself—or more, if you opt to use more expensive parts like S.T.D. or RevTech heads and S&S or Axtell cylinders, for instance.

Stage II Costs

Component	Cost (approx. '92 $)
Head work	$500 +
Carburetor and manifold	400
Cams	400
Pushrods, spring kit	200
Performance coils and module	150
Oil cooler	150
Gaskets, etc.	50
Exhaust system	350
Piston kit	200
Total parts	$2,500-2,900

Cost and Performance

The two fundamental differences between Stage I and Stage II engines are cost and performance. Both are reliable, and either can last as long as a stock engine if treated equally well. Note the "if treated equally well" qualification. In reality, chances are you will enjoy revving your high-powered Sportster to redline, which puts more strain on the engine. Fact is, it probably won't be treated equally, which is why the high-performance engine always wears out (and sometimes breaks) faster than the stock engine.

A stock 883 Evolution Sportster motor will deliver about 45 to 50hp to the rear wheel. (The 1988 and later XLH-883s have 40mm carburetors and produce about 45hp at the rear wheel; 1986 and 1987 models have a 34mm carburetor and produce about 5hp less.) This meek-and-mild engine can easily be bored to 1200cc, for a cost of about $250 in parts (piston kit and gaskets). With the addition of correct exhaust, air cleaner, and ignition module, it can deliver 70hp. That 70hp motor will have a wider power band than either the stock 883 or 1200. It will be more tractable and certainly more responsive than the original 883. And it will easily outaccelerate a factory 1200 in a low-rpm roll-on. This is a Stage I engine.

A factory 1200, with its bigger ports and valves, when equipped with the same air cleaner, ignition, and exhaust changes, will peak closer to 75hp compared to the 883/1200 conversion. Its greater power output is due solely to its cylinder heads, which have an increased airflow advantage at high rpm. The 883 ports quit working efficiently around 5500rpm, where the 1200 ports flow more air. Either conversion costs less than $1,000 to build.

The Stage II engine produces a fire-breathing 110hp plus at the crankshaft, and costs $2,500 or more to build. It will be somewhat less tractable and probably mechanically noisier than the Stage I engine. Its power will start near 3000rpm instead of 1500rpm, but will extend to over 7000rpm instead of 6000rpm.

You must build one or the other of these engines; a combination will not prove successful. A step in one stage engine, for example, may not result in commensurate performance gains when done on the other version. For instance, a larger carburetor will not substantially raise the peak power or rpm of a Stage I engine. This is because the stock intake ports will not pass enough air to take advantage of the larger carburetor. With the exception of the Mikuni HS40, the more likely result will be an engine that is less responsive at mid-rpm, and that may also have a slight stumble when the carburetor is transitioning from its low-flow to high-flow fuel delivery systems.

Fitting a set of high-performance long-duration cams to a Stage I engine may also prove less satisfactory. The long-duration cams, with their later closing intake valves, will raise the minimum rpm at which the engine begins to deliver strong performance. Instead of pulling well from the stock cams' 1500rpm, power may not begin until 2800rpm. However, there will be no substantial gain in peak power or the rpm at which it is achieved due to the airflow limits of the stock ports.

Keep in mind that to build a Stage II type of engine of 90 or 100hp, you must begin with the correct basic components. For instance, if you build a Stage I

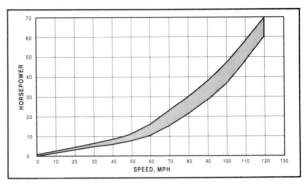

The amount of horsepower required to propel a motorcycle at certain speeds depends on its size, wind drag, and rolling resistance. The power requirements begin to increase dramatically in the 40–60mph range.

engine, then add $1,500 worth of components, it will not guarantee successful results because you have started with the wrong pistons. A high-output Stage II engine requires the correct combination of parts and services.

Experience with dozens of 883/1200 conversions has indicated that the enlarged motors are as reliable as the original 883. There are a couple of sound reasons for this. First, the Evolution XLH-1200 Sportster has proven to be reliable and dependable. Second, street bikes, even modified ones, spend a majority of their time being run at moderate speeds. A Sportster engine must deliver slightly more than 10hp to push the bike and rider along at 60mph. It doesn't matter whether it is a 1200 capable of making 90hp, or a stock 883 capable of 50hp. Fact is, 10hp is 10hp; only ten is needed, and both motors will be turning the same speed, about 3000rpm. With this small load, the stress is low and the life of the two motors is equally long.

Harley-Davidson first released the Evolution Sportster in 1986 as an 883 for several reasons. First, they were concerned about whether they could meet stepped-up emission standards. Engineering tests had determined that bore size was the most important variable engine design factor affecting mechanical noise output. The 3in bore 883 was quieter than the larger 3.5in bore. Second, the marketing people felt that a return to the original displacement of 883ci was important. Not only did this strengthen the Sportster's long-held image, but it also put the bike in a lower insurance category.

There was another concern: the gearbox. The Evolution Sportster gearbox was a holdover from the earlier iron-head Sportster which, in turn, was a holdover from way back in Harley-Davidson's past, when the engine developed 30hp as a 45ci flathead. Sportster gearboxes were known to break when abused, and Harley-Davidson wanted to do more testing before they committed the 1200cc version to production. Until complete information from the field was available, the company decided to make the larger Sportster's displacement 1100cc. In addition, the engineering department felt that a thicker cylinder liner was needed for the 3.5in bore.

Field use has since shown that the Evolution Sportster gearbox is strong enough to handle more than twice the power of the original 883. In thousands of miles of racing with engines producing up to 100hp, the stock four- and five-speed gearboxes have proven themselves—when properly set up and maintained. This includes removing and inspecting the transmission before running it in competition or in a high-output engine (see chapter 5).

The gearbox can be broken, not so much by high-performance engines, but by riding with the engine at an rpm so low that the rear drive chain jerks and snatches. There is no drive cushion built into the Sportster's rear hub, which means that sudden loads between the crankshaft and the rear wheel are delivered to the gears without any damping. This results in very high loads on the gear teeth and dogs. The answer, of course, is to keep the engine at a speed where it runs smoothly.

Harley-Davidson never intended the Evolution Sportster engine to be used for racing or hot rodding. It was to be (and is) a reliable, long-lived, and easy-to-maintain street motor. The fact that it is strong enough to survive those of us who think more power is always better is a tribute to Harley-Davidson's tendency to build strength into their products. Harley-Davidsons, after all, are typically kept for a long time, and even get passed along for generations. Knowing this, the factory engineers design for long-term use; they know that their bikes need to be durable and rebuildable in every way. We hot rodders can take advantage of that extra strength to make more power!

Any engine, though, when stressed beyond its design limits, will reveal ultimate weaknesses. Indeed, those of us who hop-up engines will push that engine's design limits until some problem slows us down or stops us. How much we are slowed down is largely determined by how much planning and problem solving we are willing to do to overcome the problem. Oftentimes, simply throwing money at the problem does not fix it; it requires a methodical examination.

Perhaps the extreme example of pursuing power at any cost is the top-fuel drag racing Chrysler Hemi motor. Through several decades, this motor has been modified so much that there is little left of it but the name and general layout of the original design. It is still a 90deg V-8, but some of the more successful examples no longer have even the hemispherical combustion chamber from which the design was given its name.

Our goal with the Evolution Sportster was to develop as much performance, both peak power and range of power, as possible without requiring exten-

sive modifications or the services of a specialty engine builder. We have stopped far before the point of having to invoke "fixes" such as those used on the Chrysler Hemi drag motor.

Unlike pure racing engines designed without regard for manufacturing costs, engineers who develop production motors like the Evolution Sportster must consider cost an important part of the design process. Harley-Davidson's engineers made a couple of choices that have haunted them. All Evolution motors, Sportster and big twin, tend to develop head gasket leaks when the engines are cold. And they tend to distort their cylinders, which in turn leads to loss of ring seal and power.

The head gasket leaks are the result of two Evolution design features that were not present in its predecessors, the iron Sportster and Shovelhead big twin. For economic reasons, Harley-Davidson chose to flatten the joint between the Evolution cylinders and heads, making machining easier. The iron Sportster and Shovelhead motors had spigots formed at the top of the cylinders that were a close fit into the heads. These spigots prevented the direct impingement of burning gases on the head gasket edge and the joints between the gasket, head, and cylinder—and that's why they did not leak!

To address the head gasket leakage problem, Harley-Davidson introduced four different head and base gaskets to the Evolution motors. The latest of the head gaskets, introduced in 1991, provides a better gas seal in a cold engine. (These new gaskets can be used on earlier Evolution Sportsters.) The new 0.017in base gasket introduced in 1992 also seems to work better than any previous gasket. These gaskets crush down to about 0.015in, so are referred to as 0.015 gaskets. These gaskets can be bought and used on earlier Evolution Sportsters

Evolution motors use long steel studs to clamp the cylinders and heads to the engine cases. The cylinders and heads are made of an aluminum alloy. Like most metals, the steel studs and the aluminum cylinders and heads expand when heated. But the rate of expansion for aluminum is ten times that of steel for any given temperature change. Between ambient and running temperature, an alloy Sportster cylinder will grow in length about 0.040in. Meanwhile, the studs that clamp the cylinder and head lengthen by only 0.004in.

The clamping pressure of the studs on the cylinders increases dramatically as the engine heats. A head gasket that allows combustion gas blow-by when the engine is cold usually seals perfectly after the engine warms. One way to minimize the risk of blowing a head gasket is to allow the engine to warm thoroughly before using it hard.

If the studs are tightened enough to ensure that the joint between a cylinder and head was gas-tight on a cold engine, it causes excessive clamping pressure on the parts when the engine is fully warmed. The cylinders tend to distort, and the studs could break or pull out of the aluminum cases. These things have happened in the field, especially to highly modified engines.

Stock Evolution engines often run with distorted cylinders, especially the 1200. The distortion has two primary causes. First, the aluminum casting that surrounds the iron-alloy liner is rather thin. It lacks enough stiffness to remain sufficiently rigid under normal running conditions. Second, as mentioned, cylinder-head clamping pressure created by the differential expansion rates of the steel studs and alloy cylinders can become excessive and lead to permanent cylinder distortion. In other words—they bend.

Modifying these engines to make more power doesn't seem to make the distortion problem worse. However, an engine operating at high rpm and with more air getting into its cylinders with each cycle (the whole point of modifying it!) will be more sensitive to cylinder distortion and loss of ring seal than a stocker rolling down the interstate making 10hp.

S&S Cycle in Viola, Wisconsin, makes replacement aluminum cylinders for Evolution Harley-Davidsons that have more aluminum surrounding the sleeve. Although these are less prone to distortion, even the S&S cylinders distort some. There are several manufacturers, including S&S and Axtell, that provide solid iron cylinders for the Evolution engines that should prevent distortion altogether. They add about 15–20lb, though, which offsets any efforts to build a lightweight Sportster.

You can build a perfectly satisfactory high-performance Evolution Sportster without spending the extra bucks for special cylinders. While the small distortions typical of stock cylinders may be important to the road or drag racer, the effects are so small in normal street use that they can largely be ignored. It does, however, become a greater concern when building the ultimate engine. The loss of ring seal can be minimized by running a tight piston clearance. This is best left to the performance shops that have lots of experience. Sending your cylinders to a machine shop that is unfamiliar with the Sportster engine may ultimately lead to more expenses.

Compression Ratio and Cranking Pressure

It is a truism that a high compression ratio is necessary for truly high performance, particularly in the lower end of an engine's power range. That certainly is true of the Evolution Sportster. This engine responds well to an increased compression ratio, and a modified engine should have as high a ratio as it can tolerate.

Perhaps the most common misconception about compression is the belief that the numerical compression ratio is the only thing that matters. It is not. What is more important is cranking pressure, which is the measure of how much pressure develops in the combustion chamber near the time of ignition.

The numeric compression ratio is merely a way of describing the relationship between the volume of a cylinder when the piston is at bottom dead center and when it is at top dead center. Cranking pressure, on the other hand, is affected more by camshaft design than by the change in volume as the piston travels along its stroke.

An intake valve is normally closed sometime after the piston has started its way up the cylinder on the compression stroke. The sooner the inlet valve closes after bottom dead center, the sooner the piston begins to compress the air-fuel mixture in the cylinder, and the higher the pressure will be when the piston reaches the top of its stroke. The later the valve closes, the lower the pressure.

If air had no weight, a cylinder could be filled virtually instantly and all intake valves could be immediately closed at the beginning of the compression stroke. However, air has mass, so it takes time to build momentum and get it into an engine's cylinder. The higher the rpm at which an engine is expected to produce its peak power, the less time there is to fill the cylinder. This then requires that the intake valve open sooner and close later in the engine's cycle.

A high-rpm cam, with its long intake and exhaust durations and overlap, develops a lower cranking pressure than will a cam optimized for lower rpm power delivery. An engine that has a high-rpm camshaft can get away with a higher compression ratio than the same engine fitted with a torque cam. As mentioned, it is cranking pressure, not compression ratio, that is important.

Every combustion chamber design has an upper limit to the amount of cranking pressure it can tolerate. While the cams control the cranking pressure, it is the combustion chamber shape that influences the amount of cranking compression the engine can actually withstand. Every tuner and performance shop have their own ideas of what shape combustion chamber works best. Some are more efficient at processing and burning the fuel mixture than others.

The Sportster engine runs well at or below 175psi (pounds per square inch), as measured by a common compression tester at cranking speeds. Harley-Davidson prefers to limit cranking pressure to 160psi, but they have to consider that their customers may not have their engines properly set up. When fitted with Harley-Davidson's own 883/1200 conversion pistons, the cranking pressure is closer to 160psi. This relatively low pressure is no doubt necessary due to the lack of squish area (more about that in a minute). While adequate, this could be improved. When fitted with Wiseco Piston Incorporated's 883/1200 conversion pistons, an Evolution Sportster will develop about 170psi with stock cams. This cranking pressure works perfectly. The engine will not be overly sensitive to gasoline quality, although it should definitely be run on the higher octanes. It will get the maximum effect of high compression at lower rpm where most of these engines spend the vast majority of their running life.

The penalty for raising the cranking pressure beyond what a combustion chamber will tolerate is destructive detonation. If you fit Harley-Davidson's 1200 piston kit to an 883 without making their recommended chamber modifications, the compression ratio would be close to 10.8:1. Detonation may destroy the engine at full throttle if poor fuel is used. Under extremely severe detonation the Harley-Davidson cast 1200 pistons sometimes break—as will any cast piston.

Squish Area

One time-honored way to both suppress detonation and improve combustion is to establish "squish" areas between the pistons and cylinder heads. Evolution engines respond very well to squish. Squish (a Britishism) is a portion of the area of a head that is fitted to within 0.040 to 0.060in of the piston. The modern two-cycle engine would not exist without squish areas.

Squish areas suppress detonation in two ways. First, they squeeze air-fuel mixture into the center of the combustion chamber just before ignition. This greatly increases gas turbulence and improves mixing and flame travel. At the same time, they prevent or limit burning within the volume of the chamber defined by the squish areas, until the piston has moved down the bore a bit. This reduces piston and combustion chamber heating and improves thermal efficiency, which in turn helps the engine run cooler.

An 883/1200 conversion using Wiseco forged pistons produces an effective squish area. The more advanced engine with ported heads and modified combustion chambers can use flat-topped pistons or 20 or 30deg domes for an even more effective squish area. Using the Wiseco kit is quick, easy, and economical; using a domed piston and modified head requires more work and money, but produces better results.

The key to building a Sportster with squish areas is setting the piston-to-head clearances (deck height) correctly. This critical detail is the single operation that requires more than assembly skills. We will talk you through the procedure in the next chapter.

Pistons

Building a Stage I Sportster can be both quick and easy by using 883/1200 conversion piston kits. Both the Harley-Davidson Screamin' Eagle and the Wiseco Pistons kits have been tested by performance expert Joe Minton. S&S Cycle also offers a kit. They each have advantages and disadvantages. Another option is to obtain a specially modified flat-top pistons offered by performance shops nationwide. The quality and result depends on the performance house, however, because each application requires different combustion chamber modifications. Many provide excellent results. Of course it is impossible to test them all, so we will talk about the two conversion kits that we have experience with.

Harley-Davidson's kit is very complete. It contains a set of stock 1200cc Sportster piston assemblies, complete instructions, and every gasket, seal, and O-ring needed. Following the instructions carefully will result in an 883/1200 conversion engine that performs nearly the same as a stock 1200, without changing to new heads.

Drag race engine developer Dan Fitzmaurice of Zipper's recommends using Speed Pro rings, which are used by engine builders in all forms of pro racing. A unique plasma-applied coating improves top ring lubrication and sealing, and helps minimize cylinder-wall scuffing. A special low-tension compression ring also reduces power-robbing friction. The hand-lapped sealing surfaces break in quickly. These rings seem to be especially effective in the standard Sportster cylinders that suffer from distortion. Speed Pro

This illustrates the extremely thin cylinder resulting from boring 883 barrels to 1200cc displacement. Cylinder distortion has always been an Evolution Sportster problem in the larger 3.50in bore size engines. Joe Minton

The greatest advantage of the Harley-Davidson conversion kit is that all the parts are genuine Harley-Davidson. When it comes time to overhaul the engine, parts can be obtained easily from any Harley-Davidson dealer or from the factory. In fact, the pistons are OEM XLH-1200 parts, so they are of proven quality. The stock piston rings are rather thick (0.050in) by high-performance standards. They tend to lose ring seal above 7000rpm, but if you are building a Stage I engine, this will not be a limitation because the Stage I engine should not be revved this high anyway.

The trickiest part of the Harley-Davidson kit involves modifying the heads with a rotary file (hand-held grinder). To get a proper compression ratio (really, the cranking pressure) down to a survivable level, metal must be ground off from the combustion chamber. This requires considerable skill and the use of a hand-held grinder, and may be best left to a high-performance or machine shop.

Wiseco's 883/1200 piston kit was designed to provide some degree of squish effect. The piston features a depression machined into its top. The depression allows use of the unmodified stock 883 combustion chambers. That, in turn, permits the establishment of squish zones between the flat portions of the pistons and 883 heads. The pistons are forged and are tougher than cast Harley-Davidson parts, although they weigh the same. Wiseco uses thinner (0.040in) rings.

The only disadvantages of the Wiseco pistons are that they cost more than the Harley-Davidson

A standard Harley-Davidson 1200 piston (left) next to a modified dished type used with standard 883 heads. This is an easy and inexpensive way to convert an 883 to a good-running 1200 that can produce 70hp or more with a minimum of modifications. For maximum performance, however, a flat-top or domed piston that combines good squish areas with optimum combustion chamber shape is essential.

parts, and they make more noise because forged pistons must be built with more clearance than cast pistons. Some people say they make *a lot* more noise, while others are not as sensitive. You make the call.

There are other flat-top pistons that can be used with modified heads. This type of piston set is well suited to a Stage-II-and-beyond motor with ported heads and highly modified combustion chambers. In this case, material is added to parts of the chamber by welding, and the chamber is completely reshaped to

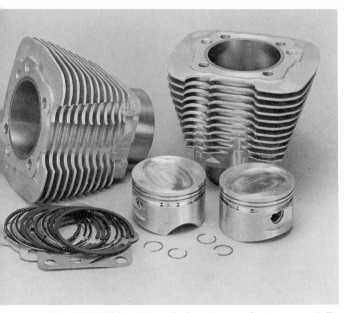

The S&S 1200cc kit includes pistons that are specially modified for installation in an 883. Its dished shape adjusts combustion chamber volume so that complicated head machining is kept to a minimum. The resulting chamber shape features a squish area on one side of the combustion chamber, opposite the spark plug. S&S Cycle

The S&S V2 Sidewinder 3⁵/₈in bore kit gives a Sportster 79ci. The barrels feature thicker liners and more material in the aluminum cylinders to minimize distortion problems. If the kit is used on an XLH-883, cylinder-head modifications are required, and both Sportster models require crankcase boring. S&S makes a dozen different bore and stroke combinations for Sportsters. S&S Cycle

The forged Wiseco pistons and rings. The Wiseco rings are 20 percent lighter than the stock rings. Forged pistons make more noise than the standard Harley-Davidson cast pistons, although they are stronger.

provide generous squish areas and a compact burning area. These pistons are provided by companies like Axtell, Branch Flowmetrics, Carl's Speed Shop, Zipper's, and others.

For ultimate performance, pistons with 20 or 30deg of dome, again with an appropriately modified combustion chamber, offer impressive performance. Given moderate cams and carburetors, this engine easily pushes the 100hp barrier and beyond.Sportster motors with this Stage I conversion and more aggressive cams produce 1.5hp per cubic inch and more (over 110hp). Add big-bore cylinders, and you get up to 135hp at the crank. The power band may be relatively narrow, however, and now we are talking about an engine more suited to racing than to practical street use.

Again, we must consider the performance-versus-cost question. Keep in mind that these high power gains usually result at engine speeds up to 7500rpm, which results in the incredible piston speed of 4765fpm (feet per minute). (A racing XR-750 at 9000rpm has piston speed of only 4400fpm.) At these high speeds, the chances of such problems as broken pistons and dropped valves increase.

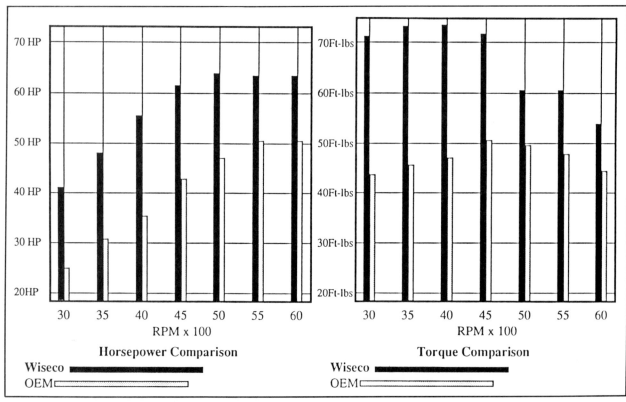

Wiseco measured a stock XLH-883 Sportster on its engine dynamometer (taking the reading from the crankshaft), then dismantled the top end, bored the cylinders to fit a Wiseco 1200cc conversion kit, and reassembled it. The results of the standard 883 and the converted 1200 comparison are shown in these graphs, which were provided by Wiseco. Wiseco pistons are forged, which makes them stronger than OEM pistons. However, they make more noise than cast pistons. Installing this Wiseco kit in an 883, using stock heads, results in a compression ratio of 9.5:1. At about $200, the Wiseco 1200cc conversion kit gives the most power and the best power-per-dollar value of any modification you can make on an XLH-883. Wiseco Piston Inc.

Head and Base Gaskets

Earlier, we referred to the fact that Harley-Davidson has used several variations of Sportster head and base gaskets. They were attempting, sometimes without tremendous success, to eliminate head gasket leaks and to prevent the base gasket from squeezing out. The latest head gasket design, although effective, is not suitable for an engine built with modified squish areas.

Extensive development and testing has established that the old, reliable annealed copper head gasket is the most satisfactory solution to the head gasket leak problem. There are several variations on the market.

Custom Chrome Incorporated, or CCI, sells a kit consisting of composite-copper head gaskets with and three thicknesses of copper base gaskets. Upon assembly, the mechanic selects the base gasket thickness that places the piston in with the desired squish clearance. The advantage of being able to set piston height with the base gaskets is, unfortunately, offset by the difficulty of sealing them against oil leakage. The head gaskets are not reusable, and the copper base gasket tends to seep oil.

HES Incorporated furnishes copper head gasket kits that includes soft-aluminum base gaskets. The HES annealed copper head gaskets, like those from CCI, are 0.040in thick. The aluminum base gaskets are a single thickness (0.010in). The aluminum gas-

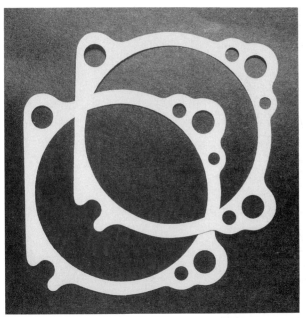

Harley-Davidson base gaskets have gradually improved over the years. The latest white gasket is marked "017" and measures 0.017in thick before installation. They crush down to about 0.015in when installed. Karl Schlei

kets seem to seal better against oil leakage than the copper gaskets. A disadvantage of the HES kit is that it makes no provision for deck height adjustment.

Bartels' Performance Products also sells a copper and aluminum gasket kit similar to the HES kit. Bartels' kit furnishes thinner 0.027in annealed copper head gaskets along with smaller diameter O-rings to match the gasket thickness. Their aluminum base gaskets are the same as the HES gaskets. The Bartels' kit also includes a tube of Hylomar brand sealant for

A broken piston results from running a Harley-Davidson 1200 conversion piston kit in an 883 that has not been properly modified. Correct head modification is essential when installing some 1200cc conversion kits. The heads must be machined with a rotary hand grinder to produce a correct compression ratio. Without this modification, a compression ratio of up to 11:1 results, and will cause detonation and damage.

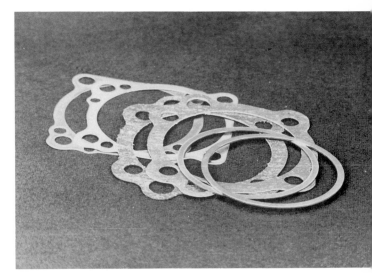

The composite head gasket sets, like this one from Custom Chrome Incorporated work very well but are more expensive to manufacture.

75

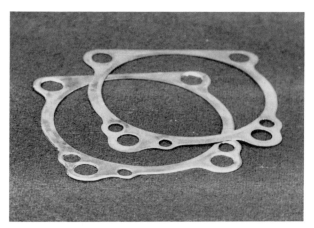

Metal base gaskets, such as these 0.010in thick Bartels', maintain consistent thickness when assembled. It is imperative that the crankcase and cylinder surfaces be extremely flat to avoid leaks when using aluminum base gaskets.

the base gasket. This sealant has proven to be very effective and is used in the factory assembly of Harley-Davidson engines. Although Sportster engines vary, the 0.027in Bartels' gasket seems to establish the correct head-to-piston clearance for effective squish height in most XL engines.

With these variations available, a skilled mechanic can nearly always establish a proper deck height without reverting to the services of a machine shop. The best performance will come from an engine with tight piston-to-head clearances, and it is worth some trouble to establish them, even if it means machine work. What works for you will be determined by measuring the deck height of your engine (see chapter 4).

Intake Airflow

To get more power, you must pump more air and fuel through an engine at a given time. This requires high-flow volumes through all the components that

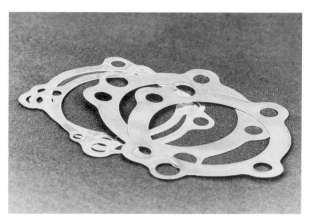

Bartels' and HES gaskets are all metal. HES supplies 0.040in thick head gaskets, while a head gasket of 0.02in thickness with O-rings of appropriate thickness are available from Bartels'.

Many tuners machine the cylinders and heads to accept special O-rings instead of using base gaskets on high-output and big-bore racing engines. Either copper or silicone materials are used. Speed shops like Zipper's can perform this modification to solve persistent head gasket leaks on street machines. Zipper's Performance Products

comprise the entire intake and exhaust tracts. To take advantage of efficient port flow, the combustion chamber and ignition system must cause the mixture to burn more efficiently and completely than it did in stock trim.

Converted to 1200cc, an XLH-883 processes more air-fuel mixture at any rpm. It also flows more mixture if the restrictive air filter assembly is replaced by one that offers less airflow restriction. The same is true for the exhaust system. The standard-

The stock 883 valves quit working by 5500rpm. Larger valves can be installed and the combustion chamber shape can be modified for maximum results. Many high-performance speed shops and Harley-Davidson dealerships can do these modifications. If not, you can send your heads to suppliers like Axtell, Branch Flowmetrics, and Zipper's, to name but a few. The head on the left, modified by Jerry Branch, has 1^{15}/$_{16}$in intake and 1^5/$_8$in exhaust valves, and more squish area than the standard head (right). Joe Minton

76

The stock 883 inlet valve is adequate to about 5500rpm before power fades completely. Larger 1200 valves add another 1000 or more rpm and with proper squish area and modified ports, opens the door to impressive performance gains up to 7500rpm. Joe Minton

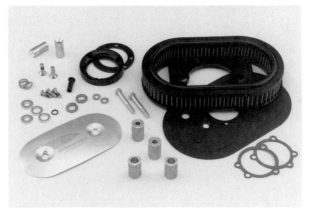

The Harley-Davidson Screamin' Eagle high-flow air filter kit, which qualifies for Twin Sports racing, includes everything needed for installation. Many other air cleaners, such as the ever popular S&S "teardrop" air cleaner, also work well on Stage I-type engines (limited to about 6000rpm) and on many Stage II applications. However, tests have proven the Harley-Davidson item slightly superior in flow volume. Harley-Davidson

production intake and exhaust systems were designed not for increased power and not even for the ultimate in styling, but to meet EPA regulations. As a result, they are the bottlenecks that block performance.

The stock intake and exhaust ports in the 883 heads are large enough to service the flow requirements of the larger 883/1200 engine up to about 5500rpm. At engine speeds above that, the small size of intake valves, and to a lesser extent the exhaust valves, restrict flow and therefore power output. A factory 1200cc engine, with its larger valves, continues to gain power to 6000rpm, with diminishing gains above that speed. An expertly ported head, such as the Branch #4 or Zipper's Stage III, maintains efficient cylinder filling up to 7500rpm.

A modified 883 head can easily be made superior to the stock 1200 head. This is accomplished by boring the seats and installing the valves from the 1200. While you're at it, you can file and sand the ports to remove any small restrictions, and do a five-angle valve job. Carefully done, with a smooth valve seat area, you will have a 1200cc Sportster that outruns a stocker in every way.

If you were to make only one modification to your Evolution Sportster, it should be to replace the stock air cleaner with a Harley-Davidson Screamin' Eagle replacement filter kit. Harley-Davidson designer Dick Parisey and his staff did a good job. The Screamin' Eagle filter gives the single largest gain in power of any bolt-on part on the market, about 3 or 4hp. This kit mounts rigidly and fits well; it should, considering that it has been engineered by Harley-Davidson. More importantly, it is so free-flowing that an 883/1200 Stage I engine will produce as much power with the filter installed as it will with no filter at all. Other filters are also available, such as the

popular S&S unit. While these filter kits will improve airflow compared to the stock air box, flow bench tests have shown that nothing currently available beats the Screamin' Eagle kit's flow volume.

Stock Carburetors

Two different factory carburetors have been fitted to the Evolution Sportsters. From 1986 through 1987, the standard carburetor was a fixed-venturi Keihin instrument with a 34mm bore size. (The big twin used the 38mm version of the same carburetor.) In 1988 the factory began using a new 40mm constant-velocity (CV) slide-type carburetor, also a Keihin. Both types are quality instruments but, for several reasons, the newer CV carburetor is the better of the two.

The newer carburetor is the better choice because it will pass more air and, when mounted to an 883/1200, will let the engine produce about 2hp more than the older version. It is also easier to tune to meet the needs of a modified engine. Accurate carburetor tuning is essential for both the Stage I and Stage II engines, and for any high-performance work for that matter.

The older 34mm unit can be easily modified to pass substantially more air than it does in its stock form. The largest flow gain will be realized by removing the choke plate in the mouth of the carburetor. The 34mm bore can also be machined out to 38mm, the same diameter as the big twin's similar carburetor, for an additional but smaller gain. However, even with a larger bore and the choke plate removed, the fixed-venturi Keihin will not pass as much air as the later CV carburetor. Depending to some extent upon choice of an exhaust system, it will also be more difficult to tune for smooth response

For maximum power output, a muffler must have a large volume. That's why the Harley-Davidson Racing Team uses those huge canisters. It's also why some of the best-looking exhaust systems and slide-on mufflers are not the best choice for high-performance use. This Bartels' two-into-one Slash-Cut system works better than most, although the other Bartels' system made for Twin Sports racing is the ultimate. Bartels' Performance Products

throughout its throttle range. In short, it would be better to find one of the later CV carburetors for your 883/1200 conversion if you own a Sportster made before 1988.

The original factory CV carburetor settings were far from satisfactory. Those first Sportsters were known to cough, sneeze, and pop back through the carburetors. The backfiring, due to excessive low throttle leanness, as well as an ignition malady which we will discuss later, was sometimes severe enough to split the rubber manifold. There were even reports of the early CV carburetors blowing off the manifold altogether. Later CV carburetors did not exhibit these problems and limitations.

It is possible to update the earlier versions of the CV carburetor by replacing its needle and needle jet with later parts. For 883/1200 and most other relatively mild applications, the needle from the XLH-1200 works well in the Stage I engine described here. It may require some fine tuning, however. Because of restriction in the stock ports, a high-flow or modified manifold is not necessary for Stage I.

Exhaust Systems

Nearly everyone who buys a Sportster changes the exhaust system, either for better looks or sound quality. Few of us consider the crossover tube that runs under the carburetor, connecting the front and rear exhaust pipes, to be an asset to a Sportster's good looks. Stock Sportster mufflers are quiet enough to please the feds, but too quiet to please the majority of Sportster owners.

Almost all aftermarket exhausts flow more air than the stock system, and therefore allow the engine to produce more power. Few of these take full advantage of the Sportster's power potential, however. The popular small mufflers that appear similar to stock simply do not have enough internal volume to take advantage of the engine's exhaust flow capabilities at higher speeds. These mufflers—Harley-Davidson's Screamin' Eagle replacement parts are a good example—are overly restrictive at full throttle and high rpm.

The problem is that small mufflers cannot be both reasonably quiet and also allow adequate flow. A set of 30in straight pipes will make almost as much peak power as a well- designed high-performance exhaust system, but few would argue that straight pipes are socially acceptable. By the way, straight 30in pipes don't work well below about 3800rpm. It is quite common for a straight-pipe, nonmuffled system to run poorly in the 3000 and lower rpm range.

The highest peak power will come with correct length header pipes (27–32in), followed by generously sized mufflers with the largest possible expansion volume in front of the silencing mechanism. Only two such Sportster systems are in production at the time of this writing: the Kerker SuperTrapp two-into-one system, and the Bartels' Performance Products two-into-one with the larger of the two mufflers available.

Both of these systems adhere to the basic silencer formula developed long ago (1911 or so) by the British to solve a noise problem they had with racing engines at the Brooklands banked oval track. Like many of today's tracks, Brooklands was built in a fairly isolated place, but gradually houses were built nearby and the owners started complaining about the noise. After experimenting, it was found that if the exhaust gases were dumped into a can that had a volume of at least ten times that of the cylinder, and then were led out through a pipe of the same diameter, the exhaust would be considerably quieter —with no power loss.

Much of the remaining high-frequency noise could be eliminated if the outlet pipe from the "Brooklands muffler" was widened and tapered to pinch the exhaust gases between the sides of the outlet pipe. This muffler design was used on many British-production motorcycles over several decades and can be found on the last of the Velocettes.

The principle of the Brooklands muffler, allowing exhaust gases to expand before entering the silencer, is still valid. Silencing requires restriction. Less restriction is required to reduce the energetic sound pulses of low-pressure gases than is needed to similarly silence high-pressure gases. An expansion chamber lowers peak exhaust gas pressures and

A divergent exhaust system capped with a convergent end cone, known as a "reverse cone megaphone," has proven to be the most effective type for maximum power output. This one is mounted on a Bartels' Twin Sports XLH-883.

Running straight pipes causes power loss below the 3500rpm range, but straight pipes are light weight which makes them popular for drag racing. Tests have shown that for maximum power using 1.75in diameter pipes with the Sportster's standard stroke, an exhaust pipe header length of 29in is ideal. A length of 28 or 30in works nearly as well. The 2in diameter Python pipes (right) are better for higher power applications, although their larger diameter requires a 23in length for best results. Python therefore makes it easier to further silence the exhaust.

Evolution engines are rather sensitive to exhaust system design. The standard exhaust pipe diameter of 1¾in is marginal for a cylinder displacing 37ci (1200cc Sportster). A 1⅞ or 2in diameter is more appropriate for high-performance work.

In order to get the noise level down to a socially acceptable level with the more popular small mufflers, it is necessary to make the silencer section more restrictive. Even these designs cannot effectively reduce high-frequency noise at full throttle and high rpm. Systems of this type are both loud and restrictive. When combined with the marginal pipe diameter, such mufflers kill high-rpm horsepower.

As an example, a 90hp Stage II Evolution Sportster motor will become an 82hp motor if its Super-

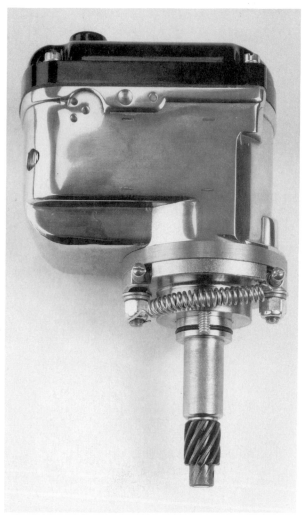

Pro drag racers often prefer to use magnetos, favoring well-proven units like the Morris magneto. The advantage is that the magneto is a self-contained ignition unit, eliminating the need for an electrical system with its heavy battery. It has no practical advantage for street use, but it looks neat. Rivera Engineering

Trapp or Bartels' pipe is replaced with a set of classic small "sausage" mufflers. It will also make more noise.

Ignition Systems

A correct ignition system—including its energy, timing, and advance curve characteristics—is essential to the optimum performance of any engine. The stock 883 Sportster does not have an optimum ignition system for high-performance use. Its energy is sometimes marginal, and although the advance curve for the 883 is far from optimum, the 1200's ignition module has the best curve available. Also, the stock ignition fires both cylinders at the same time which, while workable, is far from the best way to ignite a V-twin engine.

The question of ignition energy—how much is enough?—has been debated for decades, and tuners aren't through chewing on the subject yet. High-performance Sportsters being tested on a dynamometer have shown that weak coil energy output will limit power output.

There are many myths about the ignition process. One of the most pervasive is that high-voltage coils are better than lower voltage coils.

When enough voltage potential is generated across the gap of a spark plug, a spark arcs across the gap. How much voltage is required depends mainly upon the gap size and the pressure of the gases in the gap. The larger the gap, the more voltage required to strike a spark. The greater the pressure (cranking pressure) the more voltage required. Thus the coil

The Dyna 2000 programmable ignition module is the only ignition system on the market that can provide the optimum advance curve for the high-performance Sportster. It works with the stock Hall-effect pickup. Its switches allow you to customize the ignition advance curve to match the needs of your engine. It also gives you a choice of sixteen different rev-limiter settings and allows you to adjust the dwell period to match the coil. Joe Minton

servicing a high-cranking-pressure engine with wide plug gaps requires a higher voltage to start a spark.

Once a spark is struck, the voltage necessary to sustain it quickly lowers from 12,000 or so, to about 3,000 volts. This is because the blue-colored spark path consists of gas heated to such high temperatures that it becomes conductive (ionized). As a conductor, the ionized gas passes electricity much more easily, and much less pressure (voltage) is needed to keep electrons flowing across the gap. A coil only needs to produce enough voltage to strike the initial spark.

After a spark is struck and the voltage drops, the coil continues to dump its stored energy across the gap until it is exhausted. The greater the energy stored in the coil, the longer the spark will last.

A stock Harley-Davidson coil sometimes fails to create enough voltage to strike a spark in time to properly ignite a high-rpm, high-pressure engine. When that happens, the engine stops gaining horsepower with increasing rpm. It is not often as dramatic as misfiring or complete spark failure; instead, the power output simply flattens.

For example, in one test of an XR-1000 with extensive port work, cams, pipe, and larger carburetors, the engine stopped increasing power at a little over 5000rpm. The power output remained the same from 5000 to 6750rpm. When a higher energy, lower inductance (quicker voltage rise) coil was fitted, with no other change, the power increased steadily from 5000 to 6750rpm and peaked at 12hp greater than before the coil change. An even hotter (more energetic) coil was tried, but there was no further improvement. Experiences similar to this are fairly common. In short, higher energy and quicker reacting coils may be required when building a high-performance Sportster.

Among the coils available in the aftermarket, the Harley-Davidson orange-colored Screamin' Eagle coil has been proven to meet the needs of any high-output Sportster engine. Many other coils—such as those from Andrews Products, Incorporated, KV, and Harley-Davidson, to name a few—have been successfully tested for use in either Stage I or Stage II motors.

Ignition timing requirements are strongly influenced by the efficiency of the combustion chamber, which is mostly a matter of its shape and squish. Poor chamber shapes, such those found in the iron XL or the Shovelhead big twin motors, require more timing advance than a more compact chamber like the Sportster's.

Normal stock timing advance for the old iron Sportster was 40deg. The new Evolution Sportster models are set to 35deg for the 883 and 28deg for the 1200. Dyno testing confirmed that the 883/1200 Stage I conversion engine runs best with the stock 1200's 28deg total advance.

A street engine cannot, or at least *should not*, be run at full advance at all rpm. Until an Evolution

The standard Sportster ignition module has a rev limiter that begins to snuff the engine at about 5800rpm. Even the little 883, equipped with high-flow intake and exhaust systems, is capable of revving beyond that. The Screamin' Eagle module's limiter of 8000rpm is beyond the range of a street engine, which lets you get the most from a modified XL. Joe Minton

Sportster motor reaches about 3200rpm, it responds best with less than full advance. Extensive testing has also shown that both Stage I and Stage II type motors run best if the ignition timing at idle is set at about 10–12deg before top dead center; is advanced to near 22–25deg at 2000rpm; and reaches full advance at 3200rpm. No Harley-Davidson-produced ignition—electronic or manual—completely meets these requirements. Nor do any of the aftermarket replacement ignitions. This is one reason why some drag racing and hillclimb tuners use magnetos that can be modified to give the desired advance curve.

While all Evolution Harley-Davidson electronic ignitions are essentially the same in appearance and in fundamental operation, there is a wide variation in

If you want protection from overrevving, the Screamin' Eagle rev limiter can be plugged in for street use, then unplugged for the track. Harley-Davidson

their advance characteristics. Among all the electronic ignition modules available, the best is the XLH-1200 unit, which has a built-in rev limiter. The Screamin' Eagle module, however, features the 1200's advance curve without the limiter.

The standard Harley-Davidson ignition, first introduced in 1980, is an all-electronic system. The advance curve is built into the logic of a PROM (programmable read only memory) chip in the ignition black box, located under the left-hand side cover on the Sportster. A Hall effect sensor, located under what was the points cover, sends a signal to the ignition box. The signal is generated when one of two windows in a cup, which is attached to the end of the number two cam, passes by the Hall sensor.

When the signal reaches the ignition box it is processed according to the logic programmed into the PROM chip. Depending upon rpm and which of the two programmed advance curves are operating, the PROM then determines when to cut off current flow to the ignition coil. The loss of current through the ignition's primary coil initiates its release of stored energy in the form of sparks across the plug gaps.

All but the first (1980–1982) of the Sportster electronic ignitions have two advance curves. To be completely correct, these aren't curves at all but are, rather, a series of connected slopes that approximate a smooth progression of ignition timing advance with increasing rpm.

One curve is on-line when the pressure in the intake manifold is 3 to 4.5in of mercury less than ambient atmospheric pressure. An adjustable vacuum switch is connected to a port in the intake manifold. The switch is normally closed, but opens when the vacuum in the manifold rises to its adjusted opening point. The purpose of this high-vacuum ignition advance curve is to ensure more complete and cleaner combustion when the throttle is nearly closed and there is relatively little turbulence in the combustion chambers.

The second curve is the full-throttle curve, the one we are most interested in. This curve operates whenever the throttle is open far enough to raise the pressure in the intake manifold to near atmospheric conditions. Normally, depending upon the adjustment of the vacuum switch, the high-vacuum ignition curve operates up to about 65mph on a flat surface. By 70mph, the manifold vacuum triggers the vacuumoperated control switch to switch to the full-throttle curve. Anytime an engine is accelerated, even moderately, the full-throttle curve will determine the degree of ignition advance.

All but one of the current stock ignitions (the 1200 Sportster) advance their full-throttle curves too slowly for performance work. The 1986–1987 XLH-1100 are fail-safe curves, developed for worst-case conditions that require retarded ignition timing to prevent detonation. Thus is the extreme measure that Harley-Davidson engineers have taken to make their engines quieter and cleaner running, which has left the engines highly sensitive to air temperature, moisture, pressure, and gasoline quality.

As soon as any stock Evolution engine is "uncorked" and allowed to breathe freely, a slow timing advance curve is no longer needed. Any engine accelerates best if the timing is advanced as much as possible. The operative word here is "possible." Too much advance can lead to destructive detonation or, more often, loss of power and rough running. Considerable testing by Minton and by Harley-Davidson has led to the conclusion that the Sportster should reach full advance at or near 3200rpm for most high-performance work.

"Most high-performance work" is the key here. Harley-Davidson has used several cylinder head configurations over the years, and each cylinder head expert uses still other shapes. Add other Stage II variables to this, such as cam profiles, and you've got a situation with more uncertainty. There is no way we can recommend exact timing on each machine—with its individual components, cylinder head, and setup—without dyno testing.

Many mechanics and enthusiasts who modify Sportster engines install either the old points system or the early (1980–1982) electronic ignitions. Both the points and early electronic ignitions advance too quickly for optimum driveability; both reach full advance at near 2400rpm, which leads to high loads on the crankshaft bearings and possibly detonation, and a rougher-running engine. Furthermore, the mechanical ignition has a very high wear rate. Use antiseize compound and high-pressure, high-temperature lubricants to prevent wear.. A point system has no spark energy advantage over electronic ignition.

The popularity of the early ignition types can be attributed to dyno performance testing in 1984, conducted by Joe Minton and Jerry Branch of Branch Flowmetrics in which they found that the early electronic ignition gave best results. However, it is important to know that all testing was conducted at rpm exceeding 3000, so the early ignition was at full advance, whereas the stock ignition of that time did not reach full advance until 5000rpm, so the dyno results led to a conclusion that the old 2400rpm full-advance ignition worked better. The results of that testing were published in *Motorcyclist* magazine, and were widely read. As a result, engines are still being built based on those tests. However, subsequent modules and testing made it very clear to Minton and others that the early ignition advanced too quickly.

As mentioned, the Harley-Davidson ignition that has proven most satisfactory is the 1200 Sportster ignition. It has an idle advance of about 7deg before top dead center, 20deg at 2000rpm, and reaches its full advance of 28deg at 4200rpm. A normal 883 ignition will have only 10deg or so of advance at 2000rpm and doesn't reach full advance until 6000. The stock 883 ignition can make a well-built high-performance engine feel sluggish and unresponsive below 3000rpm.

There are four variations of the 1200 ignition module. They all have the same advance curves; however, only two are completely satisfactory for high-performance 883/1200 Sportster work. The first is the Screamin' Eagle variation sold as an off-road performance part. The built-in rev limiter (common to all Harley-Davidson Evolution ignitions) of the Screamin' Eagle module is set for 8000rpm. Since Sportsters won't create power or last very long at that engine speed, this ignition essentially has no rev limiter at all.

The second recommended module is the earliest of the 1200 modules, part number 32410-87. This module's rev limiter is set for 6500rpm, and is an excellent option for the 883/1200 Stage I engine. It acts as an rpm safety limit for the engine, which is finished making useful power after about 6500rpm anyway. However, a Stage II type of Sportster produces peak power near 7500rpm, and will need the Screamin' Eagle ignition.

As mentioned earlier, Harley-Davidson's practice of firing both cylinders at the same time was not the best way to ignite a V-twin. We are all familiar with the irregular, lumpy idle of the Harley-Davidson motorcycle. The stock ignition design contributes to this, and to their tendency to backfire through the carburetor when they are cold or too lean.

Sportsters have a double-output ignition coil. Each of the coil's two high-tension leads is connected to one of the two spark plugs. When the coil discharges, it fires both plugs. When the front cylinder's compressed air-fuel mixture is ignited at, say, 30deg before top dead center, the rear cylinder is already 15deg after top dead center and well into its intake stroke. In fact, the rear cylinder's intake valve may have been open and admitting air-fuel mixture for 60deg of crankshaft rotation. When the plugs fire, the front one ignites the compressed mixture and starts that cylinder on its power stroke. The rear plug also fires and may ignite some of the mixture being drawn into the rear cylinder.

If the mixture in the rear cylinder burns completely, the result will be a backfire through the carburetor and air cleaner because of the open intake valve. A partial burn merely adds to that rough and lumpy idle that we all know and love.

The sooner the rear intake valve opens during the engine cycle, the more likely it is to backfire. That is why high-performance, long-duration and overlap cams tend to make Harley-Davidsons run so rough below 3000rpm. Then too, some engine builders select cams that are entirely too radical for the engine's real needs.

There are alternatives. When an ignition fires one cylinder at a time, the idle evens out and carburetor

Flow tests on the SU 2in carburetor indicate that it flows less air than the standard Sportster CV-type carburetor (1988 and later). It is also very long and hangs down by the rider's leg. There was a time, however, before the Evolution engine, that the SU had a prominent place in the world of high-performance Sportsters. Rivera Engineering

backfires are virtually eliminated. Furthermore, this single-fire ignition improves smoothness and engine response below 3000rpm, and especially below 2500rpm. Single- and double-fire ignitions produce the same power, however. Single-fire ignitions are sold by Accel, MC Power Arc, and others.

Stage II Carburetors

Any number of carburetors have been mounted on Sportsters over the years. Some work very well, some don't. A list of these carburetors covers every application, from the dedicated drag racing carbure-

The Weber carburetor kit, available from Rivera, requires some expertise to tune. As supplied with these manifolds, it sticks way out, and has major restrictions in the inlet tract and air cleaner. But it looks trick! Rivera Engineering

The comprehensive Screamin' Eagle 40mm carburetor kit includes everything needed for a high-performance application. For 1988 and later models, the kit requires a 1986 style manifold, although a high-performance type from HES or Jerry Branch would be a better choice. Harley-Davidson

tor to one that serves no more purpose than to make a styling statement. Some have long, sinuous inlet tracks, some have dual throats, and some have large, bulbous housings, but many do not perform as well as the standard Harley-Davidson CV unit. A number of the carburetors that worked miracles on the iron-head XL do little or nothing for the Evolution engine.

The popular S&S carburetor is a good all-around, compact unit. However, the very features that make it easy to tune also make it more difficult to get a clean transition between the intermediate circuit and the high-speed circuit. S&S Cycle

That's because the Evolution Sportster engine flows and burns so much better. The new-technology Evolution needs an evolutionary carburetor as well.

Three contemporary carburetor kits stand out as being most suitable for the Stage II motors. Installing one of these carburetors on a Stage I engine, with the standard 883 ports, has little effect; however, installing one on an engine with 1200 heads will gain about 3hp or so. The qualifications of suitable carburetors include adequate airflow capacity, tunability , and convenience, including ease of installation, safe operation, and driveability.

Harley-Davidson sells a large (40mm) fixed-venturi carburetor kit through their Screamin' Eagle line of performance parts. The Screamin' Eagle carburetor will pass enough air to allow a Stage II Sportster motor to make over 90hp. A Stage I motor, with stock ports, does not gain much horsepower from this carburetor.

The new-style Screamin' Eagle carburetor is simple to tune. The added intermediate circuit eliminates mid-range lean running and stumbling. A complete line of alternate jets for all three circuits ensures fine tuning, making it easy to "dial-in" for most applications. It will deliver a lot more air than any other factory carburetor, which means more power output than is possible with other Harley-Davidson carburetors. The Screamin' Eagle is compact, and the installation is as sturdy as Harley-Davidson typically makes its products. Parts are available from any authorized Harley-Davidson dealer.

S&S Cycle, long known for their high-quality stroker kits, has introduced a new pair of fixed-

Mikuni carburetors have a reputation for being excellent fuel mixers. The kit for Sportsters comes complete with all necessary hardware, including an efficient K&N air filter. The more complex jetting circuitry of a Mikuni can be difficult for the inexperienced mechanic to master; however, no other carburetor can be so finely tuned to produce a crisp-running Sportster. Joe Minton

venturi carburetors. S&S has been selling their own, American-made fixed-venturi Harley-Davidson carburetors for more than twenty years. The latest versions, the E and G units, are the best they have ever produced.

The new S&S Super E (1⁷/₈in bore diameter) and Super G (2¹/₁₆in diameter) are actually more compact than the stock carburetors they replace. The quality of these kits is matched only by Harley-Davidson's. Like the Screamin' Eagle carburetor, the S&S units have only two basic tuning parts, a slow and main jet, in addition to the idle mixture adjusting screw. The S&S carburetor design is very easy to tune. It has the same basic tuning limits as the Harley-Davidson unit, so it sometimes shows perceptible transition difficulties.

Mikuni America's HS40 carburetor kit is probably the most versatile of the three. It is the most tunable, and also the most complicated to tune. It comes pre-jetted, so only a few installations will require more than minor adjustments to get it right. The Mikuni can be tuned to handle the same engine combination that might leave the Harley-Davidson or S&S carburetors staggering.

The S&S and Harley-Davidson carburetors can be made to respond as well as a Mikuni in certain applications with the addition of a ThunderJet. The ThunderJet effectively adds another fuel circuit,

ThunderJets, here installed on an S&S carburetor with a velocity stack for drag racing use, help to overcome some of the "flat spots" that some aftermarket carburetors experience. Zipper's Performance Products

This S&S carburetor has been equipped with a ThunderJet for street and occasional drag use. The ThunderJet is a unique type of "power jet" that enriches carburetion at wide-open throttle. The carburetor vacuum draws the fuel into the jet, but it is the strength of the intake pulse that draws fuel into the airstream. A rich pulse is weak; a lean pulse is strong (you can even hear this in the exhaust note). The strong pulse of slightly lean jetting draws more fuel, compensating for top-end lean running. This makes it easier to eliminate any transition jetting problems between the other fuel circuits.

This drilling operation is required when installing ThunderJets. You can do it yourself or have a performance shop do it for you. Zipper's Performance Products

which makes the existing circuits more adjustable and thus greatly improves throttle response.

Mikuni furnishes a complete and understandable tuning manual with their kit. With the manual as a guide, any special tuning needs can almost certainly be handled by a skilled and experienced mechanic. However, if you have never tuned a carburetor, you may be less than successful, depending on your skills. The HS40 is more responsive to tuning than any of the other carburetors, including the stock Sportster unit. It will not pass quite as much air as the other two, but its superior responsiveness often puts the Mikuni-equipped Sportster ahead of the others in a roll-on. The 883/1200 Stage I engine is a perfect match for this carburetor.

Installed, Mikuni's HS40 carburetor kit is more compact than the Screamin' Eagle kit, but it protrudes farther out from the engine than the S&S. The S&S setup is the most rigid of the three aftermarket carburetors, the Screamin' Eagle the least, with the Mikuni kit falling between the two.

For the ultimate in airflow performance, the S&S Super G carburetor flows much better than the Super E and it flows 15cfm more than the Mikuni HS40. Note, however, that these figures are without an air filter installed. With identical air filters, the differences between the carburetors diminish. The Super G still flows more, but only 5cfm better than the HS40. Clearly an air cleaner is the great equalizer, or bottleneck, if you prefer.

All of these carburetors flow well enough for the old iron Sportster engines.

Camshafts

Evolution Sportster engines are fitted with the longest duration (hottest) stock cams of any current Harley-Davidson. Their valve timing provides a wide power band extending from idle to a bit over 6000rpm in the case of a Stage I 1200 and the 883/1200 conversion. They can also work surprisingly well in engines with modified heads. And they are quiet mechanically due to a precise matching procedure at the time of engine assembly.

Aftermarket cams designed for the Evolution Sportster are almost universally too radical; that is, they have too much duration. In all of hot rodding, whether it be motorcycles or automobiles, the strongest tendency is to "overcam" an engine. That is especially true of Harley-Davidson tuners, who disregard engine performance below 3000rpm. That low-rpm range makes the difference between a Sportster that is docile and fun to ride, and one that is difficult and unpleasant to ride.

Without presenting a treatise on cam design, we will outline some of the critical elements of cam profiles and selection as they relate to Sportster Evolution motors. The most important valve timing event that occurs every 720deg of crankshaft rotation, is when the intake valve closes. Basically the sooner it closes, the lower the rpm at which power will be produced. On the other hand, the later the intake valve closes, the higher the rpm at which peak power will be made.

The second most important valve timing event is when the exhaust valve opens. The later it opens, the more of the power stroke can be turned into power to push the piston and therefore the rear wheel. The sooner it opens, the more time will be available for the cylinder to "blow-down."

Valve lift (its maximum distance above its valve seat) is critical in that the valve must open far enough and quickly enough to allow the port to serve a

Before the HES-Branch manifold was introduced, tuners had to weld additional material and re-machine the stock Sportster inlet manifold to get more air flow. Yet even after this extensive re-work, it still can't match the results provided by the HES unit. Joe Minton

Roller-type rocker arms have proven themselves in street and racing engines for years. Some of the benefits are a quieter, smoother running valvetrain, and a decrease in valve and guide wear. Performance shops like Zipper's can perform the conversion on your rockers, or provide an exchange set. Crane offers a set that is made from alloy steel with needle bearings. Zipper's Performance Products

generous helping of air-fuel mixture to the cylinder. When the desired valve lift, exhaust-valve opening, and intake-valve closing parameters are achieved, the other two valve timing events (intake valve open, exhaust valve close) are largely determined by the mechanics of the system. If parts didn't weigh anything, then valves could be opened instantly and at the perfect time. Since everything in the valvetrain has mass, there are limits to how hard the metal parts can be pushed without failing or wearing rapidly. Therefore, the cam lobes must be designed to move valves as rapidly as possible without causing undue wear or outright failure.

The Evolution Sportster engine is capable of turning 7000rpm with a reasonable amount of reliability. It can, for short periods, rev as high as 7500rpm without catastrophic failure. At these high engine speeds the crank pin begins to spall (chip off layers) due to the extreme loads. Many of the aftermarket cams have timings that would provide their peak horsepower when the engine is at over 7500rpm. That's fine if you are after all the horsepower you can get and don't care how many times you rebuild the engine (or replace it). But for a reliable street engine, these cams should be avoided. They usually result in power loss below 3000 or even 3500rpm, and only tend to encourage overrevving the engine.

The Harley-Davidson Screamin' Eagle cam timing matches the Sportster's mechanical limits very well, so this is a good choice for reliable street use. However, the cam lobe position provides only moderate power output below 3000rpm.

A set of new cams, such as this Red Shift set from Zipper's, is necessary to extract the most from a Stage II-type Sportster. The standard cams work well for a strong and reliable 70hp street bike, but anyone wanting to cross the 75hp barrier must change cams.

Andrews sells two cam sets that are similar to the Harley-Davidson Screamin' Eagle kit (Andrews, by the way, manufactures Screamin' Eagle cams), except that they generate better bottom-end power. The Andrews V4 and V8 XL cam sets begin to come to life at about 2700rpm, and peak at about 7500rpm, with a well-ported head. (The Andrews versions for the five-speed Sportsters are designated N4 and N8.)

The Andrews V8 cam has been part of many dyno-tested ninety-plus horsepower 1200cc Sport-

The nice thing about Harley-Davidson's XL cam kit is that it has been designed and extensively tested for use with hydraulic lifters, and to address such issues as valve dynamics, durability, and broad power band. Unlike many other cams, the Harley-Davidson cam kit was specifically designed to work well with all the other Screamin' Eagle components when installed on standard XLH-1200 heads or lightly modified heads. Harley-Davidson

The factory selects the standard Sportster cam gears to match each individual cam gear case. This keeps backlash and noise to an absolute minimum. When installing aftermarket cams, cam gear tolerances may not be ideal and some cam sets can sound like they're grinding rocks. The Red Shift cams allow you to keep your factory-installed cam gears. The Red Shift cam lobes are installed onto your original gears. You get the best of both worlds.

When building the ultimate high-output Sportster using cams with higher lifts and steep opening ramps, high-performance valve springs are required. Shown here is the

Harley-Davidson Screamin' Eagle kit. These kits are also available from Andrews, Bartels', and other sources.

sters. The V8 cam has more exhaust valve duration, which tends to cool the engine better than the V4 at high rpms. In practical terms, this only benefits a Sportster on a road race track, where most time is spent at full throttle. The V4 cams start working well at 2000rpm and peak at slightly over 7000rpm.

The Bartels' Performance Products cam set (also made by Andrews.) provides a perfect example of how the Sportster benefits from "undercamming." The Bartels' cams have slightly more moderate timing. Dyno evaluation and street testing indicate that the Bartels' cams give excellent all-round performance, and they make nearly as much peak power as the Andrews V8s.

This brings up the subject of relative performance. Some cams improve performance at moderate, everyday engine speeds. Depending on what a rider wants, this quality can more than compensate for a relative lack of peak power. A more radical cam that produces an extra 5hp at 7500rpm may not necessarily be the best choice for a street Sportster. When selecting a cam for street use, consider the mid-range, roll-on power. The best advice we can give you about cams for your Stage II engine: restrain yourself. The cams with the most duration do not necessarily provide either the most power or the widest

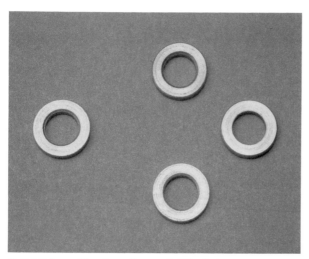

Solid lifters, like these Screamin' Eagle types, are generally not needed in the average high-performance street bike. They are preferred, however, by builders in high-output racing applications. Harley-Davidson

Valve Springs

The stock Sportster valve springs are adequate for a Stage I engine. If the engine is run at high rpm for long periods, such as in Twin Sports road racing, the stock springs lose some of their preload, and it is possible that the valves may begin floating around 6500rpm or so. In ordinary or even hard street use, the stock springs seem to hold up just fine and there is no need to replace them with aftermarket spring sets. Furthermore, most aftermarket springs are designed for a higher seat pressure and are much stiffer. These springs will place greater loads on the valve gear and can lead to higher wear rates, so they should be avoided.

A Stage II engine is a different animal because it has professionally ported heads and high-performance cams. Your porting service will almost certainly fit stiffer, more durable valve springs for the more aggressive action of the high-performance camshafts.

Lifters: Solid Versus Hydraulic

To understand the need for solid (adjustable) lifters in a street application, we must again look at the inverse relationship between engine speed and engine life. As we have pointed out, a Sportster has excellent reliability when limited to 6000rpm, and even a 6500rpm limit provides reasonable engine durability and life. Occasional bursts to 7000rpm begin to affect engine life more dramatically. For any kind of durability, it is not a good idea to use 7500rpm or more as a redline. The question is, how often do you want to rebuild your engine?

With today's hydraulic lifters, it is possible to rev a Sportster to 8000rpm. There are plenty of cams that are designed for hydraulic lifters. There are also plenty of 90 and 100hp Sportsters, not to mention drag bikes, running around with hydraulics revving to 7500rpm and beyond. The riders of these machines enjoy the benefits of hydraulics: quiet, low-maintenance performance. By keeping engine speeds under 6500rpm, they also enjoy reasonable longevity.

Solid lifters provide a slight performance advantage. Since a solid lifter is lighter than a hydraulic type, the cam design can be more aggressive, and the valve can be accelerated quicker. This helps to develop more midrange power and to reach ultra-high engine speeds. Aggressive cam designs, with quick-opening ramps, tend to collapse Sportster lifters (that's the ticking sound you hear). Engines intended for constant high-rpm use (and frequent overhauls) can benefit from solid lifters. These kinds of engine speeds never occur in street engines on a constant basis, however. In practical terms, they are limited mainly to ultra-performance applications such as racing and record-breaking attempts.

Automotive cams supplied by oil systems with 40lb of oil pressure don't have much of a problem with lifter collapse. The low oil pressure requirements of the Sportster's roller bearings present a unique challenge to aggressive cam design. Cam design technology, however, has led to ways of providing performance nearly equal to solid lifters.

Harley-Davidson found in tests that at extreme rpm, even solid lifters flex, upset valvetrain dynamics, and lead to loss of valve control.

Considering the disadvantages of extreme noise and higher maintenance—and the high performance of today's computer-designed hydraulic cams—solid lifters do not seem to provide any real advantage in street use.

Pushrods

Aluminum pushrods have only one-third the stiffness of steel rods, but they are lighter and run quieter. Steel pushrods, while stiffer, weigh 6 ounces more. The 4130 chrome-moly rods can be used in a racing engine, but the quieter aluminum rod makes a better street choice.

Intake Flow Comparison Chart

Valve lift (in)	Intake flow stock 883 (cfm)	Intake flow modified 883 (cfm)	Intake flow modified 1200 (cfm)
0.050	13.5	18.9	23.8
0.100	31.0	37.1	43.1
0.150	47.9	54.7	63.8
0.200	62.6	69.4	81.6
0.250	75.6	83.9	96.1
0.300	82.3	92.7	108.2
0.350	85.2	99.1	118.0
0.400	87.9	104.5	125.4
0.450	89.6	107.2	129.2
0.500	91.3	109.1	132.4
0.550	91.4	110.4	134.9
Open	95.9	120.2	149.4

This chart compares the typical flow in cubic feet per minute (cfm) through a standard XLH-883 head, a ported 883 (3.00in bore) with bigger valves, and a highly modified 1200 head with 1.94in intake and 1.62in exhaust valves.

All tests were performed with the heads mounted on a cylinder with the manifold and carburetor in place. The stock 883 head is an earlier sand-cast type with the bathtub-shaped chamber, and it had the early 34mm carburetor. The modified 883 head had an improved intake manifold and a 40mm Screamin' Eagle carburetor, while the 1200 head had a 44mm Mikuni carburetor.

The maximum valve lift of the stock Sportster cam is less than 0.450in. A stock 883 needs more than 120cfm at 7000rpm, and at 0.450in lift it gets only 90cfm or so. While the figures for the modified 883 may look good, the inlet velocity was down from 151fps (feet per second) to 34fps, which is too low. Adding a velocity stack gets air speed up to 149fps, which would improve low-speed running.

The 125cfm flow attained by the modified 1200 heads at 0.400in lift is more than enough to feed a

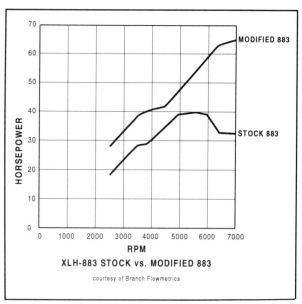

This graph compares the standard 1986 XLH-883 power output with the output of a modified 883. The modified machine had a Sifton cam set, an enlarged manifold, Screamin' Eagle carburetor and filter, and a dual Super-Trapp exhaust system with fifteen discs in each muffler. The modified heads, with their bigger valves and enlarged ports, helped the engine breathe to 7000rpm. It gained more than 50 percent more power over the stock XLH-883. This engine would undoubtedly gain another 10–15hp by installing a 1200cc piston kit.

Sportster engine at over 7000rpm. This type of cylinder head was used in the engine that produced 95.6hp (rear wheel) at 7500rpm. This equals about 110hp at the crankshaft, which is about 1.5hp per cubic inch.

Conclusion

This covers the component portion of Stage I and Stage II modifications. The actual preparation and assembly, as well as cylinder head modifications, are covered in the next chapter.

These discussions of the Sportster's design limitations are not meant to be condemnations. Rather, they are intended to reveal some of the limitations of an engine designed for reliable everyday street use, when applied to the high-performance world. It also helps to explain and support our contention that very aggressive and extensive modifications of the Evolution Sportster engine can be ultimately expensive—and successful.

The Sportster is a very tough, long-lived, reliable engine. It will not live very long, however, if it spends considerable time at engine speeds above 6000rpm, or much time pushing 7000rpm. It will endure an occasional rev to 7500, but higher speeds result in very short engine life and very large overhaul bills.

That's not to say that a more durable engine isn't possible. Ultimate reliability depends on planning and application. By completely dismantling the entire

powertrain, carefully selecting and matching components, and assembling with an expert's attention to detail, a Sportster can be made bulletproof at these high speeds. Pete Laub, for example, runs an XR-1000, which is nothing more than a Sportster with fancy heads, in drag racing. His low-ten-second runs are made at 8400rpm, which is a piston speed of over 5000fpm. It can be done, for short periods at least.

As we have noted, the Stage I and Stage II engines described here are not the only possible combination of modifications and components that produce 70 to 90hp. They are, however, highly developed and proven combinations. Either of these engines promises relative economy, durability, and responsiveness—fun machines to ride on a daily basis. They also outperform the majority of more expensively equipped and more highly modified Sportsters that you are likely to run across on the street.

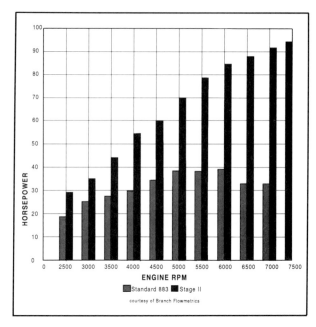

Pistons	Branch 1200cc EV Sportster 3.5in
Heads	Branch-modified #4 design with $1^{15}/_{16}$in intake valve
Cams	Andrews V-4 with hydraulic lifters
Pushrods	H-D Screamin' Eagle
Carburetor	VM44 Mikuni with 370 main jet
Air cleaner	H-D Screamin' Eagle
Exhaust	SuperTrapp two-into-one with twenty-one discs
Ignition	Dual plug, Andrews coils, timed 30deg
Spark plugs	H-D 6R12, 0.028in gap
Fuel	Standard SU2000 92 octane
Compression ratio	8.5:1; cranking compression 175psi

These are the final results of the Stage II development project by Joe Minton and Jerry Branch.

Chapter 4

How to Build a High-Performance Sportster Engine

Chapter 3 discussed the theories and bolt-on components involved in building a high-performance Sportster engine. This chapter covers the modifications and assembly, including port work and combustion chamber changes.

For the most part, the discussion of engine modifications is directed at the vast majority of riders who are interested in a powerful, yet reliable street Sportster. When you combine those two requirements, you get an engine similar to the Stage II version that produces a maximum of about 90hp, one that can be revved with reasonable safety to 6500rpm with an occasional burst to 7000rpm. The more you take a Sportster engine to this speed and beyond, the more you detract from its dependability and longevity.

For those of us who are less concerned with the preventive maintenance and frequent overhauls required by the ultimate Ninja killer, the possibilities are endless. But don't get me wrong; a 130hp Sportster does not automatically become the kind of motorcycle that must be followed around by a tow truck. Proper planning, along with careful attention to detail and setup, can help extend engine life.

Engine Blueprinting

Harley-Davidson shop-manual and production-assembly specifications are, like their ignition-advance curves, set for worst-case situations. For instance, the piston-to-cylinder clearance in the manual's boring recommendations will hover at around 0.002in. The excellent stock pistons with their barrel-shaped skirts can be run at 0.0005in, but extreme care must be taken to ensure a gentle break-in. The difference between what is possible and what is practical exists for two reasons.

First, Harley-Davidson cannot control an engine's break-in, and it is more realistic (and cheaper) to use production-assembly tolerances near the upper limit of piston clearance. Second, the factory has no control over how its parts are installed, outside of providing clear instructions. For instance, if a Sport-

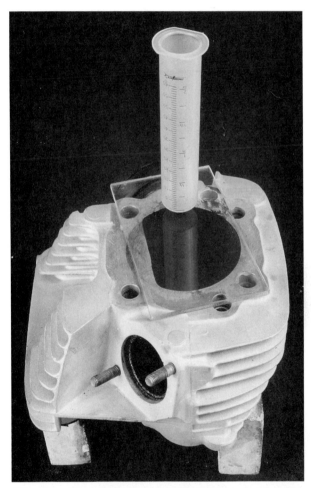

Measuring the combustion chamber volume involves the use of a plastic plate with a small hole in it and a burette (or in this case, an irrigation syringe) marked off in 1cc increments. You can pick up a burette at a medical supply house. Smear a thin layer of grease on the head and place it upside-down with the gasket surface horizontal. Put the plate on the surface and inject or pour oil into the chamber (engine oil works just fine). A chamber volume of 68cc, with the appropriate gaskets gives a 10.0:1 compression ratio in a 1200cc Sportster. Joe Minton

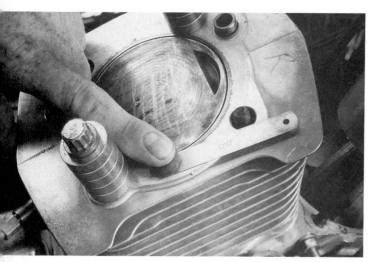

To set proper squish, the deck height must be determined by measuring the height of the piston above or below the top of the cylinder. This can be done with the simple use of a feeler gauge. Any "proud" surface can be felt with your finger. Tests have shown this to be an accurate means of measurement. Joe Minton

To measure clearances between the valves and head surfaces, use some clay to hold soldering wire in place. Install the head and tighten a couple of head bolts, rotate the engine through top dead center, and remove the head. Karl Schlei

ster's cylinders are honed without the proper use of torque plates, the cylinders may distort so much when installed and running that the pistons may bind on the cylinders and seize. Then too, not every mechanic can accurately read a micrometer, set up a boring bar, and operate a hone to end up with precision results.

Success in building a high-performance engine depends first and foremost on planning. As simple as their construction may seem, the parts have seen hundreds of hours of testing on dynos, tracks, and on the street. Seemingly small deviations from the recommended selection of components may result in large performance losses. The most notable example is using a set of popular, small accessory mufflers, instead of a large-volume type. Another would be the substitution of almost any of the small accessory air cleaners on the market. Some use foam as a filtering element, which need a larger surface area to equal the airflow volumes of the pleated cloth type, as made by K&N Engineering. A foam filter that is smaller in surface area than the Screamin' Eagle, Mikuni, or S&S filters is certain to be more restrictive.

Make no mistake, untested combinations of parts and modifications are just that—untested. Most attempts to mix various performance parts that have not been tested together result in failure. Intelligent selection based on experience certainly helps, but there is no substitute for testing. So whether you choose to follow the combination we lay out, or pick a proven package offered by a successful speed shop, the point is, *don't try to mix and match.*

The clearances can be measured with a vernier caliper or dial gauge. Karl Schlei

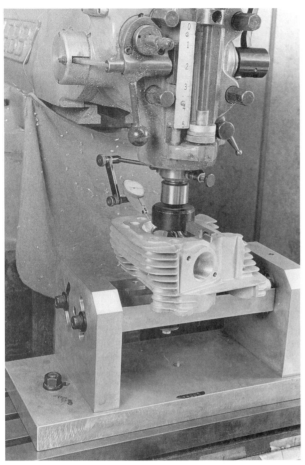

Milling a head increases an engine's compression. Head milling takes material away from the largest area of the combustion chamber, so it doesn't take a lot to increase the engine's compression ratio. Joe Minton

Surface the head to assure flatness. A piece of wet-and-dry paper on a glass surface works in the absence of a surface-lapping plate. Karl Schlei

Hone the cylinder using the desired stones. If the cylinder was rebored, it is necessary to clamp it between torque plates for final piston fitting. When breaking the glaze to fit new rings, however, this is not required. Use soft vice-jaw plates to protect the cylinder surfaces. Karl Schlei

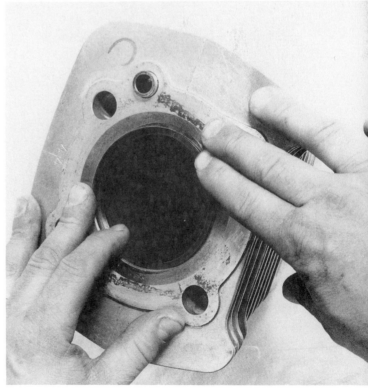

To check the ring end gap, first place the ring in the cylinder. Karl Schlei

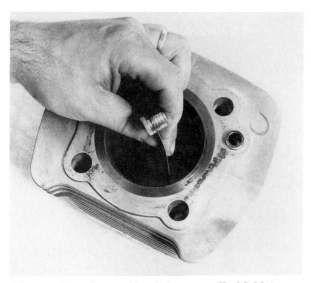

Push it down with a piston to assure that the ring is square. Karl Schlei

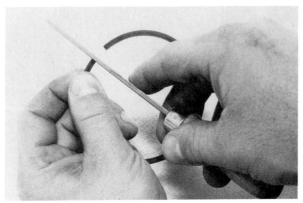

Measure the end gap with a feeler gauge. Karl Schlei

If too tight, use a file to adjust the gap. Karl Schlei

Engine Disassembly and Re-Assembly

Equally important as a correct selection of engine components is the care with which they are assembled. If you, as an amateur mechanic, work slowly and deliberately, the results can equal that of a professional mechanic. The main differences between you and that professional are familiarity and training. He or she will be able to disassemble and reassemble the engine more quickly because they know what all the parts look like and remember exactly where they go.

On the other hand, your engine may have to remain partially disassembled while you are waiting for the cylinders to be bored or while the heads are being ported. During that time parts can get dusty (or lost), and you can forget precisely where every nut

Check the piston clearance. The "quick and dirty" way is a feeler gauge. Slide it and the piston through the bore. Karl Schlei

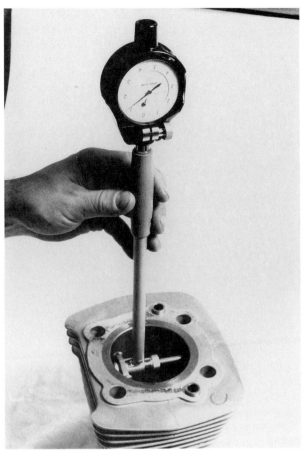

Piston clearance measured with bore gauge and micrometer. Karl Schlei

Measure the piston about ⅛in from the bottom of the skirt. Karl Schlei

When installing the oil ring, make sure that it does not overlap itself. It must butt end to end. Karl Schlei

Check the ring clearances in the grooves with a feeler gauge, then make sure the ring gaps are spaced about 90 degrees apart around the piston's circumference. Karl Schlei

Fit one clip and install the piston on the rod. Make sure the clip's groove is clean. Never re-use a piston pin clip; after removing an old one, immediately discard it so that it won't be re-used. When inserting the piston pin, always use the proper factory tool, HD-95984-32B. Karl Schlei

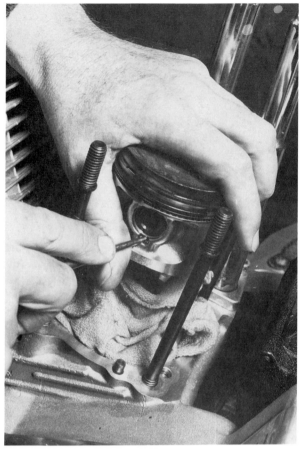

Install the other clip. Be sure to put a rag in the case openings to prevent the pin and other debris from dropping into the crankcase. Karl Schlei

Clean and check the surface of the case deck, and install the base gasket. Karl Schlei

Slide the barrel in place. If the cylinder has a large enough chamber, a ring compressor may not be necessary. Karl Schlei

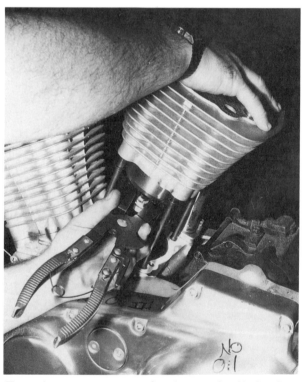

The safest way to protect the rings and cylinder from damage is to use a ring compressor. Karl Schlei

and bolt goes. Both of these problems can be overcome with the simple use of plastic bags and a permanent felt marker.

There are several methods of organizing disassembled parts. For example, when you remove the screws and washers that hold on the valve cover assemblies, place them in a Zip-Loc bag and mark the contents on the bag. Whatever bits and pieces are in that bag will then be identified as to where they go on or in the engine, and—very important—they will stay clean. Major subassemblies can be kept together in larger bags, boxes, or pans, and arranged in the order of disassembly and reassembly.

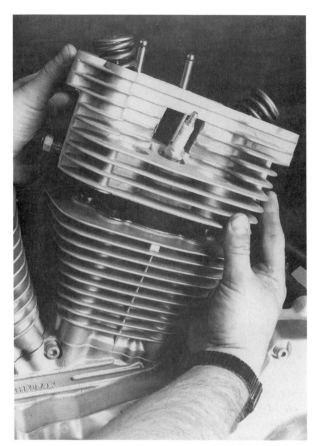

Install the head over studs and dowels. Karl Schlei

Install the correct head gasket. Karl Schlei

Some head gaskets, like those made of annealed copper, can be re-used. Even composite paper/copper gaskets can be used again providing the surfaces are in reasonable condition (right). The newer graphite-coated gaskets, however, usually stick to the surfaces and de-laminate and cannot be re-used (left). Karl Schlei

Torque the head beginning with bolt number one. Torque bolts to desired tension (see text). Install the rocker box assembly. Karl Schlei

97

Cylinder Head Nut Torque

If you overtorque the cylinder head nuts, you will increase the distortion of the cylinders. On the other hand, if you undertorque the nuts, the engine is likely to leak combustion gases when cold.

Harley-Davidson's original torque specification called for 25lb-ft of torque. However, the latest factory torque instructions involve applying 16lb-ft to the head nuts, and then tighten the nuts an additional quarter turn. This amounts to an actual 40lb-ft. We have found that 40lb-ft is a minimum reliable torque value when using any of the head gaskets discussed in this and the previous chapter. Any more torque serves only to increase cylinder distortion; any less may result in cold leaks. Extreme torque, above 50lb-ft, may lead to broken studs or ruined cases when the studs pull the threads out. Torque all the other top-end bolts to factory specs.

Before beginning, have all the parts at hand, and be sure that you have all the tools needed. It's a good idea to check the various sizes of bolts and screws, and make a dry run with your tools to see if you need something that isn't in your toolbox. Order the special tools, such as the piston pin tool and ring compressor, for example, from your dealer. Clear your bench and have plenty of clean cloth or paper towels ready to cover things and keep them clean. Many professional mechanics use antistatic cloth to help control dirt and dust, but an old clean t-shirt will do the job just fine.

Think the job through. Become familiar with the parts and procedures. Review the related sections of the Harley-Davidson service manual. Prepare, and the job will go more smoothly—and without surprises.

When you are ready to begin, thoroughly wash and dry the engine, especially around the cylinders and heads. Dirt can accumulate in the nooks and crannies and subsequently fall into the engine upon disassembly. Have fun!

This is the process to machine a head to accept dual spark plugs. The head is bolted into a jig, and is counterbored and tapped to accept a 10mm or 12mm plug. It's a fairly simple operation for a professional machinist, but requires the proper jig to assure precision results. H.E.S. can perform the service. Courtesy Andy Hansen; Joe Minton

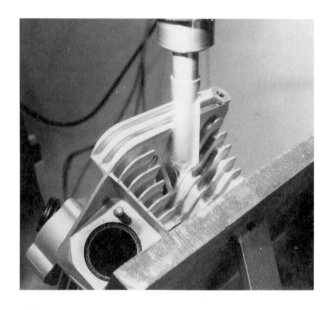

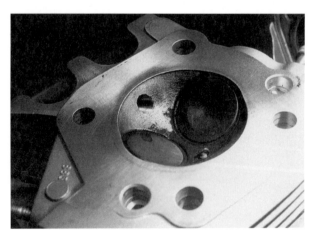

Gaskets and O-Rings

As previously discussed, complete sealing has posed some problems. Using the latest light-colored Harley-Davidson base gaskets, or using Hylomar sealant with the aluminum base gaskets, almost always seals against oil seepage. However, even this leaks if the crankcases are not completely flat.

All gasket surfaces should be flattened with a fine, smooth file. If the sealing surface has a ding, a large single-cut mill file works well to take out the high spots. While the occasional little bumps are not a problem with the stock compliant gaskets, they must be removed if the much more rigid copper and aluminum gaskets are used.

Sometimes there will be a ridge where the case halves meet. If this ridge cannot be completely smoothed with a few light file strokes, you should stick to the Harley-Davidson paper gaskets. The earlier base gaskets, dark charcoal gray in color, have a tendency to squeeze out or begin to seep oil after a few tens of thousands of miles. The new base gasket, so far, seems to do a better job of keeping the oil inside.

When installing the head gaskets, do not use substitute O-rings between the heads and cylinders for the stock ones. Harley-Davidson (and Bartels') uses the best O-ring material available and they will stand up to the pressures and temperatures of this engine. Should you use the Bartels' gasket kit, you must also use the O-rings furnished with it. They are smaller than stock to match the thinner Bartels' copper head gaskets.

Piston Rings

Neither the stock Harley-Davidson, Wiseco, nor the other high-performance piston rings require any special attention beyond setting the ring end gaps on the first and second compression rings. Both types run safely with 0.012in end gaps. The three-piece oil control rings should not require adjustment, either.

Ring end gap is easy to check and modify as required. Set the ring into the cylinder bore that it is going to be run in. Next, use a piston to push the ring down into the bore a couple of inches. This will ensure that the ring is square with the bore. Then measure the end gap with feeler gauges. If the gap is too small, clamp the ring in a smooth vise and gently file the ends with a Swiss-pattern file. Go slowly, as the material comes off quickly and you can't put it back on.

Carrillo forged rods have become a standard among many drag racers running fuel burners and maximum-output Sportsters. They are made from 4340 chrome-moly, heat *treated, and magnafluxed. A set comes complete with pre-fitted pin, bearings, and cages.*

One of the myths about engines has to do with ring gap positioning. The rings do not remain in place in their bores; instead, they rotate. The rotation rate may vary, so the relative position of the end gaps will change. Because of this, it is not critical that the piston ring gaps be evenly spaced around the pistons when they are installed. However, it is still important to stagger the gaps at least 1in or so. It is easier to coax the rings into a cylinder bore if both the first and second ring end gaps, while offset from one another, are at the front or rear of the piston.

Three-piece oil rings also rotate—as a body. The two thin scraper rings that sandwich the expander do not usually move relative to one another, and should be installed with the gaps offset.

Cylinders

When your cylinders return from the machine shop, deburr the edges where the bore meets the top of the cylinders with a half-round file. Be careful, though; these edges can be sharp enough to cut yourself. Then check the flatness of the cylinder faces, top and bottom.

Use a fresh SOS pad and hot water to thoroughly scrub the cylinder bores. Normal parts cleaning solvents fail to remove the honing oil that binds tiny chips of cylinder material and, worse yet, the carborundum particles from the honing stones to the cylinder bore surfaces. No matter how clean the cylinders may seem, they will not be free of the destructive carborundum until cleaned with soap and water. After you scrub the bores, immediately dry them and apply a thin film of oil to prevent rust. Do *not* skip this step.

Your boring professional should have cut a small chamfer around the bore at the bottom of the cylinder. The purpose of the chamfer is to make it easier to get the rings started into the bore. If the chamfer is large enough, a ring compressor may not be needed; however, to be safe it is a good idea to use one.

Deck Height

A Stage I Sportster engine may run well without squish, but it may respond just as well when the clearance between the pistons and heads is close. The relative height of a piston to its cylinder is called deck height, and it controls the amount of squish height. A tight squish height results in a more responsive and cooler running engine. A Stage II engine absolutely requires tight squish clearance, therefore this step should not be skipped.

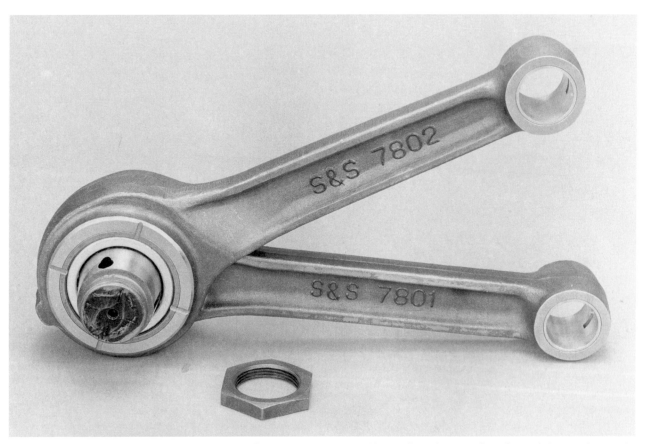

S&S offers replacement heavy-duty rods for the Sportster, including the XR-1000. Although strong, they are heavier than Harley-Davidson-made rods, and the crank must be rebalanced. S&S Cycle

Because the squish areas of the pistons and heads on an Evolution Sportster are flat, checking and setting a proper squish height is relatively easy. Simply measure the relative heights of the pistons and their cylinders, and then adjust the clearance between the pistons and heads with gasket thicknesses.

To check the deck height, install the pistons on the connecting rods without piston rings, slide the base gaskets (dry) and cylinders in place, and clamp the cylinders down lightly using two of the four cylinder head nuts and spacers. A hand-tight fit is good enough.

Rotate the crankshaft until one of the pistons is at top dead center (TDC). You can either use the TDC mark on the crankshaft, seen through the timing port, or simply position the piston by feel. Either method works.

With a piston at TDC, use a set of feeler gauges to determine the difference in height between the top of the cylinder and the top of the piston. Be sure that this measurement is made across the direction of the piston pin, not at the front or back.

Do this for both front and rear cylinders, and record the difference for each piston-cylinder set. Use a plus sign in front of the dimension if the piston is above the cylinder top, and a minus sign if it is below. For instance, $+0.007$in if the piston is above and -0.007in if it is below.

The most desirable piston-to-head clearance (deck height) is 0.040in when the engine is at running temperature. As discussed in the previous chapter, a Sportster's piston-to-head clearance grows by almost that much when it warms up to running temperature. An Evolution Sportster with a cold deck height of 0.040in runs with 0.080in squish clearance. The squish stops being effective when deck height grows to much over 0.065in.

In order to get an effective squish height in a running motor, the cold piston-to-head clearance must be set extremely close (0.020–0.025in). An engine setup this close will need to be warmed for several minutes before it can be revved at high speeds. This is because the pistons might bump the heads when the engine is cold and the revs are high enough. A great number of Evolution Sportsters have been run for many tens of thousands of miles with piston-to-head clearances set this tight without failing.

Most deck height measurements will range between -0.007in and $+0.007$in with the factory 0.017in base gasket. If it is -0.007in, use the 0.010in base gasket and the 0.027in head gasket for a piston-to-head clearance of 0.027in. If $+0.007$in, use the 0.027in head gasket with the standard 0.017in base gasket to get a clearance of 0.020in. However you shuffle the gaskets, do your best to get the piston-to-head clearances within 0.020-0.030in. If it's less than 0.020in, there may be contact between the pistons and heads; any more and the squish effect will diminish substantially.

Carl Morrow, long-time drag racer and Bonneville Salt Flats record holder, uses a Serdi machine to cut valve seats. In addition to perfect seats, the areas of the head around the edges of the seat require special attention for maximum performance. Carl's Speed Shop

When installing larger valves or different cams, it may be necessary to enlarge the valve pockets and bevel the top edge of the sleeves. Joe Minton

In preparation for installing big valves in an 883 head, this photo shows the beginning of the machining process. Larger seat pockets have been machined. Notice the proximity of the edges of the seats and spark plug areas. The start of a new combustion chamber can also be seen. Zipper's Performance Products

Copper head gaskets come in two thicknesses, 0.040 and 0.027in. Base gaskets are available in 0.010, 0.015, 0.017, and 0.020in thicknesses (see Chapter 3 for a description of these gaskets.) Remember that only the white-colored factory 0.017in, and the aluminum 0.010in base gaskets can be counted on to seal against oil seepage. Don't forget that the cases must be ultra-flat if the aluminum gasket is to seal reliably.

The combination of either of the light-colored stock or the 0.010in aluminum base gaskets, and the 0.040 or 0.027in head gaskets, will allow you to adjust deck height by 0.018in, in 0.005 and 0.013in increments, which is usually enough.

Ports and Valves

Everything else being equal, the more air that is pumped through your engine, the more power it makes. Anything that reduces airflow into and out of

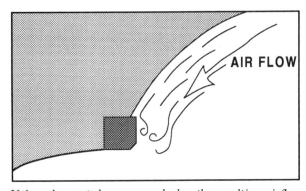

If the valve seats have a proud edge, the resulting airflow turbulence reduces total flow volume.

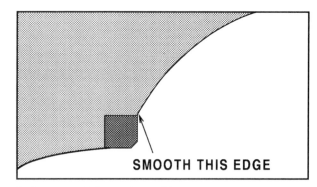

To increase airflow volume, blend the valve seats into the port walls. The seats are made of hard steel, and the ports are much softer aluminum. This work is rather tedious and care must be taken. You may want to pick up a junk head (not necessarily a Harley-Davidson head) from a salvage yard to practice on.

the cylinders reduces power output. Rough intake and exhaust ports reduce airflow, particularly if the roughness is near the valve seats; in fact, that is where it most often occurs. Sportsters have aluminum heads with pressed-in valve seats made of a tough steel alloy. These seats and ports almost never match. Small ridges usually form where they meet which create turbulence and corresponding loss of flow.

Significant improvements in airflow through intake ports can be gained by simply filing away any ridges that are upstream from the valve seats. The same holds true for the exhaust ports. After filing, smooth the areas with wet-or-dry sandpaper of 220 to 320 grade. Do not remove enough material to change the shape of the port, however.

The next step is to smooth and blend the sharp-edged machined surfaces of the seats, without touch-

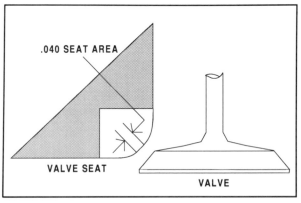

A narrow valve seat area improves flow but wears quickly. For street use, a thickness of 0.040in works well on the inlet valve; the seat areas of racing engines are much thinner. The exhaust valve, which is the hottest working part of an engine, benefits from having a wider seat. A thicker exhaust valve seat of 0.040–0.060in is necessary to help transfer heat to the head.

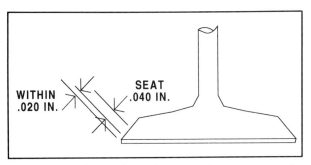

For optimum flow and maximum performance, keep the seat area on the valve to within 0.020in of the valve's edge.

ing the actual valve seating areas themselves. The idea is to smooth the machined corners immediately inside the ports and adjacent to the actual valve-seat contact rings themselves. The highly touted five-angle valve jobs you hear and read about are simply regular three-angle valve jobs with a couple more angled cuts on the inside of the ports to help blend the ports into the seats. An amateur can accomplish the same thing and perhaps do better with some careful filing and sanding. All this takes a lot of time, though, and a hand-held power grinder helps the job go smoother. Even a tiny Dremel tool helps to make life easier.

There is no magic about the actual contact area between the valves and seats. A narrow seat gives only a marginal flow advantage and wears quickly. There may be a small, low valve lift flow advantage if the seating surface of an intake valve is located at the edge of the valve. However, as the seat and valve wears, a ridge forms in the seat and in time any flow advantage will be diminished. Some tuners keep the valve-to-seat contact areas narrow, especially on the intake valve, but they also remove the heads frequently to freshen the valve job.

Valve seats cut in compliance with factory specifications will provide good flow and long operating life. The intake valve-to-seat contact width should be close to 0.040in, with the outer edge of the contact ring located about 0.015–0.020in from the outer edge of the valve. The exhaust should be 0.060in and located the same distance as the exhaust from the edge of the valve.

The exhaust valve-to-seat contact ring needs to be wider than the intake's because the exhaust valve is partly cooled by conduction across that contact surface. Exhaust valves run hot—hot enough to glow if the engine is run at full throttle and at peak torque rpm for more than a few seconds.

The shape of the valves immediately near their seating surfaces have an effect on gas flow at low valve lift heights. Stock Harley-Davidson valves are shaped well enough as they come. However, a small flow advantage can be had by filing and sanding a 0.020in radius on the edges of the exhaust valves facing the piston. A small radius here helps the hot gases in the combustion chambers turn the corner

Bob Conway, the Former Harley-Davidson racing manager who oversaw the development of the new generation XR-750 engine, describes the engine's D-shaped inlet port. Conway has a long history of development experience, and currently travels worldwide to train and qualify service personnel.

into the exhaust ports. A sharp-edged exhaust valve significantly reduces exhaust flow.

Port Work

A "ported head" is one that has enlarged inlet and exhaust ports to flow more volume. It generally includes a flow-volume check on a flow bench. But merely hogging-out a huge intake hole does not necessarily result in more power, even if the flow bench test indicates massive flow increases. It involves many factors.

A flow bench is one of the tools needed to measure the airflow through the port or ports. It is a steady-state device that applies a constant vacuum) to the port and records the amount of flow going through it. In an engine, however, the valve is only open for, at most, one-third of the time; it sits on its seat about two-thirds of the time. When the port is opened, nothing stays static: the valve is in constant motion, and its position relative to the seat changes continuously (which varies its flow restriction). In

The latest factory XR-750 inlet port shape (right) takes advantage of available airflow technology. During the mid-seventies, McDonnell Douglas experimented with port shapes. It was found that once the air begins to change direction, it tries to continue to change, resulted in airflow separation from the outside wall. By flattening and widening the port, and keeping the port's bottom relatively flat, an even pressure develops in the port's curvature. This increases the port's flow efficiency. Joe Ford

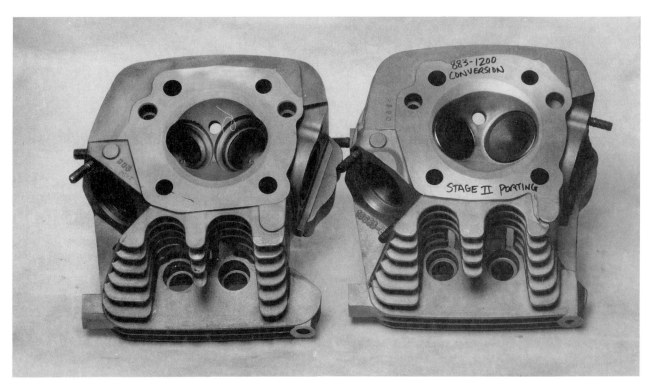

An in-process racing head (left) contrasts a finished head. Not all street riders want or need killer engines, preferring instead for moderate increases in power. By offering various stages of port work, a performance shop can tailor the level of cylinder head modifications to fit the thickness of a rider's wallet.

addition, the piston's velocity—and its corresponding pumping action—varies throughout the valve opening and closing phases.

Experienced porting specialists take these variables into account. The best port job for a particular intake and exhaust flow is the one refined through testing. Each particular type of engine responds differently to port modifications. Although a few of the most experienced porting experts may get good results without going to the dyno, they are indeed handicapped by skipping this step.

Hot rodding's most basic mathematical equation is, air equals horsepower. Extensive testing, mainly among the American stock car and drag racing communities, has established a relationship between an engine's flow volume and power. If you know the ported flow volume, the horsepower can be accurately predicted. Again, this relationship can only be accurately determined after correlating flow and dyno data for a particular engine application.

Flow volume places an upper limit on the amount of power an engine can produce. A small-displacement engine can produce the same power as a much bigger engine if their flow volumes are equal. The little motor may be running at 12,000rpm while the bigger one is at 7500rpm, but they will be capable of producing roughly equal power if the volume of air being pumped in and out is the same.

For a Sportster engine, it is possible to flow enough air through the inlet port to service the engine at 7500rpm. To do this, the flow must be increased about 35 percent more than stock. That's roughly 132cfm. Flow of 136–138cfm is possible, but the trick is getting the airflow velocities right. A bigger port flows more air at higher engine speed than a smaller port; however, the bigger port supplies this air at lower velocity, and the low velocity may inhibit carburetion at lower engine speeds. The solution is to get enough air in to service the engine's highest rpm, while keeping the highest possible port velocities.

The velocity of the gases in the port affects how the engine responds at less than peak rpm. Two different ports may have equal maximum flow and make identical horsepower, but the port with the higher air velocity makes better power at lower engine speeds; it has a wider power band than one with a lower port velocity.

There is little evidence that a highly polished inlet port improves airflow. Nor is there adequate documentation that a coarse surface improves atomizing. In fact, one SAE (Society of Automotive Engineers) engineering paper indicates that only a small portion of fuel is atomized during the intake cycle, and that most fuel atomizing takes place during the last portion of the compression cycle. However, a highly polished exhaust port can help to minimize carbon build up. Joe Minton

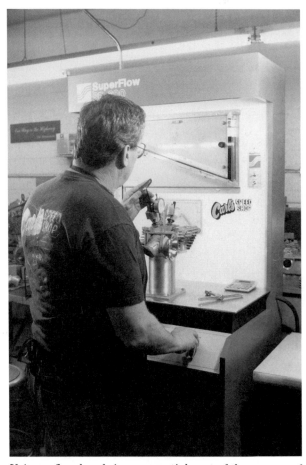

Using a flow bench is an essential part of the process of data acquisition. It also helps in development of port shapes and verifies the quality of port work. The most successful racers are "briefcase racers" that document everything and keep records and results handy. Carl's Speed Shop

The flow-volume claims, expressed in cubic feet per minute, differ from one source to another because flow through the ports is dependant on the amount of vacuum applied by the flow bench, and all testers do not use the same amount of vacuum. Also some heads are tested with carburetors and manifolds installed and some heads are tested bare. If you put a cylinder head on a flow bench without a carburetor, you'll get a much higher inlet reading than if all the components were included. It's just like comparing an engine dyno with a chassis dyno: one does not drive through the entire powertrain, while the other does. Another factor is the flow bench tester who may test an exhaust port by flowing the air into the port backwards, rather than out through it.

In terms of the entire cylinder head, intake port flow by itself is meaningless without understanding what the exhaust port is doing. The two must be balanced. That is why the Shovelhead falls flat at high speeds—its exhaust port cannot be made to flow enough to accommodate the intake flow that's possible. In this case, it is the exhaust port that limits maximum output.

An optimum cylinder head has an exhaust port with an area generally about 70–80 percent of the inlet area. However, the best exhaust port is useless with restrictive mufflers. The same applies to the carburetor, manifold, and air cleaner. Putting a modified or high-flow manifold on a stock 883 is a waste of energy because the head's ports are too restrictive to take advantage of it. On the other hand, a big carburetor and manifold won't help if they are serviced by a small foam air cleaner. The only flow test that has any real significance is one that has all the intake and exhaust components hooked up. You can't see all without testing all.

Most ports flow more air without the valves in place. Curiously, some of the best ports flow more air *with* the valves. Maximum flow is controlled by the valve; the more the valve opens, the more flow is achieved—to a point. There is a point of increasingly diminishing returns. As the flow volume approaches maximum, flow increases become less and less. In other words, there is a point where it becomes futile to continue to lift the valve further.

This diminishing return—the reason there are limits on how high a valve needs to lift—is one variable in determining total valve lift. Hitting the piston is another factor. And hitting the other valve is yet another. In the case of the Sportster, valve lifts less than 0.500in have been found to work well for all-around high-performance use. It allows a compromise between maximum port flow and valve gear life.

The Sportster's stock lift near 0.450in works efficiently with the standard ports. Port flow flattens above 0.400in valve lift. Even a Branch, Gatlin, or Mackie port will increase flow in a near-linear manner until well past 0.450in and can make full use of valves lifted 0.500in. But even these high-flow champions begin to flatten their rates at about 0.450in lift. Clearly, there is little to be gained from cams that have higher lifts for a high-powered street engine. Drag race and land speed engines may need higher lifts, but these extreme lifts shorten valve gear

A modified head (left) features big valves and ports compared to the stocker (right). Although a 96ci fuel-burning iron Sportster may develop up to 300hp, the most power you can expect from a highly developed gas-burning iron XL-1000 is about 75hp.

life. The high-lift camshafts are relegated for use in the most radical racing engines, where wear is measured in minutes instead of tens of thousands of miles.

There is a critical time during the inlet cycle when the maximum or near-maximum flow is essential. That time is when the piston is moving at its highest speed during its downward travel on the intake stroke. That point is 76deg after top dead center in a Sportster with standard rod length. It is a common misconception that this point is at 90deg, when the piston is halfway down the barrel.

It is essential that cam action lifts the intake valve so that maximum flow is occurring at or near 76deg after top dead center. The valve can reach this point (about 0.400in lift for Evolution ports) sooner than 76deg, but no later. As you can see, the design of cam timing and lift must take many things into account: flow volume and velocities, piston speed, and so on. This is why cams must be well matched to the head's capabilities.

Bottom End

A high-output Sportster engine puts a big load on the crankshaft, rods, and bearings. The standard Harley-Davidson crankshaft assembly is rugged, and if assembled and trued correctly, will withstand all but the most brutal power. In maximum-power engines for drag racing, heavy-duty connecting rods help prevent the crankcases from getting ventilated. The problem with some of these rods, however, is that they are heavier, and increase the loads on the crank pin and on all the bearings.

A 45deg twin has inherent balance problems, and it is impossible to balance the crankshaft to provide smooth running at all speeds. The standard crankshaft balance factor as it comes from the factory is 62 percent. For high-speed use, many tuners prefer to change this factor. If you ask six tuners about what percentage is best, you will probably get six different answers. Indeed, S&S Cycle admits that they have changed the recommended balance factor over the years. It appears that a factor around 55–60 percent is preferred.

The elements involved in crankshaft balance are the weights of the reciprocating piston assemblies and the rotating connecting rods. When you change these weights by installing larger, heavier pistons, you change the balance factor of the crankshaft. This is not necessarily a problem. After converting an 883 to 1200cc, you may find that you like the vibration characteristics better. If you don't, you can dismantle the engine and send the crank and piston assemblies to a speed shop for precision balance service.

The average amateur mechanic often chooses to leave the critical and precise bottom-end work to the pros. That's pretty logical, considering the expense of investing in special tooling. Balancing the flywheels requires a special arbor with pressed-on adapters, a

gram scale, and considerable balance kits from S&S range from A balance stand is needed to true th the crankcases for larger cylinders ı fixture, not to mention the boring ba time the do-it-yourselfer purchases all t. he or she could have simply paid the lo perform the work.

The Oiling System

Even if you don't rebuild your crank and bore your own cases, there are many details you can attend

When installing high-lift cams in 1991-later five-speed cases, it is necessary to remove some material from the bottom end of the lifter support area of the crankcase. A competent machinist can handle it, but you'll have to dismantle everything from the case and clean it thoroughly before reassembly. With the case relieved for clearance, check each cam to insure it clears the lobes. Zipper's Performance Products

urself. One of the most important is oil delivery management. A street bike won't need any special attention because infrequent high-speed runs do not put any unusual demands on the stock Sportster oil system.

If you are building a racing Sportster that will be used at high rpm for extended periods, you will have to modify your engine to prevent oil from pooling in the crankcase because any oil that collects in the crankcase causes power loss. Second, this results in an oil mist that clouds in the case and causes flywheel drag.

Theoretically a scavenge problem should not occur in the oil supply system, considering that the scavenge portion of the oil pump has twice the capacity of the feed portion. So much for theory. The fact is, this problem seems to occur when the engine is run at continuous high speeds. The key symptom is a loss of power after running a few minutes. Installing a windage plate helps to isolate the sump area from

the commotion of the rotating crankshaft and connecting rods. This helps to keep the pool of oil from aerating. Running an oil line from the front return hole to the rear of the sump, where the oil is delivered to the pump, helps to deliver the oil directly without exposing it to aeration.

If the oil pump drive gear wears out, total destruction results. Evolution Sportsters that are run at high speeds seem to be prone to this pump drive gear failure. It is a matter of continuous high rpm, not power output, so it affects Twin Sports and other racing applications more than street machines. If you use your bike at high engine speeds, inspect the oil pump gear on the pinion gear that drives it, inside the cam case, or replace it with the iron gear fitted on Sportrsters beginning in April 1992.

Camshaft Bearings

The camshafts ride on bushings. These bushings have proven reliable, even in racing applications. Many tuners have tried needle bearings, but there doesn't seem to be any advantage in doing so because

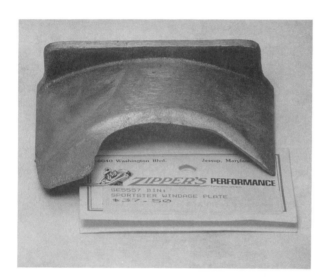

A windage plate helps to reduce drag caused by excessive oil in the crankcase. It is a necessity to maintain peak power at continuous high-speed use; however, most street riders never spend enough time at high engine speeds to require one. Zipper's Performance Products

This oil scavenging hole in the engine's sump is positioned fairly low; however, some engines may have the hole located higher. For maximum scavenging, it should be located as low as possible to minimize oil drag in the crankcase.

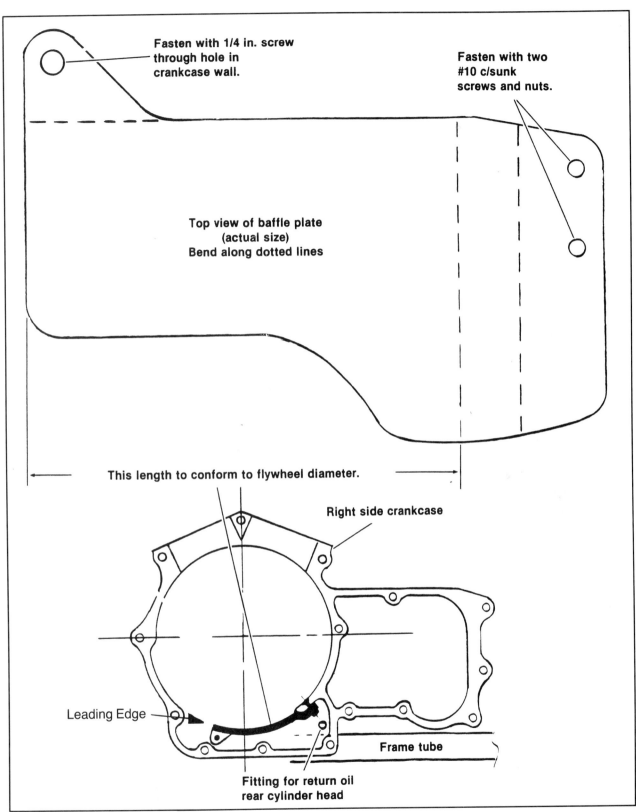

Fasten with 1/4 in. screw through hole in crankcase wall.

Fasten with two #10 c/sunk screws and nuts.

Top view of baffle plate (actual size) Bend along dotted lines

This length to conform to flywheel diameter.

Right side crankcase

Leading Edge

Frame tube

Fitting for return oil rear cylinder head

You can make a windage plate from a sheet of steel or aluminum in an annealed condition at a minimum of 0.032in thick. Install it with the leading edge positioned as close to the flywheels as possible, without touching them, to scrape oil from the flywheels. You can also install a tube from the front return hole to the rear of the sump, so that return oil will be led to the inert area without being subject to the turbulence created by the rotating crankshaft. This pattern is for an XR-750. Harley-Davidson

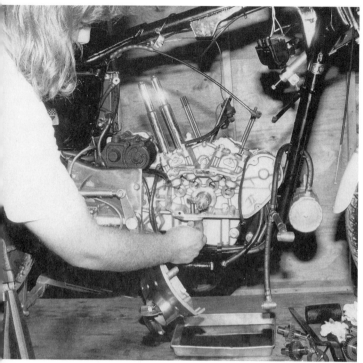

Under continuous hard use, the Sportster's oil pump drive gear is prone to fail. The result is always the same: lost oil pressure and a blown engine. This became painfully apparent to many Twin Sports racers, like this one at Daytona.

if the bearings that support the rear cylinder intake cam gear should have any excess free play, the ignition timing will bounce all over the place, and it could cause the timing rotor to break.

Stroker Kits

The stresses on a high-revving Sportster engine place practical limits on its maximum output. An option that many Sportster riders entertain is a "stroker." While commonly called strokers, most of

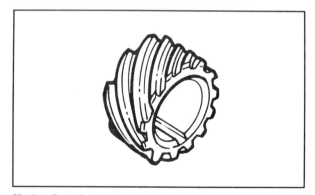

Harley-Davidson changed the oil pump drive gear's material to cast iron as a running production change on April 1992. The more durable iron seems to be holding up much better. Retrofit using P/N 26318-88A. Harley-Davidson

these kits actually increase both the bore and stroke of the engine. Stroker kits can increase a Sportster engine to as large as 110ci.

A common perception regarding strokers is that they are much more powerful than the stock displacement engines. This is both true and false, depending on how they are compared. Those who have extensively dyno tested a variety of types generally agree on two points: Peak horsepower output depends mainly on intake flow volume, and not necessarily displacement volume; and maximum midrange power (about halfway to the power peak) depends more on engine size and cranking pressure.

No matter how large an engine's displacement, its peak power is a matter of the air volume being pumped in and burned in a given time. In effect, a highly tuned engine "supercharges" itself to a degree, and the cylinder fills with more air volume than its actual displacement. This is true when the inertia of air in the inlet and exhaust tract at peak torque speed are working together. A well-tuned engine such as the Stage II type may get up to 30 percent more air than its actual displacement at peak torque rpm. Peak torque occurs in the 5000 to 6000rpm range, with the highest output of 74lb-ft at 5500rpm.

When this same engine is running at lower rpm, as most street engines do nearly all the time, the cylinders typically fill completely but do not become supercharged. At these engine speeds, power output is simply a matter of the engine's displacement. Using an S&S 89ci stroker kit as an example (probably the most popular kit), it makes more power at 3000rpm than a 74ci (1200cc) version. Its advantage is proportional to cubic volume of displacement, plus a tad more because an S&S 89ci has more cranking pressure. However, the stroker makes little more, if any, peak power unless its cylinder head air processing capabilities are improved.

The loads created by the weight of pistons, rings, and rods put stress on the crank pin and bearings. These forces are directly related to the reciprocating mass and the rod length-to-stroke ratio. Stroker kits have heavier pistons and rods, and a shorter rod length-to-stroke ratio. This essentially lowers the rpm at which damage begins to occur. The longer stroke of the 89ci stroker, even if all other factors remained unchanged, would lower permissible safe rpm by about 13 percent.

Although the 89ci stroker has a 20 percent displacement advantage and a corresponding increase in power at low engine speeds, it cannot make substantially more peak-rpm power. Its lower safe rpm limits its ability to process the air volume necessary. The smaller, high-rpm engine can take advantage of its flow and revving abilities.

What a stroker does, however, is exactly what most riders love. It provides a big power advantage in the vicinity of 3000rpm, and accelerates like no other Sportster engine configuration. At normal high-gear

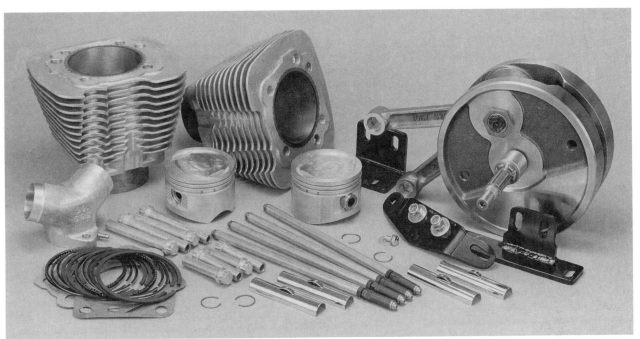

The S&S Sidewinder 89ci kit is based on a 4.32in stroke and 3.62in bore. It has proven to be one of motorcycling's most popular stroker kits. Although a Sportster with a stroked engine may be fun to ride, there are inherent disadvantages to using a long stroke. A long stroke limits engine speed, and it may also make the engine hard to start unless a special cam is used. Despite any drawbacks, the bottom line is that a stroker, with its broad torque, is a blast to ride. S&S Cycle

The Axtell 3¹³/₁₆in iron barrel (left) gives the Sportster a square bore-stroke ratio and a displacement of 88ci with the stock stroke. Used on Mountain Motors, the iron barrels tend to distort less than original equipment cylinders (right). Without resorting to a long stroke and retaining stock stroke permits higher safe engine operating speeds. S&S Cycle also offers large-bore steel cylinders.

The 88ci Mountain Motor with Axtell 3¹³/₁₆in cylinders retains the stock Sportster stroke. Frame modification is not required, and the stock piston speed helps assure good reliability. Zipper's provides big-valve head work, Red Shift cams, S&S Super G carb, dual ignition, beefed up clutch and drive system, and much more. The Mountain Motor has been in the field for several years giving both excellent service and 130hp. Not for the budget-minded builder. Zipper's Performance Products

street rpm there is nothing like cubic inches, and it will run away from the Stage II Sportster. Their top end, however, is about the same.

The vast majority of complete stroker kits comes from S&S Cycle. The company's success is largely due to the quality of the kits and customer service. The 89ci kit includes the S&S 3⅝in bore iron-lined aluminum barrels, a 4⁵/₁₆in stroke crankshaft assembly, and all the components necessary for installation. This includes the motor mount plates that are necessary because of the longer cylinders.

The Sportster frame must be modified at the rear, where the frame tubes join above the rear cylinder, to make room for the taller engine. Nearly all stroker kits require that the cases be bored to fit the cylinders, so the engine must be completely disassembled. Since the stroked Sportster motor will be as much as 1.32in taller, nearly all installations require frame modifications. Before deciding on a stroker kit, be sure to consider whether you really want to modify the frame.

The S&S 3⅝in bore cylinders are an excellent way to increase a stock Sportster's displacement to nearly that of a big twin, while simultaneously

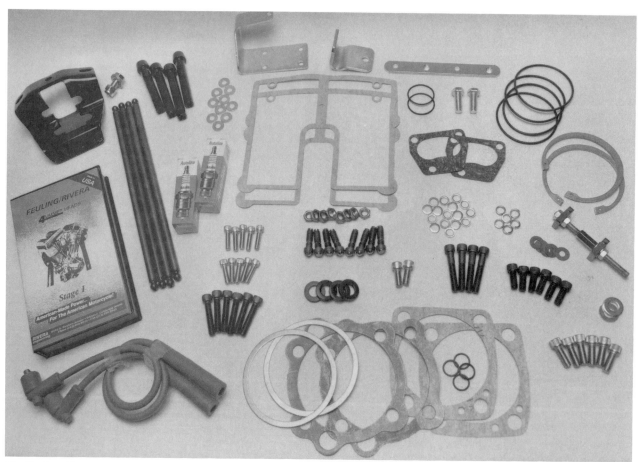

The Feuling/Rivera Stage I kit includes all related gaskets, fasteners, push rods, and ignition wires. It even includes an instructional video tape. Rivera Engineering

addressing the stock cylinder distortion problem. Again, the cases must be bored. Flywheels with strokes up to 5in are also available.

Another large-displacement option includes the Axtell iron barrels in bore sizes up to 3.81in, which produces a displacement of 87ci (1424cc) with the stock stroke. Sputhe Engineering produces aluminum cylinders with iron liners.

Exhaust Systems

Since our definition of a Stage I Sportster includes having bolt-on practicality, the exhaust systems discussed in Chapter 1 apply to Stage I. The stock XL header pipe diameter works satisfactorily on a Stage I engine, but it is too restrictive when flow improvements have been made.

A Stage II motor can produce a few more horsepower with 1⅞ or 2in diameter pipes. It will do little good to fit these larger pipes to an engine with stock 883 valve sizes. The valves and ports need to be larger—at least the size of 1200 valves—to benefit from larger pipes.

For drag race applications, where power below 3500rpm is of little value, straight pipes of the correct length provide good performance without the weight penalty of long megaphones. A land speed record machine, where weight is not such a large factor, will need the extra power available from a properly tuned open megaphone system.

Feuling/Rivera Four-Valve Heads

Four-valve heads are nothing new. Harley-Davidson introduced its version of a four-valve engine on a board-track racer in 1916. During the sixties, Ford developed a V-8 Pentroof type for Indy car racing, and it has been common in all forms of racing and street use for the past twenty years.

The four-valve design has the potential of enjoying several technological advantages over two-valve heads, if executed correctly. Probably the most important advantages are the larger overall valve area and the increased circumference area of a typical four-valve design. To visualize this, picture a column of air the size of the valve and lift diameter. The larger this area, the better the flow. For example, an Evolution engine with a single 2in inlet valve has an area of 3.14sq-in and a total valve circumference of 6.28in. With a 0.49in lift, it has a useful area of 3.08sq-in to service the cylinder.

A four-valve head like the Feuling/Rivera, with 1.49in inlet valves, has a total valve area of 3.40sq-in and a total circumference area (both valves) of 9.24in. With the same 0.49in valve lift, the four-valve head has a valve area of 4.53in—a 50 percent increase over stock.

At high rpm, the valve springs may not be able to control a heavy valve, and the valve may bounce or float and damage the engine. To prevent this, extraordinarily stiff springs are often necessary to control

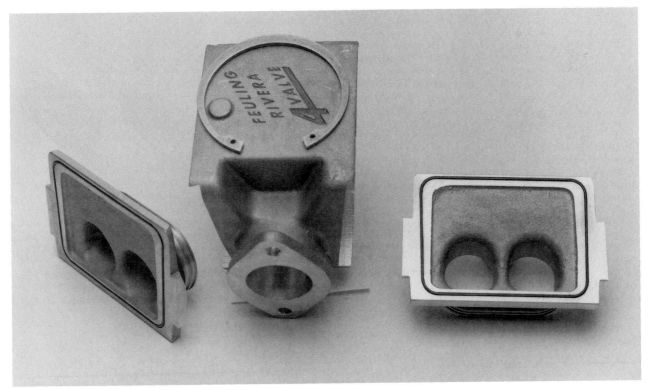

A plenum chamber, common to automotive designs, feeds the heads. Carburetors are not included in the kit. Rivera Engineering

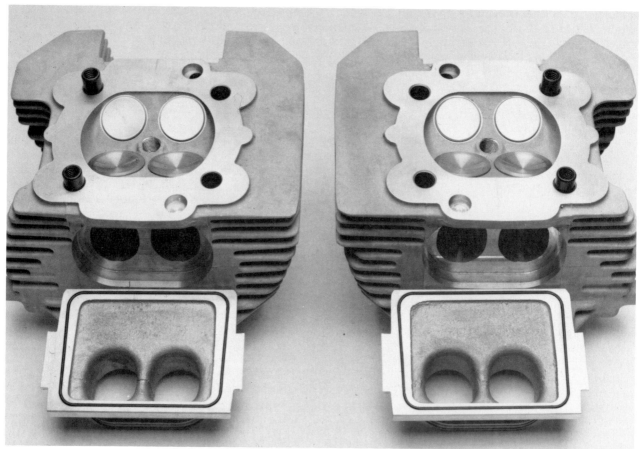

The combustion chamber features central spark plug location, low roof height, compact burn area, and large area of valve circumference. It can be seen here that a portion of the inlet valves are close to the edges of the combustion chamber wall (bottom valves). Rivera Engineering

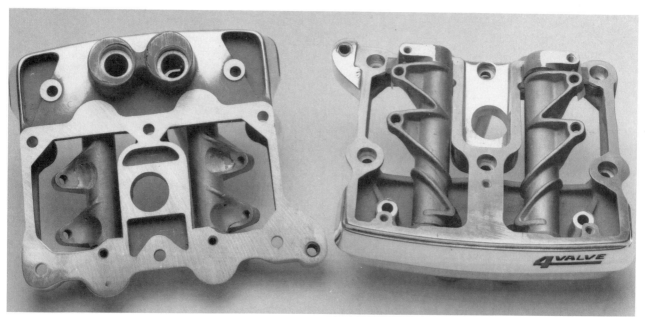

The close proximity of the Sportster's push rods (seen in upper portion of the rocker case on the left) places limits on a four-valve design. As a result, the extremely short rocker arms have unusual lever ratios (seen at bottom of right rocker case facing down). Rivera Engineering

the valves. Smaller and lighter valves, as in a typical four-valve design, are easier to control at high rpm, and lighter spring pressures can usually be used.

To take advantage of the improved flow characteristics, the two inlet valves must not be shrouded by the edges of the cylinder wall. As an example, the two-valve Kawasaki head used in superbike racing during the late seventies, despite a theoretical disadvantage, flowed slightly better than the four-valve Honda superbike head. That's because the Honda design arranged the valves in close proximity to the cylinder wall, and intake flow was restricted.

To maximize the four-valve's theoretical advantages, the concept should be applied to a short-stroke, large-bore oversquare engine. A typical oversquare bore-and-stroke ratio may be as high as 1.5:1 in engines designed to use four-valve heads. These engines spin at much higher rpm than a long-stroke engine is capable.

The 1200cc Sportster engine, however, is an undersquare design, with a bore-and-stroke ratio of 0.9:1. It does not enjoy a large area to comfortably accept four valves and, in practical street use, is limited to about 7500rpm, where piston speeds are an incredible 4765fpm! (A piston speed of 3500fpm is generally considered the maximum for longevity.)

The Feuling/Rivera four-valve head is an adaptation that had to accommodate the Sportster's existing pushrod design, so compromises had to be made. As a result, the valve side of the rocker arm is unusually short, and the pushrod side is even shorter. Without the higher leverage of longer arms, high spring tension is necessary, which places heavy loads on the valvetrain. In addition, the short arms have a high degree of fore-aft displacement as they rotate, which puts heavier side loads on the valve stem. All this would appear to cause incremental wear on moving parts, and place heavier loads on the valve guides, rocker arms, pushrods, cams, and cam bearings.

The Feuling/Rivera heads are available only in a Stage II type, with a two-carburetor plenum box. The Stage II engine, equipped with dual carburetors, produces a claimed 125hp at the crankshaft, which would give you about 105–110hp at the wheel. Twenty-five Sportster sets were made, and it has not been decided whether to produce more when they are sold out. The cost is $2,500, and does not include carburetors, cams, or exhaust system, although it does include exhaust headers so you can modifiy and mount your own pipes.

Considering its $2,500 price tag, we must talk about money and value. As previously stated in this book, it is not too expensive to get a generous horsepower gain over the stock output, but getting progressively more power from a high-performance Sportster engine is the most expensive and time-consuming process. With the Feuling/Rivera four-

valve heads, you begin the expensive part of the process after already investing $2,500.

The price of modifications (porting and flowing) to the original equipment head varies according to how much work is performed. For comparison, Branch Flowmetrics charges $760 to modify a set; Zipper's gets $500 for Stage II (street use) porting, and $750 a set for the Stage III no-compromise work. Carl's Speed Shop does a Road & Track job for $700, and unlimited heads for $2,500. A racing piston kit and intake manifold for these conversions adds another $250 or so.

There have been many successful reports of Feuling/Rivera installations; and there have been reports of people who have experienced some difficulty in installing and setting up the kit. The pool of knowledge on building high-performance Evolution Sportsters using the factory cylinder heads has been forming since 1985; by comparison, the four-valve head is a new product, so be prepared to experiment to get the right combination of cams, carburetors, and jetting.

Tuning

When your camshafts are correctly matched for the combustion chamber and the port flows of your

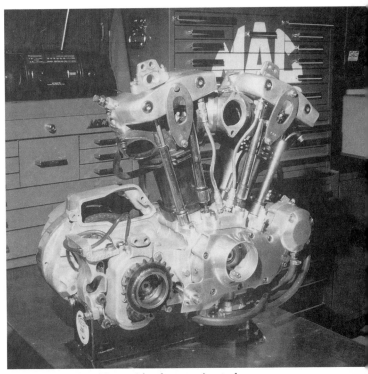

When an engine blows, it's always nice to have a spare handy. This is the back-up engine for the world's quickest Sportster pro-stock gas bike, run by Dan Fitzmaurice. Notice the modified output sprocket, which spaces the chain out farther to clear the wide rear tire. Note also the huge manifold opening leading to the iron heads. Those odd-looking brackets help to stiffen the rocker boxes.

engine, you have the perfect start for the ultimate high-performance Sportster. When you get an intake manifold, carburetor, and air cleaner to meet the maximum cylinder filling requirements of your head and cam, you have taken another important step. And when you have an ignition system that ignites these valuable gases at precisely the optimum moment, and a large-diameter exhaust system that evacuates the burnt gases without waking the devil, you are even closer to success.

Those are the basic component requirements of a hopped-up Sportster, and it is a part of the tuner's work. But like the beautiful piano that has rich white keys to plunk and pedals to push, it's all for nothing if the thing isn't in tune. Tuning is simply the act of extracting the desired performance from an engine. It starts with the things we've talked about—the correctly matched components and modifications. But it never ends, until the other variables, such as carburetor jetting and ignition timing, are correct.

Most street riders will arrive at the correct settings by seat-of-the-pants road testing. While that is not the ideal method, realistically it is the most practical approach available to many of us. This approach depends on using your senses. You will listen, first and foremost, for the rattle of detonation. You will listen to the exhaust note for the flat "blat-

Where are the fins? This is an iron head for a fuel-burning Sportster. It may look crude, but it works for fuel; this one holds a record. It is estimated that several hundred hours of work is invested in this one head.

blat" sound of a rich mixture or the sharper bark of a lean mixture. You will peer into the exhaust pipe looking for the gray color of a good mixture, and wonder what jet to change when you see that it's black.

Your carburetor should have come with a tuning handbook. Before making adjustments, be sure to read it thoroughly and understand the principles of its fuel-mixing circuits. A common tuning mistake is to associate a certain jetting circuit with engine speed or even road speed. Remember that the fuel circuits are related to throttle position and vacuum, not the position of a speedometer needle. You might want to place marks on your throttle that correspond to throttle position.

If your carburetion is rich, be conservative about leaning the mixture. Better to be safe and decrease fuel flow gradually. Make only one change at a time. Altering two or more fuel circuits, or altering both ignition timing and carburetion, only confuses the issue.

Any detonation must be evaluated and cured swiftly. It may be eliminated by simply retarding the ignition timing or enriching a carburetor circuit. The trick is knowing exactly what the problem is. If there is any way you can put your newly assembled masterpiece on a dyno, it will be rewarding. The small amount of money invested in dyno time will save you many long hours of guesswork and mistakes. Today's computers eliminate much guesswork and backtracking.

Keeping records is a vital part of the high-performance world. Never fail to write down your changes and the results for future reference. And don't forget our other important rule: Have fun!

Nitro Methane Fuel

When you change the Sportster's stroke, you change the basic character of the engine. In other words, you now have a completely different rod angle, piston speed, valve-speed-to-piston relationship, and so forth. You could think of it as moving from a small, rural town in Iowa to Los Angeles. When you start "tipping the can" and running fuels like nitro methane instead of gasoline, you are operating in a different world—like the planet Jupiter.

For those who wish to experience life on Jupiter, we will lay out the basics, and we must stress *basics*, of running fuel. It is a highly specialized area that requires considerable experience to be successful. If you want to count the people who are the best fuelers in the world on your fingers and toes, don't bother to take off your shoes.

These fuels are capable of producing powerful explosions. Elmer Trett, who raced Sportsters in the seventies, put it this way: "The difference between using gas and fuel is the difference between managing a campfire and throwing hand grenades." The Trett analogy helps to understand the difference between using gasoline and fuels. We call it "The Phone Booth Analogy."

When using a phone booth in the normal way that it was designed, you would naturally consider closing the door. In fact, to get the best performance from the phone booth (some privacy and quiet), you must close the door.

Now consider the ultimate fuel question: "If you throw a hand grenade into a phone booth, would it matter whether you close the door?" (Indeed, would you even want to be inside?) The designers never intended a phone booth for that kind of use, so all the old questions no longer apply. It's same for an engine designed to run on gasoline.

Thus, the fueled engine anomaly.

One engine developer described running a fuel dragster as "the highest form of amateur rocketry known to man." That's more true than you might imagine. Liquid rocket fuels carry fuel in one tank and oxygen in another, which is mixed together and ignited. Likewise, in a fuel dragster, oxygenated fuel is supplied to the combustion chamber, and ignited.

A normally aspirated gasoline-burning engine is sensitive to atmospheric changes, basically because it gets its oxygen from the atmosphere. Also, efficient combustion and high power require a high level of cylinder head technology, both in port and combustion chamber shape. While these things are important to a nitro engine, they are not as critical. It's all in the fuel.

To get more power from any type of engine, you have to get more air into the cylinder. Nitro methane is a mono-propellant fuel that powered some of the first rocket engines in history. In fuel racing, this nitro is added to methanol, which is about 50 percent oxygen. In other words, you're adding liquid oxygen to the fuel.

Alcohols are also about 115 octane, which allows incredible compression ratios. Although they contain about half the energy of gasoline (so you have to burn twice as much), they don't create as much heat as gasoline. This makes nitro methane and alcohol an ideal racing fuel.

There's a steep learning curve to using nitro, which is why there's still a place for the iron-head Sportster. Enormous amounts of information about iron XLs using fuel have been gathered over thirty-five years, and plentiful iron-related products. By comparison, fuel data on the Evolution is only a few years old.

With eight times the consumption rate and a price of $30 per gallon, running nitro is not cheap. If you want to build a nitro dragster, it would be ideal to spend a season helping an experienced nitro racer. For the most part, the Harley-Davidson drag-racing community is a family type of racing, and most riders are willing to help any rider who wants to get started. Because of the enormous cost of running a fuel dragster, a season's experience can be valuable and can save you a bundle later.

When building a nitro engine, there is a strong temptation to resort to the traditional American adage, "If it's big and strong, you can't go wrong." There is a problem with this approach, however. For example, an engine builder may resort to stronger connecting rods, which are heavier than the stock items. This only aggravates an existing problem: reciprocating mass. It can also be a problem when increasing the Sportster's stroke.

Detonation is fuel racing's biggest problem. The powerful nitro explosions can crack heads, lift ring lands, elongate rods, indent rod pins, and blow the pushrods right out of the engine. Adding more mass complicates the situation and creates a dilemma for the engine builder. The ideal engineering solution is to reduce reciprocating mass by making these parts lighter than stock, not heavier. However, the enormous loads on a fuel engine do not make the ideal approach feasible. This illustrates the kinds of problems facing any engine builder, and for tuners who build nitro engines, it is multiplied.

The Sportster engine makes a good foundation on which to build a nitro engine. Nitro engines respond to long strokes. They rely more on the power of each explosion rather than developing more firing pulses by using high rpm. This is one reason strokers are popular in drag racing.

Being successful in a class that allows "tipping the can" depends on only two things: money and experience. If you've got plenty of both, have fun!

Chapter 5

Gearbox and Power Transmission

In the early days of motorized vehicles, the drive wheel was normally driven directly by the engine. Although the rider could sometimes disengage the power by slackening the tension on the leather drive belt, without a clutch it was impossible to gradually reengage the engine. This meant that when the rider stopped, he or she had to kill the engine. To restart, the rider pedaled until he reached a speed fast enough to reengage and restart the engine.

The invention of the clutch put an end to this physical fitness program. Harley's first clutch, in 1912, was mounted on the rear wheel. A later clutch, on the

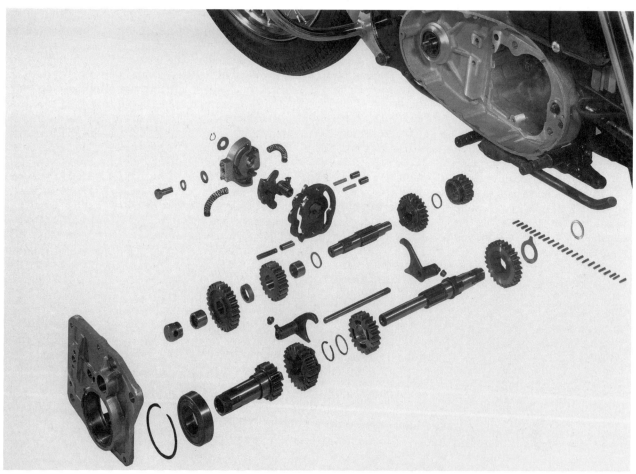

Although this photo was taken in 1954, it contains all the elements of the four-speed Sportster transmission, which remained essentially the same for thirty-five years until the 1991 rotary-shift five-speed was introduced.

1915 three-speed transmission, improved upon the original idea by offering the rider a selection of gears.

Multispeed transmissions improved performance by offering different drive ratios between the engine and the road. This allowed the rider to select an appropriate gear ratio to keep the engine in a desirable operating range. Eventually the four-speed replaced the three; and a five-speed replaced the four. These days, six-speed gearboxes are fairly common in high-performance foreign bikes. In fact, some small 50cc Grand Prix racing motorcycles have had twelve- and sixteen-speed transmissions!

Four-Speed Versus Five-Speed

The number of speeds that are needed depends on two basic speed ranges: the operating range and characteristics of the engine; and the speed range of the vehicle over the road. For street bikes that develop excellent pulling power at engine speeds as low as 1800rpm, and that operate in the legal speed range—up to only 65mph or so—a number of gears are not necessary.

For example, the standard, current-model Sportster engine produces a useful power range between about 2000 and 6000rpm. That's a 4000rpm power band, and you don't need a lot gears to keep the engine in this rpm band at legal speeds. After all, second gear alone covers it all.

Obviously, if an engine develops useful power over a narrow-rpm band, say between 4000–6000rpm, you'll need more gears that are spaced closer together. In addition, if the bike's speed range extends

The latest five-speed gear cluster and shift mechanism slide out of the transmission cavity without splitting the cases, as did the original 1954 type. To avoid missed shifts and gear damage, it's best to take advantage of blueprint- *ing and back-cut-gear services offered by machine shops that are familiar with the procedures. Zipper's Performance Products*

as high as 150mph, then more, wider-spaced gear ratios will be necessary to keep the engine within its peak-power window over this wide operating range.

Which brings us to the four-speed versus five-speed argument. A five-speed transmission gives the rider a greater selection of gear-ratio options, and it allows the rider to select a gear that puts the engine speed more precisely where he or she wants it. In other words, an extra gear helps to keep the engine speed closer to the power peak over a wider range of road speeds. Because of this, a five-speed motorcycle should be able to outaccelerate an identical four-speed bike.

Let's face it, for street riding, all this doesn't make any real difference. You can enjoy a ride through the park on a Sunday afternoon every bit as much with a four-speed as you can with a five-speed. It's only when you want high performance that the subtle difference becomes a major one.

Close-Ratio Versus Wide-Ratio

Regarding the spacing of gearbox ratios, generally speaking, the narrower a power band, the closer gear spacing that is required. When the rider shifts to a higher gear, a close-ratio gearset will keep the engine speed closer to what it was in the previous gear. A wide-ratio gearset allows the engine speed to drop to a lower speed when upshifting.

For racing purposes, the low-gear ratio is often dictated by the machine's overall gearing in high gear. For example, let's consider a standard five-speed 1991 Sportster that is geared for a top speed of 150mph at

7150rpm. This machine will peak out in first gear, revving 7150rpm, at 54mph. This tall gearing is not a serious problem for a road racer who makes one standing start and gets to racing speed only once during the course of a fifty-mile sprint. But to a drag racer who competes in an 8sec time frame, this is obviously a more serious situation.

The overall top-gear ratio for a street bike is determined by a three-way compromise—a balance between both objective and subjective factors. Engineers consider the following factors: (1) a low engine speed to provide a comfortable engine rpm that minimizes wear and tear while cruising at top legal road speeds; (2) an engine speed close to the motor's

Sportster Transmission Ratios

Four-speed (1986)

Gear	Inner ratio
1	2.52
2	1.82
3	1.38
4	1.00

Four-speed (1987-1990)

Gear	Inner ratio
1	2.29
2	1.66
3	1.25
4	1.00

Five-speed (1991 on)

Gear	Inner ratio
1	2.78
2	2.03
3	1.49
4	1.22
5	1.00

Gear Ratio Comparison Charts
Four-speed XL (34 engine, 59 clutch = 1.74:1)

Rear wheel sprocket teeth	Transmission sprocket teeth		
	19	20	21
44	4.03	3.83	3.65
45	4.12	3.92	3.73
46	4.21	4.00	3.81
47	4.30	4.01	3.89
48	4.40	4.18	3.98
49	4.49	4.26	4.06
50	4.58	4.35	4.14
51	4.67	4.48	4.23
52	4.76	4.52	4.31

Five-speed XL-883 (34 engine, 59 clutch = 1.74:1)

Rear wheel sprocket teeth	Transmission sprocket teeth		
	19	20	21
44	4.03	3.83	3.65
45	4.12	3.92	3.73
46	4.21	4.00	3.81
47	4.30	4.01	3.89
48	4.40	4.18	3.98
49	4.49	4.26	4.06
50	4.58	4.35	4.14
51	4.67	4.48	4.23
52	4.76	4.52	4.31

Five-speed XL-1200 35 engine, 56 clutch = 1.60:1

Rear wheel sprocket teeth	Transmission sprocket teeth		
	19	20	21
45	3.79	3.60	3.42
46	3.87	3.68	3.50
47	3.95	3.76	3.58
48	4.04	3.84	3.65
49	4.13	3.92	3.73
50	4.21	4.00	3.80
51	4.29	4.08	3.88
52	4.38	4.16	3.96

torque speed, for adequate roll-on acceleration while passing; and (3) an engine speed at or near the engine's "sweet spot"—a speed at which the engine feels comfortable to the rider.

Engineers usually evaluate the top-gear ratio as a team, and arrive at some sort of collective decision on the secondary-drive sprockets. For mass-produced machines, manufacturing ease and efficiency also enters the picture. For example, it's easier and cheaper to put the same-size sprocket on both the 883 and the 1200. Although this may satisfy the corporate bean counters, the fact remains that the 1200's additional torque essentially makes it a completely different animal, with a different taste in gearing.

Both secondary-drive sprockets can easily be changed, and overall gearing can be tailored to a rider's individual riding style. After all, there is no reason why a street rider must accept the gearing that factory engineers selected. Aftermarket suppliers provide both chain-wheel and belt-drive sprocket pulleys in various sizes.

Individual riding styles differ, thus it follows that different riders will make different choices in gearing. For example, some riders may prefer to downshift to a lower gear to pass traffic while others prefer to rely on top gear, without backshifting. For the first rider, a tall top gear that lets the engine loaf along at low rpm while cruising the highway might be suitable. This rider will simply select some other gear for acceleration. But the second rider, who does not wish to stir up the gearbox, might prefer a lower top gear that puts the engine speed closer to its torque peak at cruising speeds.

Another factor in riding style involves the high-performance rider who wants optimum acceleration off the line. In this case, the rider's choice of the first-gear ratio may dictate his top-gear ratio. When he or she finds themself beside a Kawasaki Ninja at a stoplight, the gearing must be right to optimize every ounce of horsepower.

The gearbox internal ratios may be changed by replacing the gears with aftermarket or Harley-Davidson Screamin' Eagle parts. Beginning with 1987 models, Harley changed the third-gear mainshaft and the countershaft drive gear to bring the third-gear ratio closer to top gear. For pre-1987 models with a wider gear-ratio spacing, stock factory-made close-ratio gears can be added.

If you want to go the other way, and replace the current close-ratio gears with the former wide-ratio units, simply see your local Harley parts dealer. Another option is to replace the standard gears with Andrews nickel alloy heat-treated gears and shafts, or HES performance products.

Harley-Davidson has made major investments to improve the quality of its gears. A new gear machining cell was installed around 1985, and the quality of gears coming from this manufacturing center has

The 1986 Sportsters can get third and fourth gear ratios closer together with a set of Harley-Davidson XL close-ratio gears.

never been better. The standard factory gears work fine in stock engines, but they are pushing their limits when power is increased. For high-output engines, such as a drag racing or even an over 80hp street machine, the tough aftermarket gears are essential.

Don Tilley adjusts the gearing on Scott Zampach's Twin Sports racer. Many factors influence a racer's decision on final gearing. Some riders may find they can reduce their lap times by using a gear ratio that other riders may find useless. The motorcycle's power characteristics and suspension setup, in addition to the rider's style, are individual factors that affect the choice of final-drive sprocket sizes.

Land speed record attempts, such as Carl Morrow's effort, require special attention to gearing. Morrow is a longtime drag and salt flats competitor with an endless string of successes. Carl's Speed Shop

Different gears are not only necessary for modified motors, but also easily available in several ratio combinations.

The standard gears can be improved, however, by back-cutting the engagement dogs on a milling machine rotary table. A rotary table ensures that each

dog's face is precisely spaced and matched to its mating gear, and this ensures that loads are spread more evenly between each dog. The back-draft angle of the cut helps to lock the gear into engagement when being driven. When the power is interrupted to shift gears, the dogs easily disengage.

Selecting Gearing

Whether it's a drag, road, or hillclimb race, gearing the motorcycle to reach optimum terminal speed is essential for maximum performance. Choosing the correct gearing, however, is no simple matter. The selection usually requires charts, graphs, calculations, and a little experience in guesstimation.

For example, let's look at Scott Zampach's gearing dilemma at Daytona Speedway in 1992. When geared for maximum speed on the banking, Zampach found that he had to drop back into third gear in the chicane, which actually slowed his drive onto the banking. The engine speed was too high for third gear, yet too low for fourth.

Zampach and his tuner, Don Tilley, decided to raise the overall gear ratio, so that the bike was actually undergeared for top speed. In other words, instead of peaking at top speed at the end of the straight, the engine reached peak power output several hundred yards sooner. This allowed "Z-man" to get through the chicane in fourth gear. Zampach felt that this allowed him to maintain more speed through the chicane and get a better drive. Despite the lower top speed, his lap times improved.

Dan Fitzmaurice, a veteran dirt-track rider, runs the world's quickest Pro Stock Sportster at 8.70sec elapsed time. Zipper's Performance Products

The world's fastest Sportster, at 153.9mph, is piloted by Charlie Hausler. In drag racing, managing the clutch and gearbox is just as essential as horsepower output. Special equipment such as air shifters and billet-steel gears are common. Larry Smith/Handcrafted American Racing Motorcycles

Manipulating a balance between clutch engagement and tire traction is the primary objective in reducing elapsed time. Here, Dan Lasenestra's rear tire distorts during his launch. Lasenestra is the 1991 ECRA (East Coast Racing Association) 11:30 class champion. Larry Smith/Handcrafted American Racing Motorcycles

Streamliners at Bonneville present another, more extreme example. It is not unusual for a long, torpedo-shaped streamliner to have an additional jackshaft between the gearbox and the rear wheel. This is often necessary to get the gear ratio low enough for the high speed that is necessary. An additional benefit of the jackshaft is the ability to split gearing into finer adjustments.

For example, let's look at a street bike that hits 120mph at 6000rpm. With a forty-eight-tooth rear wheel sprocket, a change of one tooth makes about a 2.5mph difference (120mph ÷ 48 teeth = 2.5mph/tooth). On the other hand, for a 200mph vehicle, with a forty-eight-tooth gear, turning 6000rpm, one tooth is worth 5mph (200 ÷ 48 = 4.2mph). Sometimes, with a world land speed record only 2mph away, one tooth is too much.

Computing Gear Ratios

A gear ratio is simply the difference between how fast the rear wheel turns in relationship to the engine. In other words, it is the ratio of engine rpm to rear wheel rpm. A 4.00:1 ratio, for example, means that the engine's crankshaft turns four revolutions each time the rear wheel rotates once.

To arrive at the overall gear ratio—engine to rear wheel—you need to know the sizes, or number of teeth, of all the gears or chain wheels between the engine crankshaft and the rear wheel. This basically includes three sets of gears: the primary drive; the gearbox internal gears; and the final (or secondary) drive.

Once you know the ratios, all you need to know is the rear tire's rolling circumference and we can compute top speed, or any speed in any gear, at any rpm.

There are several methods of determining the tire's circumference. The simplest is to ask the tire manufacturer for engineering data. Failing that, you can always measure it yourself. You can put a chalk mark on the tire, make a corresponding mark on the driveway, roll the bike along until the tire mark rotates 360deg, put another chalk mark on the driveway, and measure the distance between the two driveway marks.

Another method is to smear a dab of grease on the tire tread, roll the bike forward until the grease contacts the pavement twice, then measure the distance between the greasy tread spots on the floor. Another method is to measure the distance between the ground and the axle center with the bike upright, double that, then multiply by 3.14 (the constant π or pi). This is simply the mathematical way of computing a circle's circumference.

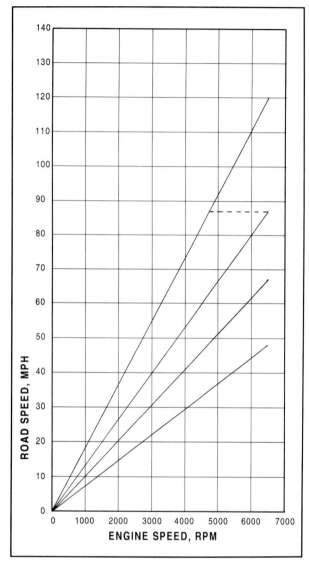

This chart illustrates the gearing of the older, early 1986 four-speed wide-ratio transmission. In this hypothetical situation, we are gearing for 120mph top speed at 6500rpm. We installed 20/48 final-drive sprockets (2.40:1) on our Sportster, for an overall ratio of 4.18:1 (4.176 rounded off). Knowing the internal gearbox ratios and rear wheel diameter, we can determine our speed in each gear by using a simple formula: 6500rpm ÷ overall ratio × 6.8ft wheel circumference ÷ 88. (The overall ratio is computed thus: primary × secondary × gearbox ratios.) By calculating top speed in each gear and plotting the speeds on a graph, we can see what the engine speed will be when we shift gears. In this case, with the older wide-ratio gearbox, when we shift from third to fourth gear, rpm drops by 1800rpm, to 4700rpm. We are at 87mph, and still have 33mph to go before we reached top speed.

Gearbox Analysis: Pre-1987 Four-Speed Wide-Ratio
20/48 Gearing at 6500rpm

Gear	Box ratio	Overall ratio	Speed
1	2.52:1	10.53:1	48mph
2	1.82:1	7.61:1	66
3	1.38:1	5.77:1	87
4	1.00:1	4.18:1	120

Keep in mind that a tire expands at high speeds, and that expansion data can help zero-in the gearing at wide-open throttle. This is especially true at higher speeds, whether it's a land speed record attempt at the Bonneville salt flats in Utah, or a top-gear run on a racetrack's straightaway at Black Hawk Farms, Wisconsin. The faster the tire turns, the more it will likely expand, to a point. To be absolutely certain, you'll need to consult the tire maker's engineers.

Getting back to computing gear ratios, in figuring the primary-drive ratio, simply divide the number of teeth on the *driven* sprocket by the number of teeth on the sprocket that *drives* it. The same holds true for the secondary ratio: divide the number of teeth on the (driven) rear wheel sprocket by the number of teeth on the (driving) transmission sprocket.

Since the Sportster has a direct-drive top gear, its ratio in high gear is 1.00:1, so you don't need to know the gearbox internal ratio to compute top-gear ratio. For computing the ratio in a gear other than top, you will need to know the gearbox internal ratios.

The overall gear ratio is simply the total of all the ratios multiplied together. For example, for a five-speed XLH-883, the 1.74:1 primary ratio, multiplied by the ratio resulting from a 48/20 final-drive sprocket combination (2.40:1), computes to 4.18:1 (1.74 x 2.4 = 4.18).

The five-speed XL-1200 has a thirty-five-tooth engine sprocket, and a fifty-six-tooth clutch sprocket, which is a ratio of 1.60:1—assuming it has been converted to chain drive, with final-drive sprockets of twenty-one-tooth transmission, and forty-eight-tooth rear wheel, which is 2.29:1. Since the gearbox is a 1.00:1 ratio in high gear, the overall gearing is 3.66:1, meaning that it takes 3.66 engine revolutions to turn the rear wheel one rotation (1.60 x 2.29 = 3.66).

Speed Calculations

Following is the formula for computing top speed:

1. Determine rolling circumference in feet: rolling circumference (inches) divided by 12 = circumference in feet.

Example: 81.6in circumference ÷ 12 = 6.8ft

2. Determine the rear wheel's rpm by dividing the overall gear ratio into the engine rpm.

Example: 7200rpm ÷ 3.84 = 1875rpm

3. Determine the motorcycle's actual road speed by multiplying the rear wheel's circumference in feet (#1) by the wheel's rpm (#2) , and divide by the constant 88.

Example: 1875rpm x 6.80ft = 12,750fpm; ÷ 88 = 144.89mph (or 145mph, for our purposes)

Notes: The constant 88 is the factor for converting miles per hour to feet per second, and vice versa. The abbreviation "fpm" represents feet per minute. Under most conditions, rounding to the nearest mile per hour is close enough.

Calculating Gear Ratios

You can see that with this gearing, your engine is revving 7200rpm at 145mph. With this knowledge, you can make minute adjustments to overall gearing. For example, let's say you feel the machine could manage

Gearbox Analysis: 1987 and later Four-Speed Close-Ratio
20/48 Gearing at 6500rpm

Gear	Box ratio	Overall ratio	Speed
1	2.29:1	9.57:1	52mph
2	1.66:1	6.94:1	72
3	1.25:1	5.23:1	96
4	1.00:1	4.18:1	120

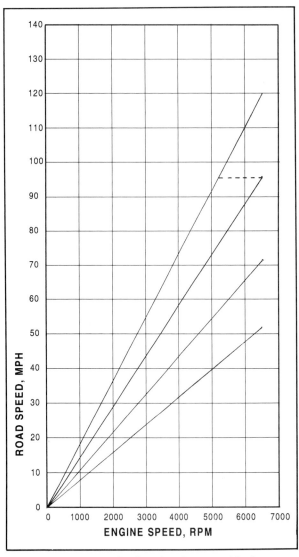

When we shift from third to fourth gear with the newer closer-ratio gearbox, we will hit top gear at 5200rpm at a speed of 96mph. With this gearbox, we drop 1300rpm, giving an additional 500rpm, and must only gain 24mph to reach top speed.

2 or maybe 3mph more, but you doubt that it would go 6 or 8mph more.

With this gearing, your bike revs 50rpm for each mile per hour (7200rpm ÷ 145mph). This means that for a 3mph increase, you'll need to adjust the engine speed by about 150rpm (50rpm/mph x 3mph = 150rpm). With a forty-eight-tooth rear sprocket, one tooth equals about 3mph (145mph ÷ 48 teeth = 3mph/tooth). In this case, going to a forty-seven-tooth rear sprocket may do the trick.

Let's say, on the other hand, you are convinced that you could get another 15mph. To figure your gearing, you must work the previous calculations. Divide engine rpm (7200) by the wheel rpm at 160mph (160mph x 88fpm = 14,080fpm; 14,080fpm ÷ rear wheel circumference of 6.8ft = 2070 rear wheel rpm;

7500 engine rpm ÷ 2070 wheel rpm = 3.62:1 overall gearing; 3.62 ÷ primary ratio 1.6 = 2.26:1 ratio; 2.26 x 20-tooth transmission sprocket = 45-tooth rear sprocket). Therefore, you need 21/45 gearing.

Sometimes it is necessary to change both of the final-drive sprockets to get the gearing you need. Assume you want to gear the bike for 159.5mph, which is a 3.49:1 overall ratio in the previous example (6.8ft tire circumference), and you have a twenty-tooth transmission sprocket and a forty-eight-tooth rear wheel sprocket already installed. By changing the rear wheel sprocket, and leaving the transmission sprocket alone, you can get either 2.20:1 (20/44 teeth) or 2.15:1 (20/43 teeth) ratio. Neither is precise, although very close, at 156.7mph (2.15:1) and 161.7mph (2.20:1). In this case, to fine-tune the gearing, you

The first Harley-Davidson motorcycles generated only 3hp. The pedals on those early machines were more than simply some parts left over from the bicycle. They were needed to start the engine and to assist in climbing hills. The hill became a rider's biggest obstacle, and it's no wonder that hillclimbing was motorcycling's first form of competition. Lou Gerencer, a Harley-Davidson dealer in Elkhart, Indiana, is a two-time National Hill Climb Champion (along with his son, Lou, Jr.). Gerencer's XR-1000 has a direct-drive gearbox that does not use oil—the bearings are lubricated by a simple application of grease, which has proven quite suitable. Gerencer keeps extensive notes on the gearing that he uses on each hill, for future reference. He also fine-tunes the final-drive ratio to suit the particular conditions on race day.

must change the transmission sprocket. You will need a twenty-two-tooth transmission sprocket, with a rear wheel sprocket of forty-eight teeth (3.49 ÷ 1.60 primary ratio = 2.18 secondary ratio).

Note also that a combination of twenty-one- and forty-six-tooth sprockets (2.19:1) gives almost identical gearing as 22/48 (2.18:1), for a speed of 159mph at 7200rpm—only 0.5mph off the mark.

This brings up the subject of overall sprocket size. Some fine-tuners theorize that using smaller sprockets results in a lighter bike, in addition to a smaller rotating mass of chain. What's more, the shorter chain that's required has less friction than a longer chain, and the friction between the chain roller

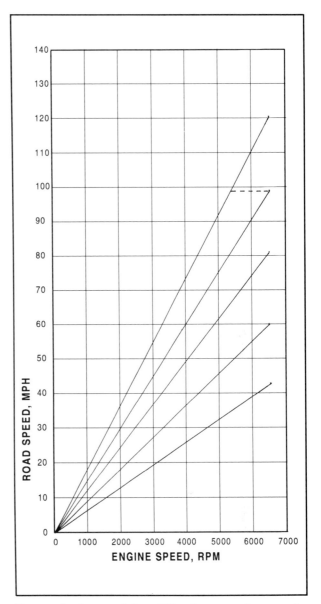

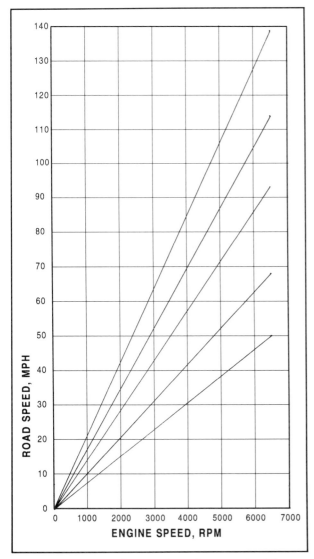

Comparing a newer five-speed gearbox, standard factory gearing produces a top speed of 139mph. When shifting from fourth to fifth gear, the engine speed drops to about 5300rpm. This rpm drop is similar to the newer four-speed box, resulting in a higher engine speed than the older version.

To gear the five-speed for a 120mph top speed, we need a gear ratio of 4.19:1. Using the twenty-tooth drive sprocket, as in the four-speed example, requires a fifty-two-tooth wheel sprocket—because of the numerically higher 1.60:1 primary ratio. This gives us a 4.16:1 ratio for about 121mph. By plotting this on our homemade chart, we can see that in the 5300-6500rpm power range, we have an effective road speed from 35mph. This gives us an advantage over the two four-speed models, which are at or over 40mph at 5300rpm. In addition, we have five gears in the 40-120mph spread, while the four-speeds must cover this 80mph with only four gears. The gear ratio that works best for your Sportster depends on the power characteristics of your engine and your riding style. If you have the stock 883 ports, for example, your peak power develops around 5000–6000rpm. In thise case, gearing must allow you to take advantage of the power range. For a Stage II engine, gear ratios that put the engine speed between 5500–6500rpm provide a nice compromise between performance and longevity, while gearing for a 7500rpm peak offers maximum performance.

and the sprocket teeth is also reduced since there are fewer teeth engaged. In other words, it's lighter and more efficient. So to get a 2.18 ratio, why not use a combination of 17/37 sprockets (149.9mph gearing), and remove about eight links of chain?

Sometimes you need to know an engine speed for a particular gear. Take Z-man's Daytona dilemma, for example. If he wanted to maintain the same speed in a different gear, he would have had to compute the engine speed needed in fourth gear to maintain that same road speed in third gear. To do this, simply multiply the primary- and secondary-drive gearing by the internal gearbox ratio, and compute the speed just as you would for high gear.

For example, with 3.84:1 overall gearing, a five-speed's fourth-gear ratio is 1.216:1, which computes to an overall ratio of 4.67:1. At 6000rpm, the top speed in fourth gear is 99mph.

Example: 6000rpm ÷ 4.76 gearing x 6.8ft wheel circumference ÷ the 88fps/mph conversion = 99mph (the abbreviation "fps" represents feet per second).

In this example, if the engine's power band comes in at 4000rpm the road speed at which the power becomes effective begins at 65mph (4000rpm ÷ 4.76 gear ratio x 6.8ft/rpm ÷ 88fps = 65mph).

These examples assume that you have a need to precisely dial-in the gearing. In some situations, you can play it by ear (although computing it before changing sprockets may save you from making a judgment error). You may feel that the bike could go a little faster, but you don't have a feeling for *how much* faster. If you find that your engine peaks too early, hang a smaller gear on the rear; however, if your engine doesn't reach redline by the end of the straight, add a tooth or two to the rear wheel. Keep doing this until peak engine speed and road speed match.

If you need to make a two- or three-tooth change to the rear, you may wish to change the transmission sprocket instead. Changing two or three teeth often involves adding or removing a link of chain. When

Stronger trap doors are necessary for high-output applications. Those machined from castings are not as strong as those machined from aluminum billet, like this 7075-T6 Bandit five-speed unit. It has additional material in stress areas and provides improved strength.

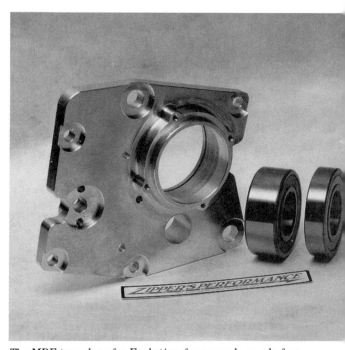

The MRE trap door for Evolution four-speeds, made from 6061-T6 billet aluminum, helps to stiffen the gearbox. This bolt-on piece is machined to accept a double-row bearing (left) for increased strength and rigidity. The standard bearing is on the right.

For ultimate quick-shifting performance, this Zipper's Bandit fully automatic RaceCase solves a multitude of problems. Although the Sportster's gearbox will withstand a certain amount of abuse, it is clearly overwhelmed by the power of drag racing, such as Pro Stock and Top Fuel applications. In addition, the Sportster transmission uses the same gear cluster to engage first and second gears. This means that the sliding dog/gear must disengage first gear, slide across the countershaft, and then engage second gear. All this results in precious time being wasted. The RaceCase is designed to house a special racing transmission developed for National Hot Rod Association (NHRA) Pro Stock racing. By using opposing gearsets, the transfer time between first and second is reduced, virtually eliminating engine kill time between shifts. The only problem with adapting the gearbox to a Harley is that to work on a Harley, the direction of rotation needs to be reversed. The RaceCase does that by using a unique drive gear system that reverses rotation in addition to reducing output speed by one-third. Zipper's Performance Products

Some of the components that make up a complete gearbox using a RaceCase. The cases are machined from 7075-T6 solid aluminum billet on CNC equipment—the main case starts with a 3ft cube weighing 75lb! The gears are made from 9310 steel billet, and various ratios are available. A rotary-type cam controls shifting, and shift action is light compared to a standard Sportster's. Zipper's Performance Products

changing only one tooth, however, you may only need to adjust the rear wheel to compensate. On the other hand, if you wish to run the rear wheel in its most rearward position—to keep as much engine weight on the front wheel as possible, for example—you may want to juggle the sprocket sizes to achieve maximum wheelbase.

Whether it's a 6sec climb to the top of a hill, or a 12sec run to 140mph, or a twenty-four-hour endurance race, the proper gearing is essential.

Transmission Rebuild

Between seasons, most tuners tear down the transmission to check for wear. It's cheaper and easier to replace a worn or suspicious gear or bearing to prevent breakage, rather than not finishing a race when you're 500 miles from home. When this happens, debris and shrapnel often lodge between the rotating shafts, which can lock up the rear end and break the cases.

Modified street bikes with hot cams, ported heads, and stroker kits should be checked more frequently. It's not a bad idea to check the primary-drive chain, pad, and clutch every 2,000-3,000 miles in a machine subjected to high-performance use.

The shift mechanism is a sensitive and critical part of the gearbox. A bent fork can cause missed shifts, an overrevved engine, and accompanying bent valves. Bent forks also cause gear failure. You should check the fork for alignment while it's on its shaft. The fork finger rollers and shift cam should be inspected for excessive wear, as well as the pawl and carrier mechanism. Four-speed boxes need more attention than the five-speeds.

You'll need to shim the gearbox when assembling the shafts. This procedure helps to minimize wear, provides positive dog engagement, and gives crisp, clean shifts. You will need to become familiar with the gear spacing and end-play thrust washers. (See the Harley-Davidson manual for further instructions.)

Once the gearbox is set up, you need only recheck it for unusual wear or damage every so often. A 70–75hp engine probably won't need any more attention than a stocker, depending on how it's ridden. Obviously if you spend a lot of time pushing redline, you might want to schedule an annual check-up. Strokers and high-rpm engines will need more attention.

While you have the gearbox apart, clean and check the entire shifter mechanism. On a racing five-speed engine, check the detent arm and plate, shifter shaft assembly, and shifter fork pins. You may also want to replace the detent arm spring and shifter shaft spring, and all the cotter pins. On four-speed models subject to hard use, watch for signs of stress on third gear—the weak link. If anything looks suspicious, consider replacing it.

The first step in installing the gear clusters is to set the mainshaft and countershaft end plays, then set the gear spacing. The mainshaft and countershaft end plays are very important.

Shimming the transmission gears and shafts requires attention to detail. The easiest method involves assembling the gears, thrust washers, and snap rings on their appropriate shafts, and measuring the gear spacing. Then calculate and write down the spacing you need to open or close up, and look up the necessary shims. Once the gears are shimmed, you will need to fit the correct shift fork. It is not generally known that Harley-Davidson supplies the forks in 0.005, 0.010, and 0.020in increments.

Before final assembly, bolt the gearbox into the cases and check and recheck the shifting mechanism while spinning the shafts. Everything should spin freely and shift precisely. Once you are confident that everything works right, you can take it apart and proceed with final assembly.

Use a good gear lube that has a high shear strength. The newer synthetics and semisynthetic lubricants, such as Harley-Davidson's Trans Fluid, have unique qualities that maintain viscosity and lubricating qualities over a wide range of temperatures, and resist breakdown and corrosion. A number of specialty oil companies offer premium lubricants, and many Sportster competitors rely on them. Spectro and Maxim are favorites.

Powertrain Maintenance

Setting up the transmission requires careful attention to detail; incorrect assembly can result in disaster. If you are not comfortable with the techniques, this is best left to a qualified technician.

Adjustment of both primary- and final-drive chains is critical for peak performance and reliability. Sportsters that produce more than standard power, and that are driven at high speeds for lengthy periods of time, put more stress on the drive chains. It's no fun to sling a chain during a race.

This pro-stock dragster, in the process of construction, incorporates a Zipper's Bandit automatic RaceCase. The Sportster engine's transmission was cut off to adapt the RaceCase, *which can incorporate a four- or five-speed cluster for gas use, or a two- or three-speed gearset for fuel.* Zipper's Performance Products

Primary Drive

The Sportster's primary-drive chain is strong enough to withstand considerable power. In fact, the part number's suffix for the standard Sportster three-row chain is a −57, indicating that the current primary chain is the same as was issued on the original 1957 XL.

Harley-Davidson tried Kevlar-reinforced belt drive in 1980–1981 on its big twins. Five years of development—which resulted in an SAE paper written in conjunction with the Gates Polybelt Company—produced a valuable drive system that works well for rear-wheel-drive. In the heat of a Harley's primary-drive case, however, less than desirable results were reported from the field.

The company reverted back to chain primary for its big twins, and there's little evidence (none, actually) that a belt works any better or lasts any longer than the standard three-row chain primary drives in street applications up to and exceeding 100hp.

After all the switching from chain to belt and then back to chain, the company stayed with chain drive. However, it did not introduce a new chain on the Sportster. This would seem to indicate Harley's confidence in the original part. Dennis Schaefer, Harley-Davidson XL model Technical Services Representative, said that the Sportster's standard primary chain has given so little trouble that he didn't expect any changes would be needed, even for a mildly hopped-up bike.

The standard Sportster primary chain will go some 50,000 or more miles, while even the strongest Kevlar Gates belts are prone to failure within 20,000 miles. The main advantage of a belt primary drive is its light weight. This is important to drag racers, but for street use the conversion is not worth the time and effort.

The most critical factor in primary chain reliability is the freeplay adjustment. It's also important to watch the shoe for wear. The normal 5,000 mile service interval is adequate for near-stock machines, but as you increase power, you should check the primary drive more frequently.

Make sure the countershaft sprocket lock screw is securely in place, and use a thread-locking compound for security—a medium strength that's hand removable, such as Loctite 242. Check the rear chain each time you ride the bike. Be sure the master link (if you are not using an endless chain) is secure.

Sportster Gearbox Noise

Like anything mechanical, the Sportster's transmission generates some whines and howls. Generally, it's not as noisy as the big twin gearbox. The quality of the noise depends largely on which gear is engaged. How much noise is normal, and how much indicates a problem?

First, let's talk about the differences in sound quality. A rattling or clattering noise would indicate a loose fit. A whining or whirring sound results from a

Notice the correct position of the transmission sprocket's lock screw—along the nut's flat—to prevent the nut from loosening. A general-purpose grade of thread-locking compound should be used. Karl Schlei

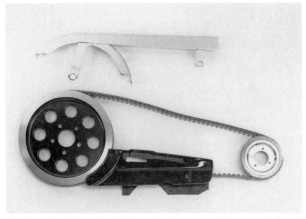

Harley-Davidson's belt kit includes everything needed and bolts on in a jiffy. It smoothes the power delivery, runs quiet, and reduces the rotating mass. However, the added weight of the pulleys, especially the rear-wheel unsprung weight, compromises overall performance and gearing choices. Harley-Davidson

tight fit. Thanks to improvements in manufacturing, over the years Harley-Davidson has made great strides in tightening the tolerances between gears and shafts. They also perform better and last longer.

Factors other than the source of the noise itself may influence a rider's perception of the sound. Fairings and windshields are examples. Their surfaces may reflect the sound back to the rider and amplify it. Wearing a helmet may also make a difference in your noise perception.

When the noise from the mufflers and the inlet tract are quieted, other sounds will seem amplified. Over the years, Harley-Davidson inlet and exhaust noise emissions have been toned down in response to EPA regulations. As a result, transmission noises in newer Harleys may give an impression of being louder than older models. That's why a side-by-side comparison of different model years may not be a valid test.

A Harley five-speed transmission case contains two shafts and ten gears (five gears are splined to their shafts, and the other five gears spin on bearings). All of these gears, whether they slide along their splines or spin on their shafts, require clearances to prevent seizure. (In other words, if the fit is too tight, a gear and a shaft can get so hot they literally weld themselves together.)

In any of the first through fourth gears, both shafts and five of the gears are used to transmit power. Three of these gears are splined, while the other two bearing gears spin on their shafts (these bearing gears turn at different speeds than their shafts). As gear selection moves from first to second, to third, and then to fourth, the transmission counter-

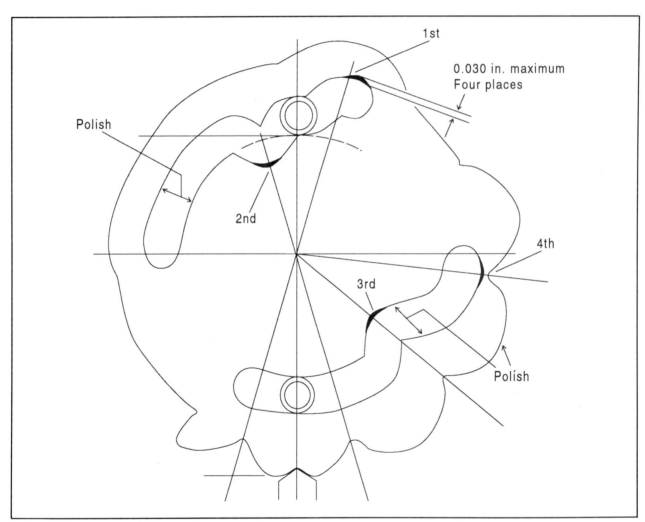

The shift forks in the four-speed gearbox take a beating when shifting at high rpm. To reduce these loads, relieve the areas of the cam plate indicated. This will allow the gears to engage more fully without unusual side loads. To determine the amount of material to be removed, with the transmission and shift mechanism assembled on the access door, shift all gears into position and check each. Remove a little metal at a time and then recheck. The gears should be completely engaged while the shift forks are centered and free of side pressure. For smoother operation, polish all contact surfaces. Harley-Davidson

shaft spins faster relative to the mainshaft. In other words, third and fourth gears make a little more noise than first and second.

Most riders probably rev their engine to higher rpm in third gear than in fourth, since high rpm in fourth gear takes you well over the legal speed limits. In this case, third gear may seem louder than fourth because as wind and road noises increase, the transmission noise will be harder to detect.

When you engage fifth gear (fourth gear in a four-speed), the mainshaft sliding gear engages the main drive gear directly. Now the power flows through two gears that are locked onto one shaft, and therefore the gears spin at the same speed as the shaft. A whole lot less is going on, so top gear is considerably quieter.

Chain Lubrication

There are many fine-quality chain lubes available, and experienced racers use just about every type of lubricant—especially the ones that offer contingency money from the manufacturer. Several of these lubes have been around for many years. Kal Guard and PJ1 are classic examples. In an independent test, Kal Guard was shown to have exceptional qualities, and PJ1 placed a very close second. (Harley-Davidson chain lube was not tested in this particular comparison.) If you want Kal Guard but can't find it, go to a Yamaha shop and pick up the Yamalube stuff; it's Kal Guard under license.

With today's level of lubrication technology, any of these lubricants will work well—*if* the chain is kept clean, the lubrication is applied, and the slack is properly adjusted. All of this is important for maximum performance. A dirty chain wears out fast; periodically or between races, it's a good idea to remove the chain, clean it in solvent, relube it, and reinstall it.

For street use, put a fresh squirt of lube on your chain every 300–500 miles—more often is better. The lubricant not only helps the chain last longer, it also helps protect the sprockets. Apply the lube between the side plates and rollers, as well as on the rollers themselves.

O-ring or "self-lube" chains have been proven to have less friction than regular types. They may seem stiff before warm-up, but after one lap on a racecourse or a mile ride on the street, friction decreases. The roller and side plate lubrication is built into the chains; however, the outside of the rollers and the sprocket teeth need lubrication to help prevent premature wear. It is necessary to apply lubricant on the sprocket teeth and/or chain rollers.

When you remove your drive chain, attach an old, worn-out (but clean) chain to it. Pull the existing chain off the gearbox sprocket, and leave the old chain wrapped around the sprocket. After you have cleaned and lubed the drive chain, you can hook it to the old chain and pull it around the sprocket.

Three types of belt final-drive systems can be fitted to the Sportster: Karata (left), Supermax (top), and original equipment.

Sportsters aren't particularly hard on chains, providing the engine is not lugged. Lugging the engine at low speeds causes enormous loads on the chain, gearbox, and engine—much more stress than running the engine at higher speeds. Riding techniques, therefore, often play a big part in driveline durability.

The Supermax belt system uses Kevlar-reinforced belts. Front sprockets are made from polyurethane, with hardened steel centers; rear polyurethane sprockets use aluminum centers. Transmission sprockets are available in five sizes, and rear sprockets in four, giving a wide array of overall gear-ratio options. Different lengths of belts are also offered, as well as custom-machined pulleys.

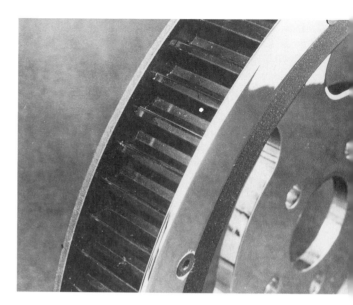

Stock sprocket teeth (left) and Supermax polyurethane teeth. Both work well and can be expected to provide good longevity; however, the Supermax sprocket teeth are more sensitive to misaligned pulleys.

Clutch

Likewise, as you add power the clutch needs special attention. So as long as you're checking and adjusting the primary chain, don't forget the clutch.

The standard Sportster clutch tends to be sensitive to overheating. Once it reaches a critical temperature, it's gone forever. If it isn't slipped or abused for extended periods, it should be OK, but it's not a bad idea to avoid problems by installing a racing clutch with the Screamin' Eagle spring. Barnett Kevlar plates have proven themselves in competition.

Twin Sports racing requires about ten rear sprockets in one-tooth increments.

134

When converting to ¹/₄in chain by machining the inside surface of the drive sprocket, a spacer will be needed for the ¹/₄in wide rear sprocket. When using wider tires, a spacer may also be helpful to move the chain outward for tire clearance. Karl Schlei

Dished-type drive sprockets for ¹/₄in chains are available from performance shops like Bartels'. Some tuners simply shave ¹/₈in from the inside surface of the stock sprocket. Karl Schlei

At this time it's also a good idea to check the bearings. If you're at the track, to remove the primary cover without draining the oil, lean the bike on its side (don't forget to remove the battery to prevent acid leakage).

Clutch Adjustment

One of the commonly misunderstood and often overlooked details of the clutch is the freeplay at the adjuster, or release mechanism. There are two clutch adjustments involved: the clutch *cable* freeplay at the

A ¹/₄in (520) chain is just as strong, yet stiffer than a ³/₈in (530) chain. It also saves several pounds. The narrow chain, however, will wear sprockets quicker and requires frequent inspection.

To make a drive sprocket that is not available from suppliers, it is necessary to cut the center from a standard Harley sprocket and weld on the sprocket size needed. Additional spacers or shims may be needed to align it with the rear sprocket. Karl Schlei

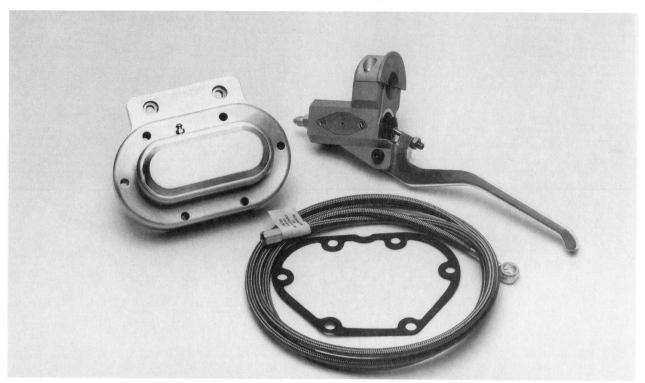

Various hydraulic clutch systems are available for Sportsters, similar to this big twin type from Rivera. In
addition, air shifter kits, like the popular MRE system, are
a must for drag racing. Just push a button, and you're in
the next gear. Rivera Engineering

The Bandit SuperClutch has proven popular for both street
and drag strip use in high-output Sportsters. It's available
in two versions, to fit 1971–1984 iron XLs and XRs, and
1984 and later Evolution alternator models (iron-type
shown). The seven-plate units adapt fairly easily (some
machining required) and accept Barnett Kevlar friction
plates. Zipper's Performance Products

handlebar lever; and the clutch *adjusting screw* freeplay at the release mechanism inside the primary-drive case.

The presence of slack in the cable does not necessarily mean that there is slack at the clutch adjusting screw, located at the clutch. Inadequate freeplay at the clutch adjusting screw will burn up the clutch. In addition, when the friction plates become overheated they may expand beyond a normal amount, reducing freeplay further. Continued high-speed use may require additional freeplay beyond factory recommendations.

The clutch screw's clearance must be set up first, then the cable slack can be adjusted. The proper procedure calls for setting the correct screw adjustment at the clutch, and then setting the correct cable freeplay. To do this, set the release mechanism by just barely bottoming the adjustment screw until there is no freeplay. Then back off a quarter turn. Once the release mechanism has its required freeplay, the cable can be adjusted so that it has $1/16$in freeplay.

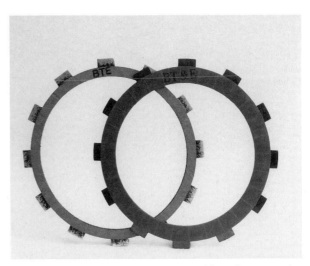

Barnett Kevlar friction plates were subjected to extensive testing and development before going on the market. The extraordinary material can be run in wet or dry environments, and have proven to be durable. Barnett

Chapter 6

Frame, Suspension, and Brakes

The basic Sportster chassis does all the important things well. Obviously, it provides mounting points for the necessary components, like a fuel tank (however small), battery, and so on. It also holds the powertrain, provides a place for the rider to sit, and links the wheels in a rigid structure.

That last point is important. The Sportster is one of the better handling and most stable motorcycles in

Author Buzzelli consulted with Harley-Davidson Styling Director Lou Netz in setting up his 1988 XLH-883. Buchanan's Frame Shop laced the American-made Sun aluminum rims to stock Harley hubs with stainless steel spokes. The 18in rear and 19in front rims, with Dunlop 110/90x19 front and 130/80x18 rear tires, have rolling circumferences nearly identical with the standard Sportster. This gives a reasonable assurance that the handling would be similar to the stock bike's. Although the bike handles beautifully and sticks well, the hard, low-profile tires give it harsher ride qualities than a stock Sportster's.

the world. Racers who ride the AMA Championship Cup Series (CCS) Twin Sports Series attest to the Sportster's stability. Several Twin Sports riders who previously competed in Supersports classes racing Japanese bikes in both the 600 and 750cc classes, have praised the XL's excellent handling. They were surprised!

The XL's excellent handling should be no surprise, however, considering the painstaking efforts by Harley-Davidson engineers to provide the optimum in stability. Harley-Davidson factory engineers and testers are sensitive about steering qualities, and all Harleys must pass strict "weave" and "wobble" tests before being accepted for production. Borderline performance flunks the test.

Motorcycle frames are designed to handle a multitude of loads. The engine's drive chain tries to twist both the frame and the swing arm; the steering head transmits loads into the top tube and the twin downtubes; the swing arm pulls and twists the rear upright tubes; the rider and rear shocks apply loads to the rear triangle section; and let's not forget that the Sportster powertrain, with its giant crankshaft, gearshafts, gears, bearings, and cases, that presses earthward with a couple of hundred pounds' force.

Coordinating the Handling Package

It's important for anyone contemplating a change to the frame, swing arm, fork, or rear suspension, to stop and consider how the change will affect the motorcycle's steering and overall handling. All of these original components were designed, engineered, and tested to work together under normal street riding conditions, with factory-approved original equipment tires.

Sometimes one simple change, such as installing a different brand or model of tire, can cause a drastic deterioration in handling. Let's not get into a major dissertation on tire engineering here. Suffice it to say that tires vary in many ways: construction, profile, material, sidewall stiffness, and tread pattern, to name a few of the obvious. The many smaller differences add up to big differences in overall performance and steering qualities.

We'll take chassis modification one step at a time, starting up front.

Front Forks

Harley-Davidson engineers did a nice job on the newer 39mm fork assembly (1988 and later). It has plenty of travel, at 6.9in; however, the damping rates

This project bike features a SuperTrapp two-into-one exhaust system, Mitchell Chicane wheels, and Performance Machine single-disc, four-piston front brake. The *combination of this exhaust, wheels, and brake saved an estimated 30lb. Joe Minton*

139

are on the limp side. In addition, the spring rate, while not bad for average street use, is too soft for hard-cornering, high-performance use. The softly sprung straight-wound stock springs allow lots of front-end dive under maximum braking, leaving little travel left to handle road bumps.

Although the fork has 6.9in of travel, the soft stock springs also sag more under cornering loads, eating up valuable ground clearance. With a set of sticky-compound tires installed, it's easy to drag the exhaust pipes on the right, and a primary-drive cover screw on the left during hard cornering.

When leaned over excessively on the left, the clutch cable may drag. If that happens, the outer sheath could be worn through, which would leak oil. The cable is open to the primary case, and is lubricated by primary oil. Be sure to secure the cable in a way that keeps it from dragging.

Pre-1988 models have 35mm fork tubes. The method of clamping the axle to the tubes makes it prone to binding the tubes, so it's necessary to take extra measures to avoid this, which is simple enough. First, leave the axle and the axle clamp bolts slightly loose, so that the axle is not clamped tightly. Tighten all other fasteners (triple crown bolts, and so on) securely. While holding the front brake on, compress the fork several times. This helps to position the axle in the lower tube clamps, and to align the two tubes. Then tighten the clamping bolts, and finally the axle nut.

Before assembling a fork, check each leg's inner tube travel for friction and free movement. With the

John Gaedke, one of Harley-Davidson's public relations managers (who once worked in the racing department) owns this XR-1000-based Cafe Racer. John rescued the tank from the scrap heap so we can thank—and envy— John for saving a piece of racing heritage from extinction. The bike was originally built as a "concept vehicle," to be displayed around Daytona to test consumer reaction. It was part of a program put together by Harley's marketing director, Clyde Fessler. One outwardly noticeable feature is anti-dive. Inside, the engine has a windage plate and special oiling system modifications to direct the oil to the crank case's pick-up point. The re-worked heads have dual plugs, sparked by Dyna-S ignition. The bike has E cams, which have the highest lift and longest duration you can use without modifications to avoid crashing valves into the pistons. (He also has a set of QC cams, which have the same lift with a shorter duration—they're not as peaky as the E type.) The E cams don't make power until 4500rpm, and Gaedke found that installing Supertrapp's Super Tips increased back pressure enough to help the low end. Now, instead of downshifting to third to pass traffic, he can just roll it on in high gear. In true KR/XL tradition, engineers were so cautious about the ability of the transmission to take the XR's 70hp, that they used the old-style clutch (which tended to slip a little) instead of the more positive-action 1983 diaphragm-spring type. Gaedke replaced his XR's clutch with the standard clutch/alternator system that was offered on the 1983 XL models.

cap off and the oil and springs removed, each leg should pump through its travel freely without binding. Then assemble the springless tube assemblies in the clamps and check the whole fork assembly by pumping it through its full travel. Binding is not likely to be caused by the fender; however, a fork brace may cause binding. Triple crowns that are bent or misaligned in some way will cause binding. You can check them by simply looking to see that the tubes are parallel.

Fork Spring Rates

The stock fork provides a cushy ride over the highway, but tends to sag under hard use. If ride quality is your goal, you may want to leave the fork alone. If you ride hard, however, you'll need to modify the fork. Most AMA CCS Twin Sports Series riders use Works Performance, Progressive Suspension, or Bartels' Performance Products springs.

Street riders who like to brake heavily and corner at maximum lean angles will find these springs essential. The progressive spring rates give a smoother ride over small bumps, while soaking up larger, sharper bumps. In addition to raising the ride height about an inch, they also minimize nose-dive under hard braking, leaving more travel available to handle bumps.

The Progressive Suspension spring is a one-piece progressively wound coil which does not offer adjustability. Its stiff rates are suitable for track use, but give a somewhat harsh ride on the street.

Works Performance features two springs: the long spring handles the soft-rate stuff, while the shorter, stiffer spring comes into play during the last bit of travel. In addition, a bolt system that separates the two springs provides some adjustability. You can adjust the amount of travel before you get into the second rate, which you can set. For those who need or

Simple bolt-on items can go a long way to giving a unique appearance. Evident on Nick Ienatsch's Evolution Cafe Racer are the Dymag wheel with Michelin Hi-Sport DOT tire, aluminum sprocket with 520 chain, Fox shock mounted upside-down, and Kerker SuperTrapp two-into- *one exhaust system. A two-into-one system like the SuperTrapp is feather light and saves considerable weight. Ienatsch later added Storz rearsets pegs. Motorcyclist*

want to take the time to fine-tune the front end, this is an advantage.

The Bartels' spring has an initial rate similar to the stock Harley-Davidson spring, which gives a nice highway ride. The increased secondary portion has a stiff enough rate to resist bottoming. For most street bike applications, this may be the best compromise.

Fork Oils

Heavier grade fork oil helps to increase the damping rate and reduce sag somewhat. While standard street bikes perform adequately with 15 weight oil, many Twin Sports riders prefer 30, 40, or even 50 weight. Although the thicker oil resists flow, which has the effect of providing slightly more damping force, it can also cause some "pumpdown" over a lengthy series of bumps. This is a condition where the fork does not rebound completely before hitting the next bump.

Some tuners who are dissatisfied with the poor rebound damping of the Sportster's front fork may choose to experiment with 80 or 100 weight gear lube. An 80 weight gear lube, besides having lubrication qualities unsuitable for damper use, is actually lighter than 50 weight oil. To reduce the risk of consumers adding gear lube to their engine, the viscosity ratings printed on a can of gear lube is double its actual viscosity. A 40 weight gear oil is labeled "80 weight," and a "100 weight" gear oil has an actual viscosity rating similar to a 50 weight motor oil.

Because a heavy, 50 weight oil increases rebound damping so severely, it is not advisable to use 50 weight oil in a front fork in the first place. There are better ways to improve handling and ride than adding heavy oils.

According to AMA CCS rules, it is legal for Harley-Davidson Twin Sports machines to have altered damping rods. Therefore, Twin Sports tuners must resist the temptation to rework the stock damper rods or to install non-OEM replacement damper rods. To prevent bottoming under hard braking, some Twin Sports riders overfill the fork tubes. This reduces the volume of air trapped in the fork tubes. When the fork tubes compress under braking, the air is also compressed, which acts like an extra spring. The less air there is in the fork, the higher the compression rate pressure. This increases the effective spring rate, which in turn reduces dive

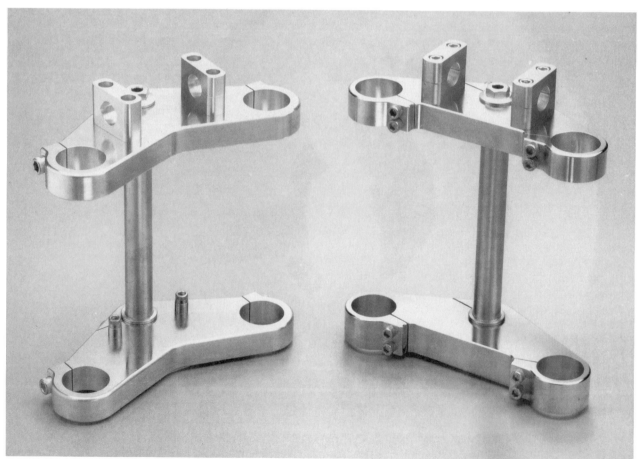

Triple clamps made from high-tech billet aluminum are the strongest and lightest types. The road race style (right) has twin clamp bolts on each leg and a thicker bottom clamp. *Dirt track or drag race style is on the left.* Storz Performance

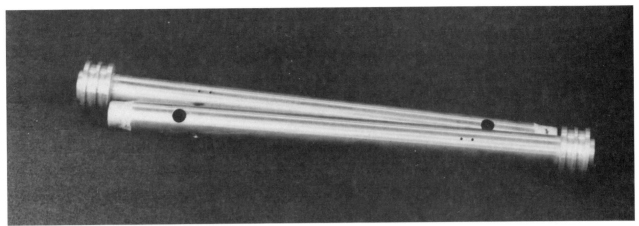

The Progressive Suspension fork damper rods are fractionally larger in diameter than standard XL units, and have smaller oil holes. They are designed for use with stiffer springs. Karl Schlei

and increases overall ride height and cornering clearance.

To get good all-around ride qualities and improved ride height, start with the progressive springs and 15 weight oil. With the springs removed from the tubes and the fork bottomed, add enough oil to fill each tube to within ⅝in from the top. For riders of average height and weight, this should not only improve suspension qualities, it will also produce quicker and more positive steering response.

Although adding more, heavier weight oil (30 weight and higher) to the fork tubes has little effect on fork action over small bumps, it reduces fork response over a series of bumps.

Fork Damping Rods

Twin Sports riders have experienced wheel hop when braking over stutter bumps—such as the area approaching the chicane at Daytona—where the front wheel can bounce and chatter. The solution to this is to alter the damping rods so that the damping force is strong enough to control the spring force.

The traditional method of improving fork damping involves removing the damper rod, and either machining new ones (more work than is really necessary) or modifying the stock units. There are two sets of holes in the stock damper rods. Welding one closed effectively doubles the damping rate. Unless you're a rocket scientist, some experimenting may be necessary. After reassembling the fork and trying it, you may discover it necessary to drill the existing hole to a slightly larger diameter. Closing off one damping hole results in a damping rate that is more suited to sticky racing-type tires than to street tires.

The real problem with the stock damping rods is the fit of the floating washer. Excessive clearance allows the oil to push past the washer rather than being forced through the rod's oil orifices. This effectively renders the oil holes useless.

Considering the work involved, most street-roaming Sportster riders will probably find it easier to buy the Progressive Suspension damper rods. They have been designed to work with progressive-rate springs. With the increased damping provided by

---

Custom Frame Builders

Following is a list of suppliers who are well-known in racing circles for custom-building frames and swing arms for racing applications. However, many other metal fabricators may be just as qualified to handle your custom frame job.

Carroll Racing/Champion Frames
Bud Carroll acquired the Champion frame business, under the name Carroll Racing Products. Address: 18700 Normandie Avenue, Unit C, Gardena, CA 90248.

C&J Frames
C&J Precision Products has been making motorcycle racing frames for many years, for road, dirt, and drag. Address: 1151 E. Mission Road, Fallbrook, CA 92028.

Kosman Frames
Kosman builds street and drag racing frames and swing arms for Sportsters, as well as wheelie bars, a front fork, and footpeg kits. A new, modular wheelie bar is in the works. Address: 340 Fell St, San Francisco, CA 94102.

Pingle Frames
Pingle Enterprise, well known for its high-flow gas valves, supplies bolt-on wheelie bars and drag bars, as well as a variety of equipment useful to racing motorcycles. Address: 2076C 11th Avenue, Adams, WI 53910.

Knight/Lawwill Frames
Terry Knight makes the dirt-track frames for Team Harley-Davidson riders. Knight has built frames under the Mert Lawwill banner. Address: 2707 Mount Baker Highway, Bellingham, WA 98226.

these units, a Sportster feels more connected to the road surface.

Aftermarket Front Forks

For projects that require the ultimate in front suspension performance, you'll find an endless array of forks available. Many are offered with the necessary mounts to bolt onto a Harley-Davidson, while others may require custom machining and special bearings. For example, complete triple clamps milled from billet aluminum are available from Storz Performance. A variable-length steering stem allows a frame builder to adapt the strong and light triple clamps to any frame.

In your quest for the perfect front end, always keep your application in mind. For example, the ultra-light 35mm Ceriani fork (only 5lb, 4oz each leg) may be ideal for a drag bike, which operates in a straight line on flat, level surfaces. But the variable adjustability of the GCB, Marzocchi, or Superbike forks make them better suited to road-race tracks, where varying terrain and track conditions require adjustments for maximum performance.

Steering Dampers

Any number of conditions can cause head shake, such as when a tire slides and then hooks up again, hitting a bump or series of bumps, or frame and

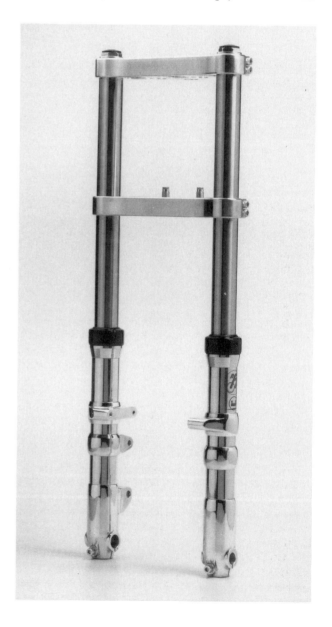

With an eye on style, Forcella Italia forks (formerly Ceriani) offers different fork units for a variety of applications. Ceriani forks have been used by dirt track riders, including many National Champions, for years. Both a Wide Glide style and a Mid Glide type is offered from Storz Performance. They offer the classic Ceriani looks combined with excellent spring and damping rates. Storz Performance

144

swing-arm flex. In any of these situations, the front end is deflected away from its trajectory, causing the fork to oscillate from side to side. In the best situation, the fork will self-center quickly without ruffling the rider's line. In the worst situation, the dynamic forces involved may result in a tank slapper, where the fork slaps from one steering stop to the other. When this happens, the rider may find himself looking for a place to land.

Sometimes head shake, when caused by a mechanical problem, can be eliminated or minimized by making adjustments. Loose steering head bearings or maladjusted rear wheel alignment are a couple of examples. Even in perfect conditions, however, head shake can be caused by forces beyond the rider's control.

A steering damper may help to reduce this. Steering dampers are simply a hydraulic shock absorber, similar to a suspension strut. Most are adjustable, some more than others. A decent universal damper might have seven click-settings with 20lb increments, while a better unit may have fourteen or more settings. Manufacturers include GCB (Enrico Ceriani, fourteen clicks), Ohlins (sixteen positions), Shindy (seven settings), Kawasaki universal (seven positions), and OEM units that are standard on many Japanese superbikes, such as the Suzuki GSXR-1000 (fourteen positions).

When installing a steering damper, it should be mounted so that the shock strut aligns with the fork's rotation. That is, the force compressing the shock should be in a straight line with the damper rod's travel. This eliminates binding. Check to ensure that the shock does not bottom or top out, so that you have full steering travel from lock to lock. The GCB damper, available from Storz Performance, permits full steering movement and is rebuildable.

Rear Shocks

It has been said that the Sportster has only two things wrong with it: the right shock, and the left shock. That may be true, and we may agree that the engineer who approved the final spring and damping rates should be taken out and flogged. The original equipment shocks, made by Showa Company, Limited, have an extended length of 13.62in, with a collapsed length of 10.00in, for a total stroke of 3.62in (pertains to 1988 and later standard Sportster models, not Huggers).

The spring rate of each is 55.3psi, which is low; and the shock's preload in its lowest setting is 146lb, which is high. This is quite an excessive preload for a vehicle under 500lb—it takes 292lb of force before the swing arm begins to move. (Third-notch maximum preload is 190lb, for a total preload of 380lb.)

Once the suspension begins to compress, it collapses easily (it only takes a force of 346lb to collapse one shock, for a total weight of 692lb). What this means is that the shock does not easily compress over small bumps, yet it does bottom easily. You get the worst of both worlds.

The shock is also underdamped, which only compounds the problem. When you run over little bumps the shocks move minutely, and these bumps in turn are directly felt by the rider. When you hit a big enough bump that compresses the shocks, with so little damping, they rebound with a bang and top out, giving the rider another jolt.

There are many aftermarket shocks that will improve the Sportster's ride, and even the least-

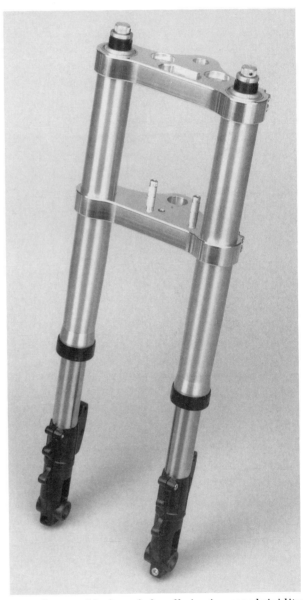

These days upside-down forks, offering increased rigidity compared to conventional forks, are regarded as leading-edge technology. This Forcella unit from Storz Performance features huge 54mm aluminum-alloy top tubes with billet triple clamps and 40mm lower sliding legs. The fork has separate adjustments for spring preload, and compression and rebound damping.

This steering damper, a GCB Ceriani, allows full lock-to-lock fork movement without bottoming or topping. Mounting the fork leg bracket outboard provides maximum leverage. For a short-stroke damper, the bracket could be rotated inward toward the center of the fork, although the damper's mechanical advantage would be reduced.

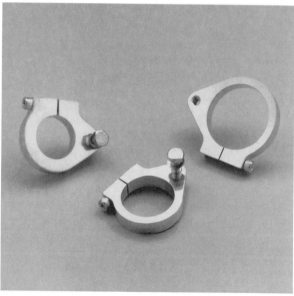

Commercially available universal brackets, such as these from Storz Performance, make the job of adapting a steering damper fairly simple. Available in various diameters, they can be utilized in a number of ways. Storz Performance

expensive units offer dual-rate springs and a nice finish. A few, like the Progressive Suspension PS series, offer little or no adjustment, but they are a better shock at a reasonable price.

For those who want or need more adjustability, there are plenty of shocks to choose from. For example, Koni's 7610 series can be adjusted without removing them from the bike. Works Performance's Alloy Street Tracker model offers screw-type preload adjusters and air-adjustable assist, and Progressive's Adaptive line gives you five-position rebound adjustment. Each shock manufacturer offers a full line of shocks with various features.

Less preload allows the shock's springs to react to the smaller bumps. It also allows the shock to sag slightly with the rider in place. A shock needs a little room for rebound so that it won't top out. In addition, progressive-rate springs give the shock a wider range within which to work. Generally speaking, you'll want an initial rate that's soft enough to provide a cushy ride over the smaller road irregularities, and a secondary rate that is just soft enough to handle bigger bumps, yet hard enough to prevent bottoming. Generally, a rate of about 80 or 90lb makes a good preliminary rate for a nice street ride. A secondary

This dragster has a threaded aluminum rod that connects the swing arm to the chassis, allowing adjustment in rear- *end ride height. This adjustment is critical for controlling weight transfer during acceleration.*

rate of about 140-160lb works well for street use, while a racing Sportster may need a rate up to 200lb or more to keep things off the pavement during cornering.

Most lighter riders will want to pick a spring that has less preload; heavier riders need more preload. Either way, take advantage of progressive, dual-rate springs. If the spring has three rates, such as Koni's, so much the better. Koni's part number 7610F-1283 adjustable dampers (1in longer than stock) and part number 250-15-1786 springs have proven to work well for many Sportster riders. Combined with the fork modifications described earlier, a Sportster becomes smooth riding and more stable.

If you find the original equipment spring rates suitable, you can install them onto 13.5in Koni shocks. They have 4.2in of travel, and superb damping. The 13.8in shock is another alternative, along with three different Koni springs, each with triple spring rates.

When shopping for springs for street use, look for an initial spring rate around 90lb; and a secondary rate around 150. For use with sticky racing tires, a heavier rate of 100 and 200lb may be more suitable.

Twin Sports racers usually equip their machines with 14.5 or even 15.0in shocks. This raises the ride height enough to keep most, but not all, of the Sportster's undercarriage from grounding in corners.

Wheels

Except for occasional checks for cracks and other damage, the standard cast wheels don't ask much. The spoke nipples on wire wheels demand a little more attention, and it is important to occasionally check for run-out.

Wherever you use your vehicle, it is likely governed by rules of some sort. For example, in AMA CCS racing, you must use standard original equipment rims; however, in drag racing, you have a wide

147

array of wheel choices. As noted in the Preface, even street riders face regulation, since altering the wheel's rolling circumference essentially violates EPA laws.

Although today's OEM safety beads are adequate in many applications, a means of positively locking the tire to the rim is essential in some forms of competition, such as drag racing. One method involves installing sheet-metal screws through the rims, into the tire bead, to help prevent tire spin. Special tire-locking wheels with rim locks are also available.

In addition to aluminum and magnesium wheels, carbon fiber wheels are available for rear-wheel drag racing applications. Carbon fiber is a material that is stronger than steel, yet lighter than aluminum.

And speaking of weight, the Sportster has a considerable amount of unsprung wheel weight. In other words, the wheels are heavy, especially the rear. The standard 16in rear wheel is the result of styling preferences, not high-performance goals. The traditional "fat" rear tire makes the back of the motorcycle look heavy, while the more open 19in front wheel gives it a lightweight appearance. This styling treatment dates back to the days of the original choppers with "ape hangers."

Sportster owners looking for more performance will want to consider trashing the 16in rear hoop. An 18in wire wheel, for example, saves more than 6lb. In addition to the weight savings, a larger variety of high-performance tires are available to fit the 18in wheel. High-quality, American-made Sun aluminum rims provide light weight with good looks. Buchanan's Frame Shop in Los Angeles can lace stainless-steel spokes to standard Harley-Davidson

No, this man is not 8ft tall. Clyde Fessler is only 6ft, 1in tall, and his Sportster has been lowered 2in. The tunneled tank, which sits lower on the frame, also lends to the bike's lowness. Fessler, vice president of Harley's general mer- *chandising department, had the entire motorcycle, including the wheels and frame, painted Burnt Orange and Cardinal Red with 18K gold leaf and silver leaf. Bob Drone, of Oakland Harley-Davidson, hopped up the engine.*

hubs (which you can purchase from your local dealer), or supply you with lighter Kosman hubs. Storz Performance is another wheel supplier.

Changing to an 18in rear wheel saves a lot of weight. More important, this is unsprung weight, and anything you can do to reduce wheel weight will pay off in improved ride and handling qualities. Even using a wire wheel with a steel rim—which is about 1.5lb heavier than a cast wheel—you can still save weight because of the reduced tire weight. An 18 or 19in tire weighs about 12lb, while the standard MT90x16 K181 weighs about 19lb, a 7lb savings.

The stock rear rim width is 2.50in. A wider rim helps to put more rubber to the ground, which helps to get more traction. However, the Sportster's rear tire width is limited by the proximity of the chain, and by the width of the swing arm and rear fender. So before planning on wider tires, carefully check your clearances. The widest tire a standard Sportster can take is about 5.6in, or the equivalent of a 130/80.

You can gain additional chain clearance by spacing the final-drive sprockets outward. Bartels' Performance Products offers dished countershaft sprockets to achieve this. As for the rear wheel sprocket, you can move it outboard slightly with a spacer. But again, you will find that you're limited in how much you can move it. Be sure the two sprockets are properly aligned.

By changing the secondary-drive chain to a ¼in width (520 size), you can gain enough clearance to open up new options for wider tires. You can do this by simply machining ⅛in off the backside of the countershaft sprocket and spacing a new ¼in rear wheel sprocket outward ⅛in. This is common in AMA CCS Twin Sports racing. It allows the use of a 150/80x16in tire.

If you change the rear wheel size and mount a new tire, make sure the tire matches the front. Tires are designed to work together in matched sets, and mixing a rear tire of one manufacturer or series with a front tire of another can result in poor handling.

Special Application Wheels

Special wheels that are designed for a specific application are often required by racing organizations. Tire locks and safety beads allow drag racers to run very low tire pressures while preventing the tire from spinning on the rim. This results in quicker starts off the line due to a large contact patch. It also reduces vibration and shake, which helps the rider to manage and control traction.

One particular MRT (Marsh Racing Tires) wheel, available from Rivera Engineering, features carbon fiber rims with CNC-machined 7075 aluminum-alloy hubs and spokes. Another nice feature of this particular system is that it allows changing wheel width without purchasing another complete wheel—you simply exchange the carbon fiber rims.

Wheel Bearings

The wheel bearings are especially critical. Sportster wheels ride on tapered roller bearings and the freeplay adjustment is crucial, especially to achieve

This particular MRT wheel (Marsh Racing Wheels), available from Rivera, features carbon fiber rims with CNC machined 7075 alloy aluminum hubs and spokes. The rims are available in either safety bead or "tire lock" styles, and they are made of carbon fiber. Carbon fiber wheels have been around automotive drag racing and advanced aircraft for years, but the technology has been slow to find its way into the motorcycle drag racing market. The material has a tensile strength greater than steel with a weight lighter than aluminum.

Mitchell offers custom lightweight wheels in a variety of styles. Made from 6061-T4 rolled aluminum heat treated to T6 condition, they save an average of 1 to 14lb per wheel, depending on the application. These are the latest Mitchell Aero wheels. Performance Machine

maximum braking efficiency and to eliminate brake drag. Twin Sports mechanics focus much of their attention on reducing friction and drag. Since all the engines are stock and produce about the same horsepower, theoretically, small details become important. One of those details is bearing clearance.

Three inner bearing spacers are available in 0.014in increments. Tuners with an eye on perfection have been known to shave a slightly long spacer to within plus or minus 0.001in. This gives a finer degree of bearing adjustment.

Other than striving for perfection in tolerance, the only other bearing variable is lubricant. Some nit-picking mechanics ask the oil companies for specs to determine the lowest coefficient of friction, among other things. Short of becoming an expert on grease, your best option is to select a high-quality water-resistant lubricant, such as lithium grease.

To check the final installation, put the bike on a stand to elevate the wheels, and spin them. Be sure to disconnect the rear chain. A wheel should rotate freely, without resistance.

Tires

The Sportster, under normal street conditions with standard DOT-approved street tires, performs in a known and accepted manner. However, a simple change to high-performance tires, made of sticky compound rubber, changes the game. Racing tires provide higher cornering speeds and lateral acceleration, which in turn subject the chassis to higher loads. Whether you are accelerating in a lateral direction (cornering loads) in a road race, or accelerating forward in a drag race, all the loads are multiplied.

Tire manufacturers recommend replacing tires in matched sets. Matched set refers to using a combination of tires that were designed, engineered, and tested to work together. Dunlop's D401 Elite S/T tires, for example, were engineered to be used as a matched set. Both Dunlop and Harley-Davidson recommend replacing tires in sets; both front and rear tires should match. It is not a good idea, for example, to replace one K181 with a D401 and not change the other K181.

If that doesn't complicate the picture, there are other variables that affect the stresses on tires: inflation pressure, load, speed, road surface, ambient temperature, wheel spin, and power. The wrong combination of these elements can result in heat build-up and total failure, such as a blowout.

With this in mind, to preserve the bike's original handling qualities, it's best to stick with known quantities. For example, installing a 16in front wheel may quicken and lighten the steering, but it may also produce a bike prone to "tank slappers." On the other hand, many people have reported running 18in fronts with little change in overall stability.

Lou Netz, director of Harley-Davidson's styling department, is a Sportster fan. His personal commuter XL has 18in rear and 19in front rims, with low-profile tires. A combination of 100/90 front and 130/80 rear tires results in rolling diameters only fractions of an inch different than stock. In terms of steering and handling qualities, the combination works well.

Netz' other Sportster is radically lowered, using a short Ceriani fork, 18in wheels, and an ex-Cal Rayborn swing arm. This alters the steering geometry. The steering qualities are anything but standard, yet the bike handles well.

Brakes

The stock Sportster brakes can be dramatically improved with two simple add-on components: Teflon-lined stainless-steel hoses, combined with pads specifically designed for high-performance applications. These add-ons can reduce the amount of lever pressure required, as well as improve stopping performance.

The stainless-steel brake line kits, such as Russell's Cycleflex, have an extremely high burst strength (15,000psi). Their reduced expansion under high fluid pressures minimizes fade and provides increased braking "feel." For special applications, preassembled lines are available from 9-51in, in 3in increments.

A set of replacement brake pads with a higher friction coefficient helps reduce lever effort and provide consistent, controlled braking. Sintered metal pads resist fade much better than standard pads, in addition to providing superior wet performance and consistency. Although these pads may transfer more heat to the fluid, the higher boiling point of DOT 5 helps reduce fade. There are a number of pads on the market, the most prominent brand names being Dunlopad, Ferodo, SBS, Russell, EBC, Emgo, and Vesrah.

The Sportster disc is made from hard stainless steel, and it works well with these pads. However, brake rotors, made from stainless-steel alloy and riddled with lightening holes, provide the benefit of reduced weight and improved water dispersion. Russell and Sudco rotors are surface ground, ensuring optimum flatness. For Twin Sports racers in search of a legal setup, the Screamin' Eagle slotted rotors are lighter than standard. When using your standard Harley-Davidson rotors, you must have them surface ground to eliminate pad drag and improve overall pad contact.

If the standard Sportster front brake is used hard for an extended period of time, several things may happen. The rider's right arm may begin to pump up and get tired; the brake fluid may boil, which produces a spungy feeling and fade; and the brake disc may warp like a potato chip.

Many Sportster riders like to install the dual-disc front brake. This is a good choice for lowering brake-lever requirements and for increasing stopping power when using a high-traction tire. However, keep in mind that adding a second disc and caliper also adds a lot of weight to an already heavy unsprung mass—it adds about 11lb—and affects handling and ride qualities.

Dual discs can improve braking performance over billiard-table road surfaces, but on rough, bumpy surfaces a lighter single-disc will outperform it. Designer Erik Buell is a firm believer in reducing unsprung weight, and the latest Buells use a six-piston single disc in place of the former dual-disc system. This resulted in an unsprung weight reduction of 7lb. The better solution to the braking

dilemma includes light weight as well as braking power.

Performance Machine offers a 12in floating disc with four- and six-piston calipers. Installing this disc involves a little less expense and effort than the twin-disc route, and it saves considerable weight. The caliper does not enjoy the benefit of seals that work so well on OE Harley-Davidson brakes, so they require a little more maintenance.

Brake Fluids

Sportsters are designed to use DOT 5 silicone-based brake fluid. DOT 5 has a higher boiling point than DOT 3 or 4, and does not affect paint and other surfaces. There is a new, improved nonsilicone-based brake fluid on the market for systems designed to use DOT 3 and 4. It is labeled DOT 5.1, and although logic would say that it could be used in a DOT 5 system, it is *not* suitable for Sportster and other DOT 5 applications. When adding brake fluid, be sure its label indicates that it is silicone-base DOT 5.

The 1991 Buell RS-1200 was the world's first production motorcycle to incorporate a six-piston brake caliper as standard equipment. The caliper is American-made by Performance Machine of Paramount, California. The new single-disc, six-piston brake replaced the Buell's previous twin-disc system. Erik Buell, the president and engineer of the Buell Motor Company, said that the resulting 7lb decrease in unsprung weight provides improved ride and braking performance over rough surfaces. The RS-1200 also has a White Power upside-down fork, which reduces overall weight another 3lb. Because the wheel assembly and bottom fork tubes are lighter, the suspension is capable of responding better to road irregularities.

A dual-disc front brake system stops well, resists fade, and provides good lever feedback to the rider. The penalty is the addition of over 10lb of unsprung weight, which has a negative affect on handling qualities. Notice the clear plastic tube covering a strand of safety wiring, which prevents the wire from rubbing the caliper.

151

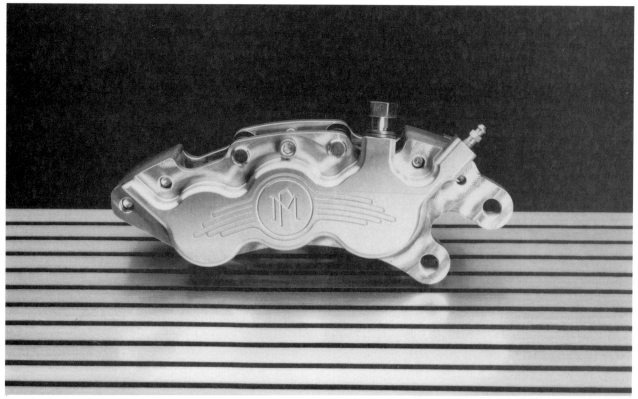

Performance Machine's beautiful six-piston caliper is the first of its type to be supplied as original equipment on a production motorcycle, the Buell RS-1200. Performance Machine

Performance Machine offers a variety of brake systems and components, including the world's first production six-piston caliper. This four-piston type is mounted with a Sudco disc rotor mounted to a wheel with a Sun aluminum rim. Sudco rotors are induction hardened with 14 percent chromium content to resist wear. The rotors are then computer drilled and surface ground for flatness. Notice the braided steel line, a must for high-performance work. Zipper's Performance Products

Purging and replacing the standard DOT 5 fluid with DOT 3 or 4 results in more positive feedback at the brake lever. DOT 5 fluid is more compressible than DOT 3 or 4.

Fairings

There's more to fairing design than simply reducing wind resistance. We can learn from an interesting story about Suzuki factory GP fairings of a decade ago. The factory team used two fairings, a "clean" low-drag model and another "dirty" fairing that had a much higher drag coefficient. The low-drag model, however, also had a pressure center located higher off the ground. This means that the wind force acting against the front of the fairing applied pressure at a point higher from the road surface than on the other fairing. The result was that at high speeds, the motorcycle had a tendency to pivot around the rear tire's contact patch, and lift the front wheel off the road. That's just about the worst thing that can happen to a bike traveling at high speeds, especially in a 150mph turn.

The high-drag fairing, with its lower center of pressure, was stable at high speeds. The dirty, slower fairing was actually more suited to a high-speed track than the slick fairing.

A small fairing might seem like a low-drag prospect, but only if its size completely shrouds what it's supposed to streamline. Before selecting and mounting a fairing, consider the size of both machine and rider. For example, a rider who is 6ft, 2in tall and weighs 220lb, will need a fairing wide enough to shroud his tucked-in frontal area. Mounting a fairing that's suitable for a 5ft, 120lb rider will not do. This is why the XLCR Cafe Racer fairing, however sporting, serves no real aerodynamic usefulness.

The same rule applies to the windscreen. A short, small window may seem efficient, but if the rider's shoulders and arms are flapping in the breeze, the fairing is not doing its job. Big bikes and large riders need more streamlining to keep the airflow smooth.

Twenty years ago, when Harley-Davidson was developing the road-racing fairing for the factory road-racing team, Harley-Davidson racing boss Dick O'Brien, along with engine developer Jerry Branch and fairing maker Dean Wixom, went to the Cal Tech wind tunnel in California for testing. The Cal Tech people had just finished work on a DC-10 project, so the XR-750 factory racer provided quite a contrast.

All tests were done at 160mph. After the first run on the bare-bones bike, the Cal Tech people looked over the results. They were flabbergasted. One of them said something like, "It's the worst piece of aerodynamics in our history. We have never seen anything so dirty." Apparently the frontal area of this little motorcycle was the equivalent of trying to push a flat board, measuring 3sq-ft, through the air!

They discovered that the air does not see a small frontal profile of a motorcycle. The air sees the front tire, the fork legs, all the cylinder fins, the engine cases, the rider and his appendages, the frame tubes, the rear shocks, the back wheel, and so on. By the time the air has passed over the entire vehicle, it has bumped into enough obstacles to create tremendous drag.

Branch went to some Hollywood supply outfit and got a life-size dummy that weighed 160lb. The group dressed it up in racing leathers and a helmet, put it in a riding position, and taped its hands and feet to the bike. Then they uncovered another astonishing fact: With a streamlined fairing mounted, the rider not only created considerable drag, it was the biggest factor involved.

The conventional wisdom of that era believed that a small frontal area would pose the least drag.

A dual-disc front brake offers two key advantages: it helps to lower brake lever pressure requirements, which means you get more stopping power with less hand effort; and it dissipates heat faster, which helps to reduce brake fade. This benefits riders who use their Sportsters in long-distance road racing, where rider fatigue can reduce performance. Like anything, it's a compromise that carries negative consequences. The additional disc and caliper increase the unsprung weight of the front wheel, putting the already under-damped standard fork at a further disadvantage. For most applications, adding racing-style pads and braided steel brake lines should prove satisfactory. A side note: adding another disc may not necessarily decrease stopping distance—it might increase it! A brake can only stop a motorcycle as quickly as tire traction allows, and if a single disc can lock the brake, a double disc simply makes locking it easier. Once a wheel locks, valuable stopping distance is eaten up while the rider regains control (assuming he doesn't crash). Additionally, when braking over bumps, the unsprung weight of a dual-disc system taxes the fork's ability to keep the tire on the road. The increased unsprung weight may cause braking problems over bumps and increase braking distance.

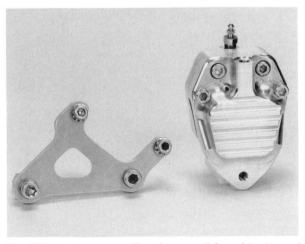

The GMA brake system offers the powerful combination of aircraft-quality billet aluminum calipers with SBS high-performance brake pads. This lightweight unit fits post-1984 Sportsters, and all the mounting hardware is included, from Rivera. GMA is based in Omaha, Nebraska. Rivera

Steve Storz is a former successful XR dirt track tuner and the proud creator of his XR-883. All the components that make up this machine are available through Storz, includ-ing items like the ML-051 lug kit that holds the turn signal lights and mounts the FGL-150 fiberglass seat and pad.

True enough, except that the rider is a part of the problem. With a tiny fairing, which theoretically creates less drag than a bigger one, the rider's helmet, arms, and legs hang out in the breeze, grabbing the air. A larger fairing, however, diverted the air more smoothly over the rider, creating less drag.

The other major source of drag came from everything inside the fairing. An opening at the front is necessary to cool the engine. The air hits the cooling fins and other parts, causing severe drag. Just for the sake of curiosity, Branch taped a piece of cardboard over the front opening, and they saw a dramatic drop in drag. They surmised that although an air-cooled engine needed the opening for cooling, a slicker design for a liquid-cooled engine was possible.

After a week's work, the team came up with what has proven to be one of racing's most successful fairing designs. Other racing teams adapted the shape, and many speed records were set at Bonneville using the fairing. Copies of this shape are available from Bartels'. Mounting hardware made specifically for Sportsters is not available, however. Universal mounting hardware is available, but the brackets must be modified or even custom-made to fit the Sportster.

Troubleshooting Handling Problems

Twin Sports machines need long shocks (14.5 or 15.0in) to gain additional cornering clearance. This alters the standard steering geometry, reducing trail and increasing rake angle. Combined with the stan-dard fork's somewhat limp damping, the result is a tendency for the machine to shake its head over bumps, especially a series of bumps.

The series of bumps at the entrance to the chicane at Daytona International Speedway in Florida provides a perfect example. This area of the track usually causes a modified Twin Sports machine to shake its head. A steering damper can help minimize this. But if there's a problem with a particular bike that affects handling in the slightest, a rider will find out about it when he arrives at the chicane.

Keep in mind that often a handling problem is not the result of a single large problem; rather, it may be due to several components that are only slightly out of spec. When a soft damping rate is combined with a slightly out-of-balance front wheel and a barely misaligned rear wheel, anything can happen. Following are some troubleshooting suggestions to help avoid some of the more likely problems that may occur.

● Wheel alignment: Proper rear axle adjustment requires a method of mechanically checking alignment of the front and rear wheels. There are special wheel-alignment tools available, but most experienced tuners simply rely on string, straight boards, or angle iron.

● Wheel balance: There are two types of procedures for balancing wheels: static and dynamic. Although dynamically balancing a wheel is considered the most accurate, most race tuners rely on the static method. Sportsters are very forgiving of many things, but an unbalanced wheel can result in poor, and even dangerous, handling.

● Wheel runout: For racing purposes, both eccentricity and sideways runout should be held to under 0.031in whenever possible.

● Bent components: Check the frame and swing arm by aligning the wheels using a method described above and by plumbing the wheels vertically. Check axles and swing-arm spindle for straightness. If you should crash, be sure to carefully inspect your wheels before using them again.

● Overloading: The weight that your Sportster applies to the road affects tire stability and life. Too much weight can cause a tire to overheat, resulting in a blowout. Check the tire's sidewall for its maximum carrying capacity.

The lines of Storz's XR-883 creation combine the looks of the dirt track XR-750 with Evolution power. Is this what Harley-Davidson's XR-1000 should have looked like? It does not matter; if you want a Sportster like this, Storz makes it possible.

● Underinflation: This has the same effect as overloading. Too little air increases running temperature and effectively reduces the tire's load-carrying capacity. Note the maximum inflation pressure indicated on the sidewall. A tire's overheating is usually caused by underinflation and/or overloading. When the ambient temperature is high, so is the tire's pressure.

● Improper wheel alignment: Misalignment of the rear wheel is just about the easiest thing a

This is a rider's eye view of Paul Wiers' gasoline dragster. Note the hydraulic clutch, which helps the rider to control the machine's launch. Wiers handmade it by grafting two standard Harley brake master cylinders together. Wiers works in Harley-Davidson's vehicle engineering department.

Sportster rider can mess up. When adjusting the chain, count the flats that are turned on each adjustment bolt. Then before riding, get out the string or angle iron and check the alignment.

● Incorrect tire mounting: Make sure the tire bead is concentric with the rim. It is also important not to overinflate when mounting a tire. Never exceed the maximum inflation pressure recommended on the tire sidewall. Some people have been known to pump a tire up to 50lb or more just to seat the bead. This can damage the tire.

● Abrasive road surfaces: An abrasive road surface will wear a tire faster than a smooth surface. Some surfaces provide more traction than others, which may accentuate a marginal handling problem.

● High speeds/heat build-up: Heat can build up for a number of reasons, such as already described. Excessive speeds can also heat up the tire, although if within the design parameters (inflation pressure, load, and so on) it should not become a major problem.

● Wheel spin/hard use: The reason drag racers do burnouts is to bring the tire temperature up to running levels. That's fine for a cold tire, but not so good for a tire that is already hot.

● Skidding or hard braking: Braking can "spin" the tires, in the opposite direction as power sliding. It's not so hard on the front, but the rear tire gets spun one way by the power, and skidded the other way by braking forces. Add the loads and skidding of lateral acceleration while cornering, and you can really beat up the tires, especially the rear.

● Radials: Sportsters were never intended to run on radials. Check the tire manufacturer's fitment data. Better still, call the tire maker's customer service people.

● Clearance: When mounting sizes other than original equipment, physical interference between parts is a dangerous possibility. For example, a fatter rear tire can drag on the chain guard, rub brake lines, and catch the underside of the fender.

● Rim size: The rim width determines the size and shape of the tire's contact patch. Consult the manufacturer's data chart for appropriate rim and tire fitment. Increased tire size may require increased wheel rim width.

● Tubes: New tubes should be installed in new tires, along with new rim bands. Remember, no tubes in radials; and no radials on tube-type rims.

● Repair: Punctures cannot be safely repaired. Permanent plug-patch repairs of small tread punctures by a qualified repairperson may be adequate for street use, but not for racing.

● Sealants: Liquid sealants are not recommended for any racing motorcycle. They add unsprung weight at the outer circumference of the tire, which can negatively affect handling, and they are generally not considered safe for high-speed applications. They can be used on street machines that are ridden conservatively, however.

● Spokes: Broken or loose spokes in a wire wheel will cause wobble and instability.

● Installation: Only trained personnel should handle tire mounting. If you have never mounted a tire, or have never been trained in the correct techniques, either don't try it or get proper training.

● Bearing wear: Check the bearings for proper adjustment and looseness. This includes wheel, steering head, and swing-arm pivot bearings. Remove the shocks to check swing-arm slack. Proper inner spacer length is critical.

● Loose fasteners: Check all wheel axle, fork, and shock attachments. On wire wheels, check spoke nipples.

● Damping: Check rear damper rods and stroke action; check fork damper for damage, and oil quality and weight rating. Watch for oil leaks.

● Wrong tire choice: Mixing tire brands and types may result in unusual handling. Combining a fresh tire with a worn tire can also negatively affect handling.

● Tire wear: Irregular wear, or wear that has altered the tire's profile, affects handling. On treaded tires, always check tread for sideways and eccentric runout before mounting the wheel. Ozone rots tires. Generators create ozone, so don't park your bike or store you tires in a room with a generator. The sun's rays also deteriorate rubber. Best to park your rubber in the shade.

● Steering geometry: Any change to shock or fork length changes the motorcycle's original design. Altering the standard steering geometry essentially presents a completely new engineering challenge.

● Road surface: Sometimes the conditions in a particular portion of a racetrack can upset a normally stable machine. The solution may be as simple as altering the cornering line, or as complex as making minute adjustments to the rear suspension's spring and damper rates.

● Loose nut behind handlebars: Sometimes a change in riding techniques, such as altering the cornering line, lean angle, braking, corner exit speed, and so on, can solve or minimize a problem.

● Insufficient information: Before making any changes, all the variables should be isolated, questioned, and inspected. Too often the real problem is simply a piece of missing information.

● Bad advice: Remember that although discussing the problem with other riders may be helpful, not every racer shares all he or she knows! Beware the rider or tuner who may deliberately mislead you.

Chapter 7

AMA CCS Twin Sports Racing Series

The American Motorcycle Association Championship Cup Series (AMA CCS) has become an impressive success. The Twin Sports class accommodates more-or-less standard XLH-883 Sportsters in the AMA's road racing program. More and more riders and Harley-Davidson dealers have become involved, and the inexpensive format enticed the AMA to consider and institute another type of "stock 883" class in dirt tracking. In essence, it is a return to the original principles of the "run-what-ya-brung" AMA Class C rules.

Twin Sports and Other Road Racing

Stock motorcycles have long been the cornerstone of American racing, since the days when Walter Davidson won an endurance race in 1908. Before the advent of high-performance speed equipment, riders drove their street bikes to the event,

You can easily see the differences in combustion chamber shape between the sand-cast head (left) with its "bathtub" chamber and the later die-cast head with its "hemi" chamber. The castings came from different vendors, and there were times during 1986 and 1987 that the company used both vendors simultaneously.

stripped off the lights, ran the race, then drove their bikes home for dinner. It was quite a sight to see a bunch of 61 and 74ci big twins blasting through the woods and the sand and the mud, and over jumps! This run-what-ya-brung racing was the foundation of the American Motorcycle Association's Class C racing, which still remains today, in one form or another.

The AMA's premier road racing class accommodates 750cc four-cylinder engines and 1000cc twins. Technology has taken these machines to an unbelievable level of complexity and cost. Obviously, with so many other, less-expensive motorcycles around, there are plenty of other options for racing, and the AMA has classes to accommodate this. (In addition to the AMA, there are about fifteen or more other organizations that sanction road races, such as WERRA and AFM.)

In road racing, the AMA's Championship Cup Series has classes allowing all displacements, two-stroke or four-stroke, two-valve or four-valve, overhead cam and pushrod, and box stock to Grand Prix. There are National Championship Series and regional events, as well as sprints and long-distance endurance races.

The AMA CCS professional road racing Super Twin class is for Sportsters and other four-stroke, twin-cylinder machines of 451 to 1200cc. The AMA CCS Harley-Davidson 883 US Twin Sports Series is for professional riders competing on stock XLH-883 Sportsters.

The Championship Cup Series includes fifteen regional championships. In addition, there are classes for two-stroke and four-stroke singles and multicylinder bikes. The class structure that applies to Harley-Davidson Sportsters is as follows:

- Heavyweight Supersport (unlimited V-twin displacement)
- Unlimited Supersport (unlimited displacement, experts only)
- Middleweight Superbike (unlimited)
- Heavyweight Superbike (unlimited)
- Lightweight Super Twins (up to 900cc)
- Heavyweight Supertwins (unlimited)
- Middleweight Grand Prix (unlimited)
- Unlimited Grand Prix (unlimited, experts only)
- Sportsman (production machines only, unlimited)
- US Twin Sports (standard 883)

CCS events usually include all of these categories. Except for the Twin Sports race, they are open to other types of motorcycles. For example, Heavyweight Supersport pits unlimited-displacement V-twins against 750cc fours; the Heavyweight Superbike pits Sportsters against unlimited-displacement two-cycles and four-stroke singles, and 750cc four-cylinders. Most Sportster riders sign up for several classes just to get in some riding time and have some fun.

The biggest difference between classes is the amount of modification allowed. For example, Supersport classes allow V-twins to have unlimited engine modifications, so an 883cc Twin Sports machine is at a disadvantage; Superbikes may use fairings; and Supertwins and Grand Prix bikes are unrestricted as long as they meet certain other rules.

The Philosophy Behind Twin Sports

With Harley-Davidson's support, the AMA introduced the CCS 883 Twin Sports in 1989. The rules for this class were based on a combination of previous Battle of the Twins (BOTT) and current 600cc and 750cc Supersport classes.

Major modifications are not allowed in the Twin Sports class, such as the use of expensive components, cylinder and head work, and other extensive engine and chassis mods. As a result, massive amounts of time and money are not required. No other form of road racing offers so much fun for so little resources.

Without question, the relatively small investment is one of the reasons for so much interest in the class. All it takes is one XLH-883 (a used one will do),

Is racing a Sportster fun? Ask Nigel Gale, 1989 Twin Sports champ. As you can see, he uses both hands for clutch work, one for gripping the trophy, and the other....

159

and about $1,000 to prepare it. With a few hundred dollars more for gas, motels, and entry fees, you can get your Sportster to the starting grid. If you decide to quit racing, the bike can be put back to stock condition and used on the street, or sold for all—or nearly all—of the original purchase price.

Certainly another possible explanation for the class' success is that it presents a unique challenge to tuners and riders alike. Since the rules require "box stock" engines, the machine's speed and quickness depends more on the abilities of the rider and tuner. In addition to careful preparation and setup prior to the race, the final adjustments on race day are critical.

According to Harley-Davidson's dynamometer, a stock 883 produces 55hp at the crankshaft. This translates to, maybe, about 45hp at the rear wheel. The rules permit a few power-boosting accessories, such as the Harley-Davidson Screamin' Eagle high-flow air filter kit and ignition module, and a high-flow

exhaust system. These add about 6–10hp, depending on attention to small but important details such as ignition timing and carburetion.

All this can transform a 100mph Sportster into an over 130mph machine; some 883s have been clocked in excess of 132mph. In this chapter we will look at all of the engine, drivetrain, and chassis enhancements being made to Twin Sports machines.

Rule Book-Legal Modifications

Because, as the rule book states, "all internal engine parts must be stock parts and must remain as produced," there are few things a tuner can do to increase a Twin Sports machine's actual horsepower output. There are, however, many things that can be done to reduce friction and to ensure maximum efficiency.

An engine oil treatment is one such technique. Added to fresh oil, these chemical additives bond to engine parts, forming a low-friction coating. It can be

Nigel Gale wore the Twin Sports number-one plate in 1990, here at Loudon, New Hampshire. Gale, a long-time

Bartels' team rider, is a tough competitor and can always be counted on to set the pace.

American Harley-Davidson entered its bone-stock 883cc Twin Sports racer in the 1991 twenty-four hour endurance race at Nelson Ledges Raceway, and finished sixth. "When the Harley went around, people stood up and watched," said Jim Bailey. "It was definitely the crowd favorite." The bike made 852 laps without any mechanical problems. Since then, they bored the engine to 1200cc and hopped it up for long-distance racing. "When we pass the Ninjas, it gets their attention," said Bailey. Left to right, riders Tom Rose, Roy Nicholson, and Dave Bloom.

Nigel Gale, 1989 Twin Sports champ, here at Road America in June 1990, has always been a strong Twin Sports contender. He usually maintains his own machine, as well as helping other Bartels' riders.

Here's a fairly typical 883 Twin Sports bike, showing the oil cooler, oil breather catch tank, and a steering damper. Note that the battery is turned around for easy access to the terminals, and a custom mounting plate for the choke lever (left), ignition toggle switch, and a starter button (right).

as common as Slick 50, which can be found in hardware, department, and automotive stores.

Another such treatment used by some tuners, including National Association for Stock Car Automobile Racing (NASCAR) racing teams, is Poly Dyn TX-7. It is made by Polymer Dynamics, Incorporated of Houston, Texas. The product contains a Teflon fluorocarbon resin. A Mobil Oil Company engineer who had tested TX-7 said that it contained the finest quality Teflon that Mobil had ever seen.

If engine treatment sounds like a lot of hocus-pocus, stop to consider that in racing, little things add up. As one tuner said, "You don't get a yardstick with one big inch. It takes a lot of little inches."

Although AMA rules forbid "removing metal," there are no rules prohibiting a worn-out engine—or

Gene Church, riding Lucifer's Hammer, *was a three-time BOTT champion, 1984-1986. The bike was prepared by Statesville, North Carolina, Harley dealer Don Tilley, who* *has tuned Sportster-based machines to dozens of wins and many championships.*

rather, a loose engine at the looser limits of tolerance. Some tuners have been known to subject certain parts, such as shafts and bushings, to accelerated wear, to set the clearances at maximum factory standards. One method involves spinning shafts in their bushings with a small amount of valve-lapping paste. The increased clearance between shafts and bushings can help to reduce internal friction.

Another example is the oil pump. A brand-new pump may be so tight that you can barely turn it by hand. But after putting it in a pan that contains a thin mixture of solvent and grinding compound, and spinning it with an electric motor for a while, the pump will loosen up and turn freely.

Which brings us to the pump drive gear. Under the loads imposed by constant high- speed running, this gear has shown a tendency to fail. When that happens, the entire motor fails, with expensive results. Anything that can be done to reduce loads on this gear will improve durability. Some tuners send both oil pump drive gears to companies that offer low-friction surface treatments, such as Advance Materials Innovations for Tribonite, or Kal Guard for molybdenum disulfide. In the spring of 1992, Harley-Davidson introduced a new gear made from iron which lasts longer. Because the engine's life depends on these gears, they should be frequently inspected for wear or damage.

Perhaps the most important single element in revving a Sportster at high engine speeds is oil viscosity. Theoretically, the scavenge side of the oil pump is supposed to pump all the oil out of the crankcase. Problem is, at sustained high engine speeds, the sump can fill up with excess oil.

An "excess" of oil amounts to only a few ounces. A heavy oil mist in the sump causes a lot of drag on the crankshaft wheels, which dramatically and noticeably diminishes a Sportster's power output. A few ounces of oil can cause so much drag under continuous high-speed running that the engine will not even reach 5500rpm. If a racer reports that the bike lost power and won't rev after a lap or two, chances are the sump has loaded up with excess oil. In the Sportster engine, oil control of the sump means everything.

Because a thin oil pumps faster, it is more likely to pool in the sump, get past the rings, and blacken spark plugs. If you see the dark evidence of thin oil, and you are using a lighter, 5W-30 grade, try switching to 15W-50.

Some of the fastest Twin Sports machines have oil coolers installed, while others do not. One reason often cited for not using a filter system, with its additional oil lines, is that it tends to put more resistance on the oil system and strain on the oil pump drive gears. Another reason is that it may reduce crankcase scavenging and power output.

AMA Rules: What You Can Do to Improve Your 883

Here's a brief list of what the top riders are doing to their 883 Sportsters to be competitive in Twin Sports racing.

- Do a good, multiangle valve job.
- Bead-blasting the head with very fine beads to clean up carbon is permitted.
- Install Screamin' Eagle ignition module and high-flow air cleaner kit; install high-flow exhaust system.
- Change the carburetor's internal metering jets; install Dynojet carburetor kit.
- If carb is 34mm unit (1986–1987), replace with 40mm CV carb (1988 and later).
- Install larger 3/8in oil lines to and from oil filter, and install oil system vent with catch can.
- Replace stock tachometer with more accurate or reliable unit, or one that will not kill the ignition on failure.
- Install high-performance ignition wires; disconnect VOC.
- Replace stock ignition-key switch with an on-off switch, or rewire to use the stock Engine Off switch to kill the electric system.
- Remove as much wiring as possible to simplify and fool-proof the electrical system.
- Install the battery backwards, so that the terminals are more easily accessible.
- Replace the push-pull twist grip and cables with a simple one-wire throttle; replace clutch cable with a Barnett unit.
- Use racing brake pads and braided-steel brake lines.
- Drill the brake discs with lightening holes; or replace with lighter Harley-Davidson Screamin' Eagle slotted discs.
- Surface the discs to ensure flatness to reduce brake drag and maximize braking.
- Use stiffer progressive-rate fork springs, and longer 14.5 or 15.0in rear shocks with adjustable damping and springing.
- Use 40 or heavier weight fork oil.
- Install fork brace and steering damper.
- Offset the transmission drive and rear wheel sprockets to clear extra-wide tire.
- Use 1/4in wide #520 chain instead of standard 3/8in wide #530 type.
- Install DOT-approved racing tires.
- Install clip-on handlebars and rear-set controls.
- Mount the front number plate in a way that enhances streamlining, so the wind pushes it into a convex instead of a concave shape.
- Remove everything nonessential that the rules permit.

For a CCS rule book, contact AMA Championship Cup Series, P.O. Box 447, Skyland, NC 28776.

However, if the oil temperature rises to levels that cause the oil to break down and lose lubricating qualities, an oil cooler may be essential.

Keeping the oil cool helps improve power output, and keeps the oil from breaking down. Today's oil can easily withstand continuous temperatures of about 240deg Fahrenheit. When oil reaches temperatures higher than 260deg, it begins to break down and oxidize. When that happens, it causes overheating and, eventually, engine failure.

A street XLH-883 Sportster, even when equipped with a high-flow air box and exhaust system, normally develops engine oil temperatures no higher than about 180deg F. The relatively low power output, massive aluminum fins, and remote oil tank are features that keep a Sportster's oil temperature down to safe levels. To determine if an oil cooler is needed, simply check your normal operating temperature. You can do this with the simple, yet effective Screamin' Eagle oil tank dipstick temperature meter. Install it, and check it after a hard run. If it's lower than 220–240deg, your oil should not be destroyed. (It's a good idea to check the meter in a pan of water, comparing it with another thermometer, to verify its accuracy.) If you want a lower running temperature, install the cooler, but remember that running too cold (under 160–180deg) can also cause problems because the oil does not flow readily.

When constantly revved over 6000rpm, a Sportster engine can get hot enough to cause the oil to break down. The oil temperature of a Twin Sports Sportster can reach 350deg during a race, enough to destroy the oil's lubricating qualities. Installing a low-restriction oil filter, such as the Harley-Davidson or Lockhart (Lockhart makes the Harley filter) can drop oil temperature by 50deg F. or more. Whether you use an oil cooler or not, it's a good idea to change oil after every race.

Due to normal manufacturing tolerances, cam timing can vary as much as 5deg arc each way. It is possible, theoretically, that the right combination of cams can provide 10deg of additional opening, and possibly 10deg of additional overlap. To achieve this, a tuner may have to test an extensive number of cams, and select the stock cams that have just enough manufacturing tolerance to provide a difference. Chances are, however, that a little tuning finesse will result in greater improvements. For example, an old XR-750 tuning trick is to check the cam timing with the followers in the 180deg position. When turned around, lifter manufacturing variation may add a few degrees of valve opening.

The Sportster's vacuum-operated-control (VOC) switch does not operate at high engine speeds, so it has no effect on high-speed performance. However, on tracks that have low-speed corners, the vacuum-operated switch may help acceleration from the

Like anything mechanical, under continuous high-speed use, the Sportster engine will explode. The photos show the results of a Twin Sports engine that was used too long between preventive maintenance checks. One rod broke in two, while the other broke into three parts. The cases were not repairable. To prevent this, a Twin Sports machine should be rebuilt mid-season, if not more often. Karl Schlei

slowest corner, depending on the gearing and the minimum rpm the engine may be producing. It's easy to plug or unplug the wire. The method does not affect how the engine runs at high speeds.

To gear the bike correctly at the racetrack, a rider must know the actual speed that the engine is turning. A standard factory tachometer may not give the rider such accurate readings. The needle may point to 6000rpm, but that does not necessarily mean that the engine is actually turning 6000. Before relying on what your tach tells you, have it calibrated by an instrument shop. If the needle waggles at high speeds, toss it into the nearest recycling bin and get a tach that indicates the correct engine speed.

Some tachometers provide a computer readout of a run, such as those made by Stack Tach Action

Dave McClure, 1985 BOTT Champion, aboard his XR-1000-based racer. You can see how the high XR exhaust *system stays out of the way, providing McClure with ample cornering clearance.*

One of the Bartels' team bikes, equipped with the Bartels' reverse-cone megaphone. Extra lightening holes have been drilled in the brake discs to reduce unsprung weight. Discs should be surfaced to assure flatness.

The rider of this Twin Sports machine made the left footpeg bracket with a provision for moving the peg's location. Karl Schlei

Replay and Auto Meter Pro Cycle. These tachometers allow you to record and play back a run for later evaluation.

If you use the standard tachometer, keep in mind that if the tach fails, it kills the engine. It's a good idea to route the tach wire to a place where the rider can reach it, to disconnect it while running, so he or she can stay in the race.

Preparing a Twin Sports Sportster

It's relatively easy to build a Twin Sports XL. It's more difficult, however, to be competitive with some of the other riders, like Twin Sports champs Nigel Gale and Scott Zampach—or ex-champ Randy Texter, Mike Hale, Dick Koehler, and all the other pro-quality riders whom you can meet on any AMA CCS starting grid. But not everyone races to become a champion. Many Twin Sports riders race just for the fun of it.

Current rules allow the use of any stock 1986 and later Evolution Sportster parts. That's an advantage for someone starting with a pre-1988 model, for example, which has the smaller, 35mm diameter fork legs and more restrictive carburetor. With a 1988 or later CV carburetor, a Sportster will produce about 50hp standard, which is about 4hp more than an XL equipped with the earlier 1986 or 1987 unit.

You may swap internal transmission gears, providing they are the Harley-Davidson parts, and any final-drive sprockets and chain may be changed. It will be necessary to offset the sprockets and use a 520 chain (0.25in width) to allow clearance for the

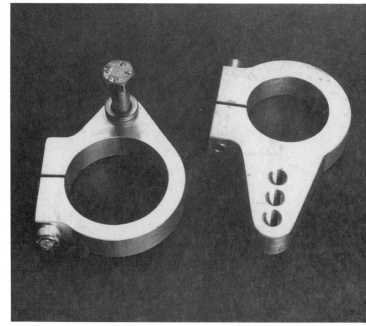

Brackets such as these from Storz Performance are useful for mounting steering dampers and number plates. Karl Schlei

wide rear tire. Using the narrower chain and aluminum sprockets saves as much as 7lb.

You must remove the headlamp, taillight, turn signals, and jiffy stand (that's the side stand that flips

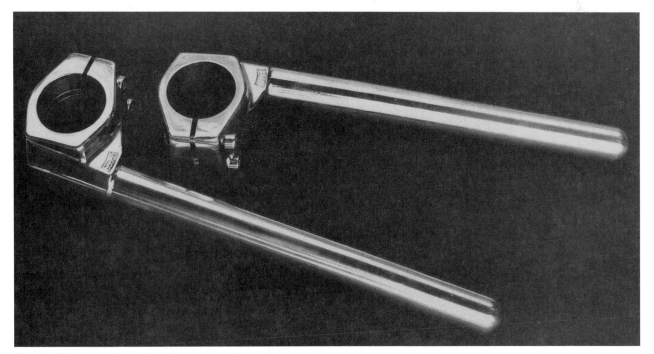

Classic Magura clip-on handlebars are ⅞in diameter, requiring the standard Harley-Davidson controls to be sleeved. Karl Schlei

up when you kick it). All oil drain bolts or plugs must be safety wired. The front fender mounting rivets must be replaced with bolts because they are prone to loosening. Appearance items such as the (steel) tank and fenders must remain stock. Any standard Harley-Davidson seat, including parts and accessories, may be used. You may also replace the stock 2gal tank with the Harley-Davidson 3gal unit.

Most riders take advantage of the option to install a twin-disc front brake, because a single-disc front brake is prone to fade, and the disc will warp under hard racing use. Additionally, the rider's high front-brake-lever squeezing requirements are enough to physically exhaust him or her within a short time. The Harley-Davidson Screamin' Eagle lightened discs are a good item to add because they save a lot of

To be competitive, Twin Sports riders need front and rear sprockets in one-tooth increments. Karl Schlei

unsprung weight. Braided-steel lines and alternate pads are also legal.

Any rear shock may be used, and the front fork springs may be changed. Most riders use 15in rear shocks, although some opt for 14.5in. Taller shocks alter the steering geometry and quicken the bike's handling qualities. Currently, modifying the fork damper rods is not permitted, but officials have been considering allowing modifications. You may use any amount or weight of fork oil in the fork tubes.

Most Twin Sports racers use Dunlop 591 Sport tires, a 110/80x19 front and 130/90x16 rear. There are other choices, however. Nick Ienatsch likes Metzelers, and more than one rider has been seen sporting the brand. It's a personal choice, and what works for you may be the tire you get for free through a tire company's promotional programs.

Clip-on style handlebars and rear-set footpegs are needed so that the rider can tuck into a streamlined position. Some riders use flat drag bars or upside-down stock bars, but most prefer the type that clamp to the fork legs. These are somewhat adjustable to suit the rider. You can move them up or down for height adjustment, and within the region permitted by the gas tank, they can be adjusted fore-and-aft.

Although most riders prefer to install the bolt-on Bartels' or Storz rear-sets, a few riders chose to handmake their own. The Bartels' pegs fold, while the rigid Storz pegs don't. Folding pegs offer an advantage in crash situations, but some riders will argue that rigid pegs help to protect the machine is a crash-and-slide situation.

Note: Before proceeding with preparation of a Twin Sports machine, be sure to get the latest AMA CCS rule book in case any rules have changed since this book was written.

Preparing the Engine

Inside the Twin Sports engine, it is illegal to remove metal from any surface; only as-manufactured parts are allowed inside the engine cases. The exception are the valve seats: You can touch up the seats with a high-quality valve job, but the rules forbid removing aluminum from the ports or altering valve shape.

The air cleaner, exhaust system, and ignition module may be changed. These, and other tuning modifications, will improve the Sportster's power at the rear wheel from about 45 or 50, to 60hp.

The most popular and best-performing air cleaner is the Screamin' Eagle kit. This results in the single biggest horsepower gain of any add-on item. Dyno tests have shown a gain of 4hp or more. Many racers swear by the Dynojet carb kit, which further improves power and throttle response when properly installed. Even so, fine-tuning is required for optimum performance, and this will require dyno work.

If you want to build your carburetor from scratch, you can change the main jet, use a needle from a 1990 or later 1200 Sportster, and open up the hole in the bottom of the slide with a No. 33 drill bit. This seems to work well for both street and track.

Any exhaust system may be used, provided that it passes the AMA's tech inspection and noise restrictions. A good exhaust system will add about 3hp. Walk through the pits at any Twin Sports event and you'll see that the Bartels' pipe is the most preferred, used by most front-runners.

There are other options, however. Kerker's Mike Wymer found that a 29in header pipe made the most power on the 883 Evolution. Actually, any length between 27 to 32in works nearly as well. Wymer's testing found that the longer the megaphone, the more power the engine made. Wymer also tested a two-into-two system and saw a 1hp gain. However, the two-into-one had a 3hp advantage in the 3000–4000rpm range, which gives an advantage when coming off corners.

The Screamin' Eagle ignition model, which has a rev limiter of 8000rpm, permits an 883 to rev as much as its little restrictive ports will allow. That's about 7000rpm, if you do everything right. Ignition timing is one of those things. Advancing the timing 5deg from the stock 35 makes another horsepower or two. But

there are other ponies to be gained with careful dyno work—and subtle adjustments in carburetor jetting and ignition timing.

After an Evolution 883 has run several hundred hard miles, the cylinders distort and take a "set." Reboring the cylinders at this point helps to improve ring seal. A racing 883 can be run at 0.002in clearance. Some tuners set clearances much tighter, but careful run-in is necessary. Tight clearance helps the rings seal better, which in turn helps the engine run cooler, make more power, and last longer.

When it comes to honing the cylinders, tuners differ in their preference of stone grit. Some prefer a fine, 600 grit surface, which takes more time to run-in, while others prefer a coarser 400 grit or less, which seats rings more quickly. When sizing the cylinders for new pistons, you must use torque clamping plates for boring and honing operations. When breaking the glaze for new rings, however, this is not necessary.

A good multiangle valve cutting job can improve flow. When the valve begins to lift, a smoother radius streamlines the incoming fuel charge, and it gets more mixture into the cylinder faster. Keep the actual seating area as far out to the tip of the valve head as possible (see Chapter 4).

This Sportster is built to compete in the new 883 dirt track class, which the AMA launched in 1993. The rules regarding modifications are patterned after the AMA/CCS Twin Sports class regulations. The exhaust pipes are Storz Performance. Karl Schlei

When performing a valve job, you must smooth the areas leading to and from the valve seat face. With properly narrowed valve sealing areas and smoothly shaped entries and exits, you can get another horsepower. Keep in mind that although the rules allow cutting the valve seats, you may not touch the ports. The current valve stem seals supplied by the factory, which are blue in color, don't seem to last as long as the previous black ones. They should be replaced frequently.

The Bartels' rearset kit features easy bolt-on installation. Storz Performance also offers bolt-on rearsets. Both kits reverse the shifting to a "down for up" pattern. Although this may seem backwards at first, most production racing motorcycles use the "push down to go fast, pull up to slow down" pattern.

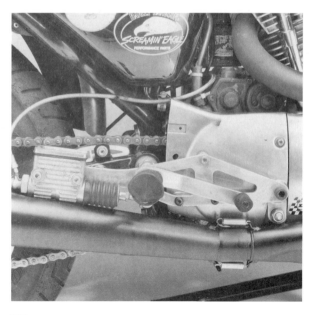

Because the loads on a Sportster are so stressful when constantly revving to 6000rpm or more, it is important to perform more preventive checks and maintenance. Most serious competitors tear down the top end before a major race for inspection, and to perform a fresh valve job. Some tuners even prefer to re-ring the engine after every few races.

Constant high-rpm use takes a severe toll on the entire engine, and it should be torn down after five or six races, with careful attention to the rods. Running at high speeds tends to stretch the rods and they have been known to break. It is better to replace them midseason, than to have to replace the whole engine later.

The oil pump drive gear should also be checked, at least by midseason. If there is any wear at all, replace it.

It's a good idea to run a new Sportster for a couple thousand miles using a standard petroleum-based motor oil (such as Harley's premium oil). This will run-in all the parts and let the cylinders take their set. After stripping the engine and checking all clearances, you can perform a high-quality valve job, and rebore the cylinders to get them straight. Some tuners, however, simply re-ring the standard cylinders.

Most Twin Sports racers prefer synthetic motor oils. When breaking in new rings or other parts, however, use regular motor oil until the rings seat and then change the oil. Some professional tuners use an

You don't have to spend hundreds of dollars for a rearset kit if you are capable of building your own. Here is an example of a Twin Sports racer with handmade rearsets. The foot peg mounting plates can be cut from 1/4in aluminum plate. Either 6061-T6 or 7075-T6 will work well; 7075 is the strongest. Notice the good use of safety wire.

engine treatment to help reduce friction, such as Poly Dyn TX-7.

Synthetic motor oils have several advantages over petroleum-based oils. They flow quicker when cold, which reduces severe wear during start-up. They also contain esters which coat engine parts for reduced friction. And they can withstand higher running temperatures without breaking down. That last point is very important to an engine like the Sportster's, which reaches very high temperatures when run hard.

When you get to the track and begin running your fresh engine, it is important to consider how you set up your Sportster. Tight piston clearances, for example, will require some finesse and more run-in time.

Cylinder Head Modifications

Since the AMA insists that no metal be removed from the original parts, you might be led to believe that all Twin Sports vehicles are equally matched. No way!

As mentioned in Chapter 2, the Evolution Sportster went through periods of interchanging heads from different vendors. As a result, there is no way to determine which 883 motorcycle came off the production line with which head during the first two years of production.

Tuners who have measured the combustion chamber volume of these various heads discovered that the original sand-cast heads had a lot of variation. Some have compression ratios approaching 10:1. The diecast heads, however, are more consistent and have a lower compression ratio, usually in the area of 8.1:1 to 8.4:1. (The factory offers no official explanation for this.)

One enterprising tuner decided that, because one combustion chamber volume was smaller than the other, why not make them both the same? So he shaved a little material off the "large" head to equalize them. While this may seem like a logical and acceptable approach to setting up a Sportster for Twin Sports racing, according to AMA rules, it is not legal.

The AMA CCS rule book states: "No metal removal or internal engine modifications, including surface treatments or blueprinting, are permitted" (Rule F-4). However, there are times when the factory

Katsuyashi Kozono, of Sakado, Japan, rode the Sundance Daytona Weapon *in the 1992 Super Twins race at Daytona. The one-time international effort was sponsored by Nordica Japan, Sanyo Electric, Motul Oil, and Mr. Donut, as a promotional event. A huge TV crew followed the event during the week, so that an advertising video could be aired in Japan. Although ignition troubles allowed only a* *few laps of practice, Kozono managed to qualify in sixteenth place. The problem was eventually traced to a faulty cam bearing, which were of a needle type. The machine showed a lot of promise, but during the race, a mechanical problem forced Kozono to drop out. David Dewhurst*

may machine a head's surface to correct a manufacturing problem (such as an unacceptable scratch on the gasket surface). This may leave a Twin Sports competitor in a vulnerable position: the head may be "as produced," but illegal. The AMA admits this poses a problem and, at the time of writing, is reviewing the issue.

Flow bench tests have shown that the diecast 883 head has a slight flow advantage over the sand head. The diecast head's shallow roof allows a little more flow around the valve, while the sand-cast head's deep bathtub chamber walls shroud the valve slightly.

Twin Sports tuners have differing opinions of which head is best for combustion and power output. Some will say that the squish area of the sand-cast head offers better turbulence and burning, while others insist that the lower roof of the diecast head improves the flame front. Considering the manufacturing variation, it's a moot point.

Due to manufacturing variation, not all heads flow the same. Some heads have ports that flow slightly better than others. One method of building the optimum Twin Sports machine is to hand-select the heads. A big Harley-Davidson dealership has the benefit of being able to order a large number of heads, flow test them all, keep two good ones, and return the rest. After all, the prize money for a single race win would pay for the restocking charge.

The rules, alas, do not permit anything that would increase compression, such as installing taller seats to get the valves deeper into the chamber. If allowed, this would not only increase compression, it would also improve flow. Milling the top of the spark plug hole area, to drop the plug farther into the chamber, is also outlawed. No fair leaving the base gasket off, either!

It is possible that an extraordinary combination of manufacturing tolerances could result in exceptional compression. For example, combine the follow-

The Daytona Weapon's *components were sourced all over the world. The frame and swing arm were handmade in Japan, and the engine, of course, is an American Sportster XLH-1200. Other pieces include Lockheed front brake calipers (England), Brembo front and rear discs and rear caliper (Italy), PVM magnesium wheels (Germany), and Öhlins inverted fork and rear shock (Sweden). The 4.5 gallon aluminum fuel tank, 3.0 quart oil tank, and carbon fiber and Kevlar fairing were all made in Japan. The cast-iron liners of the 1199cc Sportster engine were removed and replaced with Nikasil-coated aluminum liners. The engine also has Red Shift cams, Baisley valves and roller rockers, S&S adjustable steel pushrods, Screamin' Eagle ignition module, Bandit clutch, and downdraft Keihin flat-side CR carburetors. Primary drive is a 40mm AT10 Syncroflex belt. T. Shibazaki, who owns and runs Harley-Davidson Custom Works in Tokyo, designed and built the machine. It features a unique six-link engine isolation system, similar to the Buell four-link system. Wheelbase is a short 57in, and rake and trail is 25.4 degrees, 3.94in. It weighs 370lb, and is claimed to produce 110hp at 6500rpm, with 85ft-lb of torque at 5300rpm. At first glance the engine appears to be an XR, although it's an Evolution XLH-1200. That's because Shibazaki is a big fan of the XR series. When he decided to create new, stiffer rocker boxes, he fashioned them to look like the XR's rocker boxes, even down to making nonfunctional rocker spindle plugs.*
David Dewhurst

ing: a long distance between mainshaft to connecting-rod pin; long connecting rods; tall pin-to-crown pistons; short cylinders; and low case deck. With enough cranks, cases, rods, cylinders, and pistons to compare, anything is possible.

Riders who want the Number One plate, and all the prize money they can get, pay close attention to some of these details. But some riders participate in Twin Sports for the fun of it, and these sorts of things don't interest them. Still others may cry "unfair!" But as that little-known Chinese philosopher Ken Lee once said, "What kind of a sissy word is 'fair' anyway?"

Racing regulations usually require the securing of certain attachments, especially anything related to oil, brake and safety systems. Some examples of this are: all drain plugs (engine, transmission, fork tubes, etc.); oil filler and inspection plugs; axles and axle clamp bolts; brake caliper mounting bolts and nuts. In addition, the list should include any fastener of critical importance, such as a tachometer gearbox bolt or a throttle-adjusting screw.

Safety Wiring

Racing regulations usually require securing certain attachments, especially anything related to oil, brake, and safety systems. Some examples of this are all drain plugs (engine, transmission, fork tubes, and so on); oil filler and inspection plugs; axles and axle clamp bolts; and brake caliper mounting bolts and nuts.

In addition, the list should include any fastener of critical importance, such as a tachometer gearbox bolt or a throttle adjusting screw.

Under most conditions, the most suitable wire is 0.032in corrosion-resistant stainless-steel wire, in condition A (annealed). There are some cases where 0.020in wire will work, such as for wrapping a chain's master link. Safety wire is normally available in 1lb spools. If you can't find it at a common hardware store, you can always find it at local airport supply houses.

Other methods can also be employed, such as cotter pins, safety pins (sometimes called hair pins), or bent tabs. A cotter or a safety pin is normally inserted into aligned holes through a shaft and its nut, such as a standard Sportster rear axle. When using a safety clip, it is inserted until the first "hump" clicks over the fastener.

A bent tab is usually used on a nut. It has an ear that locks into a hole or notch, and once the nut is properly torqued, another tab is bent over one of the nut's flats.

Small screws provide another way of securing things. For example, a #10 screw with a large washer can be inserted into a drilled and tapped hole next to a seal. This helps to prevent the seal from popping out. (Always use a thread-locking compound.)

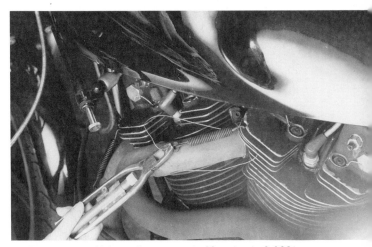

Under most conditions, the most suitable wire is 0.032in or 0.040in corrosion resisting stainless steel wire, in condition A (annealed). There are some cases where 0.020in wire is suitable, such as wrapping a chain's master link. Safety wire is normally available in 1lb spools. If you can't find it at a hardware store, you can always find it at local airport supply houses.

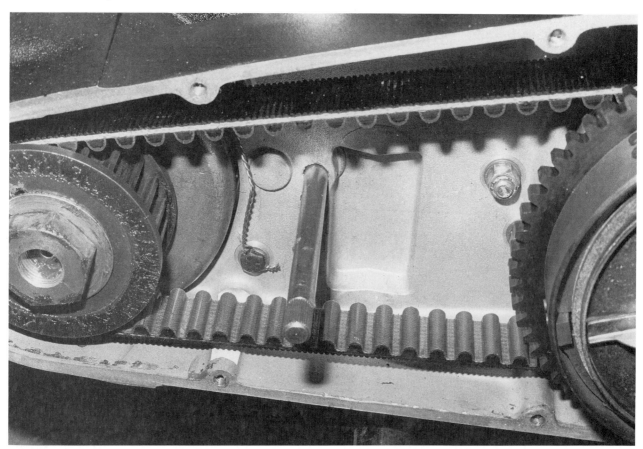

Other methods can also be employed as well as safety wiring, such as cotter pins, safety pins (sometimes called hair pins), or bent-tabs. A cotter or a safety pin is usually used by inserting it into aligned holes through a shaft and its nut, such as a standard Sportster rear axle. When using a safety clip, it is inserted until the first "hump" clicks over the fastener. A bent tab is usually used on a nut. It has an ear that locks into a hole or notch, and once the nut is properly torqued, another tab is bent over one of the nut's flats. Small screws provide another way of securing things. For example, a #10 screw with a large washer, can be inserted into a drilled and tapped hole next to a seal. This helps to prevent the seal from popping out. Always use a thread-locking compound.

Chapter 8

Managing a Sportster Racer

Racing a Sportster is similar to being the chief executive officer of a large corporation. A CEO goes to the office, attends meetings, and uses some tools to help manage the work day, like a dictaphone and a telephone.

Likewise, a racer goes to the office in the pits; then attends a "meeting" with other racers at high speeds out on the track, and uses some tools to get the job done. The only big difference between the racer and the CEO is the speed at which their chairs are traveling.

Keeping a Race Record

CEOs also carry important papers in a briefcase. Racers should too, but surprisingly, many do not. Being organized is an important part of managing the

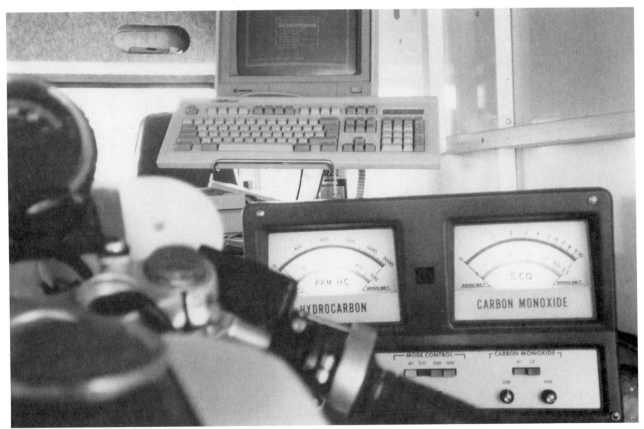

The Bartels' mobil dynamometer visited a number of events on the racing circuit in 1992. It's simply a trailer containing a self-contained computer-monitored dyno that can measure bikes to 180hp. The dyno can be rented on a per-run, hourly, or private lease rates. Bartels' Performance Products

Harley-Davidson has a dozen dynos used in engine development and testing to meet future EPA requirements. Most of the dyno rooms are adaptable to simulate a variety of running conditions. In some cases, a computer can be programmed to run the engine through a cycle to simulate a certain type of riding. The ambient environment can also be adjusted from freezing to boiling.

art of racing. Riders who keep notes and records are generally better prepared to deal with managing the mayhem politely referred to as "race day."

Let's imagine a road racer who did not write things down. He or she goes to the same track he or she ran last year, and thinks they may have run 21/45 gearing. . . or was it 22/46? On the first lap of practice the driver arrives at the chicane. "Where is my breaking point? Do I use first gear or second?" Without notes on the day's events, you have to start all over.

It's a good idea to take notes both during and after a day of practicing or racing, recording the machine's setup, and writing down details about things like the jets in the carb, the gearing, tire pressures, and any other unusual aspects. Notes on running the event are also important, such as details about the track, the weather, sequence of events, how the bike handled, results of changes that were made, and so on.

When you have a notebook filled with this kind of information, you always have a reference point. Keeping a record of everything you do to the bike will help you from repeating the same mistakes twice. If

A flow bench in Harley-Davidson's EPA lab supplies data vital for engine development, especially in complying with EPA requirements. A flow bench and dynamometer are part of the information-gathering process, whether you manufacture or race motorcycles.

you don't have a notebook, you are prone to making mistakes that could be avoided, and finishes lower than your capability.

To avoid confusion at the track, it is helpful to have fill-in-the-blank check lists. You can create these yourself, and run extra photo copies. For example, you might want an inventory of the equipment to take to the race, or of the bike's initial settings before the race. Another is a race-day record with spaces to list things like the date, track, ambient weather, tire pressure, and any changes to carb, gearing, shock settings, and so on.

The information-gathering process actually starts before the machine is prepared, with the acquisition of data through a flow bench, dynamometer, and computer. Without this, trying to set up, build, and race a motorcycle is like steering a boat in the fog without a compass.

The data provides you with evidence of what works and what doesn't. The facts will either support what you already have in mind, or will show you what ideas might not be workable. In fact, data acquisition can be a humbling experience—it can make you aware of how little you know, or prove that what you know is wrong.

Dan Fitzmaurice of Zipper's Performance Products made an interesting observation. He calls it his "Cows in the Field" theory. If one cow heads for the barn, others will follow. Racing motorcycles are not like cows. Each machine is unique, and without

This tachometer has rubber straps that isolate it from vibration. Tachs are sensitive instruments vital to successful racing. It's pretty simple: lose a tach mid-race, and you lose the race or blow an engine.

The Auto Meter Pro-Cycle Memory tachometer can provide valuable data that can be analyzed to improve performance. By knowing the engine rpm at particular points in a quarter-mile run, a rider can make informed decisions about such details as clutch adjustment, traction management, and gearing.

The Halonite line of fire extinguishers offer excellent flame-snuffing "firepower" at a reasonable cost. Every transport vehicle and pit area should be equipped with one. This little portable unit is capable of handling just about anything but a forest fire, and can be purchased at a Harley-Davidson dealership.

177

knowing what another rider's goals or motives are or how the bike is set up, following his lead can often *reduce* your performance, not *improve* it. Racers who have no solid data to guide them, sometimes react like cows.

A simple example is the final gearing. Spying on another competitor's rear sprocket size won't help you if you don't know what countershaft sprocket is on the bike. And how do you know that he didn't stamp a misleading number on the backs of all his sprockets, and run them facing wrong-way out?

Problem Solving

Solving problems is more of a cerebral exercise than a physical one. Before understanding *what* needs to be done, you must first understand *why*.

Don McCaw, who already held a 190.796mph record in MPS/PAF (fully streamlined) class, re-broke another of his records by posting a speed of 172.476 in class MPS/PAG (partially streamlined). The streamlining of his Sportster-powered Buell RR-1200 lends an important advantage. With several miles to run up to top speed at Bonneville, a vehicle's weight and acceleration is usually not a critical factor in the streamlined classes. "Airflow is really number one," McCaw said.

"What is the problem?" The bike is slow.

"Why is it slow?" Ignition timing? Carburetor jetting? An air leak? Improper gearing? Wet-sumping?

"If the bike is doing something that is not right, how can it be fixed? Change my approach to riding? Change the bike's setup? Change a component?"

This brings us back to data acquisition. Without enough data, we don't know what to do. That's why we write down everything. Data acquisition begins before the motorcycle ever gets to the track. Information such as flow rates is necessary if you need to know whether your engine is producing all the power you can get from it.

Computers can help to configure a machine for a particular track. For drag racing, a program called Quarter lets you set up certain parameters, programs the bike's setup, and tells you what your speed and time are likely to be. Dan Fitzmaurice has compared the computer's results with actual on-track performance to correlate the computer with reality. This helps him come closer to the correct initial settings for such things as gear ratio, launch rpm, slipper clutch setting, and so forth.

A dynamometer is useful for more than measuring your final results. It is the tool that helps you extract the final ounce of power from your engine. For example, while at the Daytona races in Florida, Damion Gregory, a California-based tuner, took his Twin Sports XL-883 to a dyno. After making a base run to determine where the machine was at, he began to experiment with carburetion and ignition timing. He settled on a 4deg ignition advance from where it was originally set, to 44deg, and gained 4hp. *Free horsepower.* Gregory was able to understand what needed to be done because he knew where he was coming from, and in which direction he should go.

The top tuners make a point of not changing two variables at once, such as gearing and jetting, or jetting and ignition timing. Many times, a small variance masks another problem. By changing a second variable, you often create another, completely different problem.

For example, let's look at a bike that has over-enriched carburetion, and does not reach redline. A rider might be tempted to change both jetting and gearing. However, leaning the fuel mixture will give it

Warner Riley ran a Sportster at Bonneville for ten years, 1967–1976. In seventeen record attempts, he set sixteen land-speed records. His is the fastest non-streamlined Sportster ever. It was run in various configurations, on fuel and gas, with and without fairing, in engine sizes from 76 to 96ci. The fastest time was 212mph, with an all-time record of 206.544mph. Because of the ultra-close gearbox ratios and high overall gearing, this motorcycle could go 165mph in second gear.

more power, possibly enough to reach redline. If you add a few sprocket teeth you may end up overrevving, and find yourself changing it back again.

Using the Ol' Noggin

The first step in doing anything to your bike on race day is to think. When you make a change, think carefully about the steps involved before doing the work. This will help you organize the tools and the work process. Most important, when the job is done, check every component that you touched. It is not unusual to be interrupted during the task, and this can easily lead to a forgotten step.

Here's an almost unbelievable true story. A mechanic had been interrupted several times while changing his rear sprocket. When he finally thought that he had finished the job, he relaxed and had a soda. Imagine his surprise when the time came to

Several short track three-wheelers have been built for competition, like this unusual critter. It is designed to run clockwise, rather than the traditional left-hand direction, on Speedway tracks, although this type of vehicle also run on ¹/₄ and ¹/₂ mile tracks. Powered by an XR-1000 engine, Ken Ohrt pilots the thing, and Doug Whitson is the "monkey." When Ohrt and Whitson changed to alcohol fuel, they encountered a new world; changing fuels is like installing a different motor, and requires starting from scratch. That "duck's beak" over the front wheel is a 2-plus-gallon fuel tank. Hot Bike

take his bike to the starting grid, and he discovered that he had forgotten to put the chain on! Other true stories include such calamities as forgetting to replace warmup spark plugs with colder racing plugs, and the all-time classic of forgetting to add enough fuel.

Airplane pilots walk around their aircraft, performing an organized system of inspection before every flight. They usually use a check list that includes items of critical importance to both safety and performance. Many of the items simply involve *looking* at the components to make sure they are in place, and that they look *right*. This procedure is also a good idea for a racing pilot who is about to travel at very high speeds.

Race Preparation

On race day, a rider who is free to concentrate on racing always has an advantage over riders who must preoccupy their minds with details other than operating the machine. Operating the motorcycle is the rider's primary job, so anything that relieves the rider of other details will be beneficial. This is well explained in Keith Code's book, *A Twist of the Wrist*.

According to the Code model, you only have a given capacity of concentration. Certain racing, such as launching a bike at the drag strip's lights or peeling off for a 120mph corner in a road race, require a high level of concentration. Distractions can rob you of your ability to concentrate. Nagging questions such as "Did I tighten that bolt?" or "Is it geared right?" are best answered in the pits when going to the starting grid.

For this reason, when a machine arrives at the starting grid with correct gearing, its tires fully pumped up, all its safety wire in place, and everything ready so go, then the rider arrives with his or her mind set 100 percent on racing. That makes for a better chance of winning, instead of just placing.

Race Day

It's no fun to get to the track and realize you left your helmet in the closet. You can do a few things to

minimize these types of disasters. It helps to make a check list so that you won't forget anything.

Every rider has his or her own approach to getting organized. Some stack all the necessary items in a corner of the garage. Then on race day, they simply rely on a mental check list to ensure that they have everything they need.

Even if you use the stack method, it helps to have a written list. This is especially true if it's your first race. Loading the equipment and rushing to the track is enough to have on your mind, without wondering if you filled up the gas can.

Remember, although your first priority is to race a motorcycle, there's no reason you can't be comfortable. Take a chair, a tent, a cooler, refreshments. Some riders like to have their spouses or friends along; others find this a distraction. You may have to devise a plan to keep your loved one occupied while you attend to racing matters.

Your list will probably include these items, at a minimum: Full gas can; helmet, leathers, boots, gloves, pads, jock strap; bike stand; wheel alignment

What Time Is My Race?

How much time do have before your next race? Some local events may run fourteen or fifteen races. Your's might be the eighth and thirteenth. Here's a simple method of organizing your race day.

Tear the day's schedule from the program, and tape it to your tool box lid or van window. When the first race is flagged off, note the time. Make a note of how long it takes to run it, and how long it takes to get the next one started. You can extrapolate the approximate time your races will start from this. As each race is run, put a line through it so you can keep track.

tool; drinking water; lunch; milk crate; stool, lawn chair, umbrella; tools.

Registration

It is always most convenient to preregister whenever possible. Sometimes, however, when you're not sure if you can get the day off or if you'll get the

Leo Payne, a Wisconsin drag racer, shocked the Bonneville scene in 1970 when he set a world land speed record of 202.378mph on his dragster. Carl Morrow built the bike, *and they both had a part in producing the film* C C Rider. *Morrow also set dozens of Bonneville records. That's Morrow astride old number 67A. Carl's Speed Shop*

new motor in the van in time, you'll find yourself signing up at the track.

When you arrive, bring your crew along with you to the registration booth so they can sign any liability releases. Make sure you've got your membership card, ticket stub, preregistration form, and whatever else the club might require.

Remember that these people process a lot of riders in a short time. Anything you can do to speed things up will make them happy. It may save time if you bring your own pen, so you can fill out a form while standing in line. Fill in all the blanks so there won't be any technical difficulties.

Oh, and don't forget the entry fee, if you must pay one.

Last, but not least, pay attention, and smile!

Tech Inspection

A technical inspection of the motorcycle and the rider's protective gear, sometimes referred to as a safety inspection, is part of the racing tradition. The purpose is twofold: to ensure that the vehicle con-

forms to the organization's basic rules; and to ensure that the vehicle is safe.

Some of the things the tech inspector looks for include proper drain plug safety wiring; anything loose or suspicious; adequate tire tread; properly mounted fairing; adequate handlebar clearance (does it hit the tank?); and compliance with often-overlooked regulations.

Some organizations require the rider to bring along the entry form or a tech slip. They want to make sure the leathers, helmets, and gloves are in good shape. Torn gloves are useless in a crash.

It's normal to become irritated when a tech inspector sends you back to the pits to fix something. You stayed up all night preparing the machine, and you're tired and irritable, and practice starts in a few minutes, and he's just being a jerk, right?

Don't expect the tech inspector to give you a break. His purpose is to make sure the equipment that goes out on the racetrack at high speeds is safe. Safety is the primary concern. Besides, if you had done it right to begin with, he wouldn't call you on it.

You don't have to be Joe Pro to enjoy racing a Sportster. This rider, out of Biff's Harley-Davidson, launches his Stock-883 class Sportster. Even with a standard engine, all the critical elements of drag racing come into play, such as preparing the machine before race day, making changes to the bike's set-up during the course of the day, and managing traction during the run. Notice that this machine appears qualified to run in 883 Twin Sports road racing with its clip-ons, steering damper, long rear shocks, and rearsets. You can also see the safety wiring on the front end.

Proof that the "iron barrel" still lives. When Dave Zehner and Dan Fitzmaurice built this 102ci Sportster, they had a goal in mind: to push the V-twin iron head into the 8sec bracket. The engine generated a claimed 160hp on gasoline, proving that tuners can use Evolution heads, XR-1000 heads, and even four-valve heads, but in the end, it's not the head that breaks records. It's the determined application of technology and rider skills. Fitzmaurice, the rider, holds a number of records in several racing organizations with this machine.

Doug Morrow, of Carl's Speed Shop, has run his 105ci five-speed through the quarter in 10.47sec at 130.35mph. The bike is streetable, right down to its electric starter. The heads flow 180cfm, about 20 percent more than the best worked-over XR-1000. Carl's Speed Shop

Sometimes, however, riders forget or overlook something. This is why it's a good idea to check the bike, with the tech inspection in mind, before you ever put it on the trailer. It's also a good idea to get there as early as possible, so you don't panic if he flunks you.

If the rules require something like a safety wired sump plug, don't go to the races thinking that they'll let you off. That's not the way the system works. The rules are there for everyone's safety, not just yours. Your transmission oil can put other riders on their heads.

Here's a technical inspection check list:
- Bring your bike.
- Bring your riding gear, if required.
- Bring any required paperwork.
- Have a pen and paper with you.
- Make sure your bike is ready before you go.
- Pay attention.
- Smile.
- Have a nice day.

Remember, it's not nice to bug officials with questions that the day's program answers.

AMA Amateur and Semi-Professional Programs

The American Motorcycle Association offers about twenty forms of amateur competition—not counting all its professional programs—from dirt track to road race, from hillclimb to hare scrambles, from ice racing to Scottish trials.

The additional categories in each form of racing, including categories for women, veterans, seniors, super seniors, four-stroke, limited wheelbases, stock, modified, mini, and—did I forget youth groups?—add up to hundreds of options in AMA racing.

Unfortunately, Harley-Davidsons no longer compete in most forms of AMA racing. Instead, you'll usually find lightweight, single-cylinder imports competing in the dirt events, and high-revving, multi-cylinder imports ruling the pavement races. Motorcycles like Harley-Davidsons, powered by long-stroke engines with big pistons, no longer present a challenge in many types of racing.

Every so often, however, a gallant competitor brings a Harley-Davidson Sportster to the starting grid of a race that's infested with foreign bikes. The reaction from officials and other competitors is always the same: "You're going to race *that*?!" Following the smirks and stifled guffaws, someone usually starts a pool to decide which lap the Harley will break.

Take the 1986 Baja 1000, for example. David Farrow, Jim Jackson, and Jeff Kaplan entered a stock XL-1100 engine wrapped in a custom C&J frame. No one took the effort seriously. One competitor joked that the Sportster might not make it across the starting line. However, as the team approached the end of the 1,000 mile torture test, and appeared to be a strong contender, everyone cheered them on. Some people even pitched in during the team's gas stops. They finished fourth in the big-bike class.

When Jim Bailey, of American Harley-Davidson in Ann Arbor, Michigan, entered a Twin Sports 883 in a twenty-four-hour road race at Nelson Ledges, Ohio, the officials were certain he had made a mistake. "This is the endurance race," an official said, "your race is next week." Members of other teams started a pool to predict when the bike would drop out. Before the race was over, the Harley-Davidson pool was changed to a Yamaha pool because several Yamahas had broken gearboxes. The Sportster proved to be the crowd favorite, and finished sixth.

Sportster-based machines compete regularly in only a few types of AMA events: dirt track, hill climb, and road race. Harleys run in drag races, of course; however, currently the AMA seldom sanctions drag races. Because it's difficult for a twin to compete against four-cylinder machines, several all-Harley-Davidson drag racing organizations have developed.

There are several tiers of AMA rider classifications. For example, an amateur meet offers only prizes and awards, in what is generally open to B and C class riders. In the A class, when a limited amount of prize money is distributed, the meet is considered to be a semi-pro event. If a larger purse is offered, the event is a Pro-Am meet. (Professional meets for experts, that pay still larger sums of prize money, are obviously not in the same class as amateur or semi-pro events.)

Following is an overall look at the AMA amateur and semi-pro programs. As you will see, the average 480lb Sportster is not at home in some of these events.

• Dirt track and short track: Everyone knows what oval-track races are, but did you know that there are categories for Veteran riders (over thirty years old), Senior riders (over forty years old), and Vintage motorcycles (pre-1975)? A Sportster is too large and heavy for short track.

• Hillclimb: These races can be run against time or distance. The typical Harley-Davidson is a long-wheelbase, open-class machine. Some are direct-drive.

• Drag racing: Drags can be time trials or the classic two-rider runoffs. Either way, they're always run against a clock to determine the winner. Lowest time wins. Diverse categories offer something for everyone. This sport has enjoyed growth every year for a decade.

• Road race: Road races are run on closed, paved courses at least one mile long, with a variety of left and right turns. Classes may include Showroom Stock, Modified Production, Grand Prix, and Vintage, in every displacement from 50cc to open. Classes may also be restricted to engine types of two-stroke or four-stroke, and single, twin, or multicylinder

David Clayton runs an 88ci Mountain Motor in Class C. All he needs to do is take off the wheelie bar and rear struts, *and he's got a street bike!* Larry Smith/Handcrafted American Racing Motorcycles

184

types. Usually at least two classes are suitable for a Harley-Davidson. Some riders enter two events at a single meet.

- Sidecar classes: Yes, there's a special category for "chairs," in 650 overhead cam and 750 pushrod twins, two-cycles, singles, multicylinders, and open displacements.

- Off-road field meet: Off-road field meets are a series of contests involving speed and/or power (sled pulls, drags, and so on). Sportsters are quite suited to this, but few events are well publicized.

- DTX: DTX is dirt-track racing at its cheapest, for more-or-less stock motocross machines from 85 to 500cc. It originated from a desire to provide an

Sam Plih and his custom-framed 96ci iron-head Sportster are strong competitors in Pro Stock class. Larry Smith/ Handcrafted American Racing Motorcycles

inexpensive form of entry-level dirt-track racing. It allows competitors to run machines that, although outdated for motocross competition, are perfectly suited under the AMA dirt-track rules. Not open to V-twin Harleys, though.

• Enduro: Speed is not the determining factor in enduro competition; rather, the winners are determined by maintaining a time schedule. It's run over all types of terrain using various checkpoints—timed, secret, gas stop, and so on.

• Reliability enduro: This is an even more restrictive form of enduro, including special tests that conform with FIM rules. It is designed to measure machine reliability and rider skill. Competitors for the International Six Days Enduro are selected during this event.

• Closed-course enduro: This is simply an enduro with a few alterations, mainly that riders must travel a shorter course of two or three miles, lapping at least two or more times. What makes it interesting is that all checks are secret.

• Grand prix: A closed-course meet that includes both natural and graded or paved terrain, run as a multi-lap race.

• Hare and hound: This is held on a marked course over natural terrain, with a dead-engine start. At the flag, everyone starts their engines and takes

off. It can be point-to-point, or run in loops of at least thirty miles, minimum sixty miles total. This forms the basis for classic desert racing in the Southwest. Big twins used to compete.

• Hare scrambles: Similar to a hare and hound race, except this event is conducted on a closed course using trails and paths over natural terrain, between 2.5 to 40 miles in length. First rider home wins.

• Scrambles: A scrambles Involves left and right turns over a prepared course, including hills—and jumps are permitted. It's intended to measure rider skill rather than motorcycle speed. Also called TT (tourist trophy) racing.

• Ice: Ice races are limited to a half-mile oval or shorter, for studded and nonstudded tire categories, in all displacement classes including sidecars. Studs are sheet-metal screws with single-slot hex heads between sizes #7 to #10, screwed into the tire from the outside. Nonstudded means you fall down a lot. A Sportster would saw a hole in the ice!

• Motocross: By far the most popular form of (foreign) motorcycle racing, the only engine displacement classes in motocross are 125cc, 250cc, and open. Many rider classifications are provided.

• Observed trials: In observed trials, also known as English trials, the riders must traverse observed

Dave Feazell, American Motorcycle Racing Association 1991 number-one Pro Stock record holder of 9.104 ET. Larry Smith/Handcrafted American Racing Motorcycles

sections containing natural obstacles, while losing as few points as possible. Competitors lose points for "dabbing" a foot, "footing," and failing to complete or start an observed section. The typical bike weighs, maybe, 180lb. (Have you weighed your Sportster lately?)

● Scottish trials: This is an intriguing combination of enduro and observed trials. Either type of course may be used, long or short format. It includes timing, check points, and observed sections.

● Off-road reliability run: This race is run over any terrain that can be traveled by a single-track vehicle (highways, backwoods trails, and so on), following a designated course with a maximum average speed of 30mph. Checkpoints and multiple speed averaging may be utilized, and enduro scoring is used.

● Off-road trail ride: This one's just for fun. Similar to a reliability run, it's run on any single-track terrain, but it's not a speed event. A poker run or other nonspeed contests may be included.

● Speedway: Limited to a flat oval track less than 2,250ft in circumference, the competition includes handicap, scratch, or team events for machines in 250, 350, and 500cc classes. They run on

fuel. A few Sportster-based single-cylinder bikes have competed in speedway, by blocking off one cylinder.

Sportsman Drag Racing

Any motorcycle rider can participate in Sportsman drag racing. At every drag race event, even at major National Championship meets, the day's racing program always includes a class of competition referred to as Sportsman. It has a category for every type of motorcycle and even if a rider shows up with a totally unique bike, "bracket" or "handicap" racing accommodates everything.

The Sportsman class is an entry-level category, and it presents an excellent opportunity to get started in drag racing. In addition, requirements for prior experience and protective gear are more relaxed. For example, riders competing in the slower classes may wear jeans rather than full-body leathers, and prior racing experience is not required.

Most professional drag race riders got their start in the stock classes, beginning with a more-or-less standard motorcycle. As riders gain experience and get used to the speed and the full use of maximum power, they usually get power hungry. Then they start hopping-up the engine with head work, big displace-

Bill Lace on his 141ci Evolution Sportster. He is an ECRA Super-Modified Street record holder, with an ET of 9.205sec. Larry Smith/Handcrafted American Racing Motorcycles

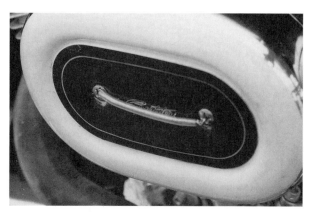

Sliding a small, clear plastic tube over the wire protects metal surfaces. Always use clear plastic, so you can inspect the wire for breakage.

ments, cams, and carbs. Next thing you know, they're tipping the can (using oxygenated nitro methane fuel).

Dan Fitzmaurice of Zipper's Performance Products said, "Once you get engaged in this, it rolls from there. You get the rush of drag racing, and it snowballs." Although Zipper's does some performance work on dirt-track and hillclimb machines, the vast majority of its racing business is drag.

Most Americans are hot rodders at heart, especially motorcyclists. According to Fitzmaurice, given an easy method of improving performance, most riders seriously consider modifying their machines to run in the high-speed "professional" classes.

It's not unusual to see dealership personnel helping their riders at a drag race. Mechanics who work on stock bikes every day sometimes like to dabble in a sport that challenges their tuning ability, by assisting their customers.

Drag racing is probably the most family-oriented form of competition. You'll find spouses and kids helping out in the pits. It's quite unlike the closed fraternities of other types of motor sports, such as road racing, where a woman's involvement in preparing and assisting with machinery is more of an exception.

Ask Phyllis McClure, wife and manager of racer Jim McClure. Jim is a record-holding world champion who set an unprecedented string of twenty-one consecutive drag race wins. Phyllis practically runs the whole program, assisting with machine preparation, maintenance, overhauls, and fuel mixing. Together with their major sponsors Rivera and Primo, they are a family team.

Anyone interested in trying their hand at drag racing will be surprised how easy it is to get started. All you need are a helmet, a good jacket, jeans, gloves, and boots. Oh yeah, bring your street bike.

This Twin Sports racer has all the brake attachments, axle, and fork drain plug wired.

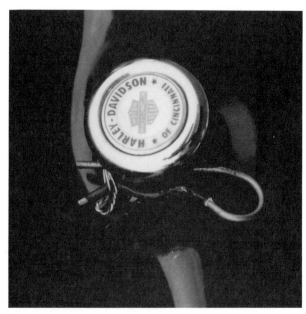

Here's a good way to safety wire the oil cap: with a hot wire coat hanger, pierce a hole through the rubber plug that corresponds with a hole drilled in the filler neck. Insert a hair-pin safety clip, and safety wire it.

Appendix

High-Performance Parts Suppliers

Accel Performance Products
175 N Branford Rd
Branford, CT 06405

The newest Accel entry is the Thunder Twin fuel injection system, available in a variety of configurations to fit stockers or strokers. Featuring simple bolt-on assembly, Accel claims the system delivers more power and better fuel mileage. The electronic control units (ECUs) are individually calibrated for specific applications, although an unlimited ECU that is programmable for racing applications is available.

Other new products include a Mega-Fire ignition module, U-groove spark plugs, dual-stage foam PowerFilters, points conversion kits, and the SuperCoil, which is claimed to produce up to 67 percent more voltage than stock coils.

Accel produces high-performance ignition, charging, starting, fuel, and lubrication systems and components.

Andrews Products, Inc.
5212 N Shapland Ave
Rosemont, IL 60018

Although best known for its cams and cam kits, Andrews also produces a wide array of camshaft drive and transmission gears and shafts, belt drive pulleys, and high-output ignition coils.

The Andrews transmission gears allow tuners to change the internal gear ratios for wider or closer overall gear spacing. Shot-peened for longer life, Andrews gears feature lead-in ramps and beveled drive dogs for smoother shifting.

Andrews also offers valve checkers and dial indicators for measuring valve travel and setting guide-to-spring clearance on Evolution and Shovelhead Sportsters and big twins, and a high-flow accelerator pump kit for stock Keihin carburetors.

Axtell Sales, Inc.
1424 SE Maury
Des Moines, IA 50317

Axtell manufactures finned and finless cylinders and kits for street or track use, as well as pistons. Everything is made to customer order. If you send lower ends and heads, Axtell will also build engines from scratch, dealer direct.

Barnett Tool & Engineering
9920 Freeman Ave
Santa Fe Springs, CA 90670

A leader in clutch innovations, Barnett now offers its Series K clutches, made from Dupont Kevlar material, for Harley-Davidson motorcycles from 1941 on. Kevlar is claimed to possess better strength, thermal stability, and wear resistance than other clutch base materials. Barnett's own testing showed that its Kevlar-based friction plates last three times longer than semi-metallic and twelve times longer than asbestos materials.

Bartels' Performance Products
3237 Carter Ave
Marina Del Ray, CA 90292

Bill Bartels, owner of Bartels' Performance Products, has a long history of racing and high-performance involvement. His current offerings for Sportsters include cams, pushrods, gaskets, exhaust systems, intake manifolds, and complete engine services.

Branch Flowmetrics
5556 Corporate Dr.
Cypress, CA 90630

Jerry Branch's head porting and modifications are certainly well known. Branch Flowmetrics offers modification services on your cylinder heads, and also stocks some ready-to-ship heads for quick same-day turnaround.

Carl's Speed Shop
9339 Santa Fe Springs Road
Santa Fe Springs, CA 90670

With a history of setting speed and drag records that spans three decades, Carl Morrow offers a complete line of high-performance parts, accessories, and engine services. Products include unique CDI magnetos, engine conversion kits, extended swing arm kits, and speed equipment from major suppliers and manufacturers. Evolution frame modification for installing taller stroker engines also available.

Crane Cams, Inc.
530 Fentress Blvd
Daytona Beach, FL 32114

Crane manufactures cams, tappets, and other valvetrain and ignition system components.

Custom Chrome, Inc. (CCI)
One Jacqueline Ct
Morgan Hill, CA 94037

CCI's RevTech line includes an array of high-performance components designed and manufactured under CCI's close scrutiny. Among the company's most notable items are cylinder heads that come with a statement verifying each head's flow. A unique carb with interchangeable venturis, in 38, 42, and 45mm sizes, allows customizing to individual needs. It has an accelerator pump, and the main jet can be changed quickly by simply removing a plug from the float bowl. CCI also distributes Andrews, Crane, S.T.D., Delkron, Axtell, and other high-performance specialties.

Drag Specialties
9839 W 69th St, Box 9839
Eden Prairie, MN 55344

Drag Specialties offers its own line of air cleaners, tappets, crank pins, connecting rods, pinion shafts, valves, guides, and piston sets. They also distribute products from Accel, S&S, Bendix, SU, Ness, Wiseco, Hastings, and Manley, to name a few. In addition to the famous Drag Specialties exhaust systems, including the Python, they also offer a wide array of bearings, carburetor jets, and other replacement parts.

Flo Dynamics
1150 Pike Ln, #2
Oceana, CA 03445

Flo Dynamics offers both products and services. In addition to an extensive line of tool steel valves and ignition system components, the company provides dual-plug head conversions, lubrication system modifications, and three-bolt exhaust flanges for Shovels. Flo Dynamics also provides its Super Port Flow for Evolution heads, and intake and exhaust porting service.

Harley-Davidson, Inc.
3700 W Juneau Ave
Milwaukee, WI 53208

Harley-Davidson manufactures a complete line of Screamin' Eagle components, ranging from air cleaners to camshafts.

Head Quarters
P.O. Box 119
Komoko, Ontario
Canada, NOL 1RO

Head Quarters does cylinder-head repair and modification work, including no-lead conversions, bathtub and hemi chambers, and porting. The company also offers its own line of high-performance and OEM-type replacement valvetrain parts, from cams and gears to seats and seals. In addition, HQ is the Canadian distributor for Crane, Andrews, Rowe, Velva-Touch, Hastings, Gapless, S&S, Mikuni, SU, and SuperTrapp.

Holeshot Performance
311 Chestnut St
Santa Cruz, CA 95060

Holeshot manufactures a product by the same name– Holeshot. It's not an air shifter, but it's compatible with one.

When installed on a five-speed, the Holeshot lets the rider speed-shift gears without using the clutch or letting off the throttle. It can be disengaged if desired, and kills the engine until the next gear is fully engaged so the engine won't overrev in case of missed shifts. An Evolution Sportster unit is adaptable to other models.

Holeshot also offers a molybdenum-disulfide dry film coating that reduces friction by 200 times when oil is present and reduces wear. The coating impregnates metal and requires no additional running clearance.

House of Horsepower
1190 Griffith St, #2
Louisville, KY 80027

House of Horsepower specializes in motor work, heli-arc welding, and machining, in addition to its line of cases, covers, and cylinders. The cases feature beefed-up wall thicknesses and reinforced motor mount areas. Cylinders are offered in both finned and finless configurations, in bore sizes up to 4in.

Jammer Cycle Products
6417 San Fernando Rd
Glendale, CA 91201

Jammer's markets brand-name systems, such as Joe Hunt and Morris magnetos, SU and Dell'Orto carbs, S.T.D. cases, and Andrews gears.

Kal-Guard Coating and Manufacturing Co.
16616 Schoenborn St
Sepulveda, CA 91343

A long-time aerospace supplier of specialty antifriction treatments, Kal Guard's MOS/2 moly dry film process is popular among racers. Send them your shiny metal parts, and you get back dull-finished pieces that are many times lower in friction.

Karata Enterprises
3 River Rd
Conshohocken, PA 19428

Karata has been in the belt drive business for seventeen years. It is one of only two aftermarket companies licensed to distribute Gates Kevlar reinforced Poly Chain. Various sizes of pulleys offer a wide array of gearing choices. Front pulleys are made from one-piece chrome-moly steel; rears are hardened aluminum alloy.

Kosman Racing Division
340 Fell St
San Francisco, CA 94102

Kosman makes frames for Sportsters and distributes such other racing components as Akront rims and Grimeca brakes.

Mikuni America Corp.
8910 Mikuni Ave
Northridge, CA 91342

In addition to its complete line of carburetor accessories, Mikuni America offers its bolt-on HS series smoothbore 40mm carburetor kits for Evolution Sportsters. The kits come complete with adapters, clamps, cables, air filter, and cover, as well as a tuning manual.

Morris Magnetos, Inc.
103 Washington St
Morristown, NJ 07960

Morris magnetos are self-contained units that do not rely on battery power. They provide up to 200 percent more voltage than stock ignition systems. In addition to other ignition-related components, Morris markets a dual magneto system, and an electronic EDI device that fires twin plugs from one mag.

Performance Machine, Inc.
16243 Minnesota, Box 1739
Paramount, CA 90723

Performance Machine manufactures and sells high-performance brake components.

Rivera Engineering
6416 S Western Ave
Whittier, CA 90606

The four-valve head kit is perhaps Rivera's most earth-shattering new product. Rivera also offers its exclusive Eliminator II SU carburetor system for the four-valve head (as well as for Panheads, Shovelheads, and Evolution big twins), and a dual-throat Dell'Orto carburetor kit. Rivera produces its own line of valvetrain and other performance items, in addition to being a distributor of such established lines as Delkron, Sifton, Crane, Leineweber, Andrews, Velva-Touch, Rowe, Manley, Hastings, Arias, Dyna, and Morris.

S&S Cycle
P.O. Box 215
Viola, WI 54664

S&S Cycle has been making engine parts, carburetors, oil pumps, and stroker and big-bore cylinder kits for thirty years. The S&S Sidewinder kits give displacement options from 79 to 103ci. Some are recommended for street use, others for track. Steel cylinders for fuel-burning drag racing, with bore sizes to $5^{1}/_{8}$in, are also available. American-made S&S butterfly-valve carburetors feature fully adjustable idle screws and interchangeable jets available in venturi sizes up to $2^{1}/_{4}$in (57mm). S&S supplies everything from velocity stacks and air cleaners to control systems and jets. Other replacement parts include heavy-duty rods, pistons, rings, and all valvetrain components.

S.T.D. Development, Inc.
P.O. Box 3583
Chatsworth, CA 91313-3583

S.T.D.'s specialty is high-performance cylinder heads. The Evolution Sportster head features the traditional two-valve layout, with bathtub chamber, twin plugs, unleaded-style seats, and raised ports for improved airflow. Because the heads are made from better metal than the original-equipment heads and have more metal around the port areas, they have more power potential.

Sputhe Engineering , Inc.
11185 Lime Kiln Rd
Grass Valley, CA 95949-9715

Sputhe Engineering has been in the business of designing, pattern making, testing, and manufacturing for over twenty years, and has been making alloy cylinders with cast-in liners since 1977. They also offer a wide array of bore-and-stroke displacement combinations for Sportsters in sizes from a 3.5in short-stroke 883, including a 5in stroke two-liter monster (125ci). They also market dual-carburetor Lectron and Mikuni carb systems.

Storz Performance
239 S. Olive St.
Ventura, CA 93001

Perhaps best known for his XR styling treatment for Sportsters, Steve Storz also offers his own cam, which was used in Don Tilley's *Lucifer's Hammer* race bike. Storz Performance also distributes Bullet Proof crank pins and tappets, Axtell's "drop-in" cams, and Mikuni's unique flat-slide carbs that are pre-jetted for certain applications.

Thunder Products
P.O Box 61
Patascala, OH 43062

Thunder Products' Dial-A-Jet kits install quickly and help cure the stock carburetor's lean staggers. The patented system also offers an adjustable tuning solution to carburetion problems caused when adding low-restriction exhaust systems and other performance parts.

Zipper's Performance Products
8040 Washington Blvd
Jessup, MD 20794

Zipper's offers a comprehensive line of performance products, combined with hands-on racing experience. In addition to their own products and services, they market other brand-name components as well. In-house services include flow testing, porting, boring, crank rebuilding, and head work. Some unique Zipper's items are Red Shift cams, Thunderjets, custom valve train components, Zipper's-Bandit Machine "race case" gearbox case, and oil-cooled clutches. In addition, Axtell pistons, Andrews products, Carrillo rods, MRE air shifter kits are also available.

Index